GRASSROOTS RULES

CHRISTOPHER C. HULL

Grassroots Rules

How the Iowa Caucus Helps Elect American Presidents

STANFORD LAW AND POLITICS

AN IMPRINT OF STANFORD UNIVERSITY PRESS

STANFORD, CALIFORNIA

Stanford University Press
Stanford, California

Printed in the United States of America on acid-
free, archival-quality paper

Library of Congress Cataloging-in-Publication
Data
Hull, Christopher C.
    Grassroots rules : how the Iowa Caucus helps
elect American presidents / Christopher C. Hull.
       p. cm.
    Includes bibliographical references and index.
    ISBN 978-0-8047-5803-1 (cloth : alk. paper)
      1. Primaries—Iowa.   2. Presidents—United
States—Nomination.   I. Title.
JK2075.I82H85 2008
324.5'209777—dc22   2007032914

Typeset by Newgen–Austin in 10/14 Janson

To Richard Clayton Hull, my long-lost father

Contents

Figures

Tables

Acknowledgments

It's funny how you think all acknowledgments are trite until you write a book. Then suddenly you realize that all those authors actually meant it when they thanked people without whom the work might not—or certainly would not—have been completed.

Anyway, I've got my own list, now. So here we go.

This book would never have been possible without the support of my family and friends. It was the powerful emotional and professional backing of the people I am about to name that pulled me through.

Among my family, the first acknowledgment is due to my dear friend, football buddy, and consigliore, my uncle, John Ogle. He has had to serve *in loco parentis* out on the East Coast, with the rest of our family back in Montana (and a couple in Iowa, of course)—and with my father gone since before the mists of my memory were lifted. A kid without a dad could have no better uncle in the world, and I've sure leaned on him to get through this project. Thanks, Unc.

Thanks are also due to my mother, Janet Hull Goldberg, as wise and ebullient a mom as anyone could hope to have. I occasionally take her boundless enthusiasm for wisdom for granted, and I shouldn't. Her unconditional love never wavers and is much appreciated.

And among my friends, I cherish the day I met each one of my college friends: Jonathan Funke, Rana Dershowitz, John Merz, Pete Schmidt, Charlie Reece, and Nick Darnton. They have brought joy to my existence since I was a mere lad, and bearing up under the strain of a new firm and a book deadline is a lot easier with them around. They are loyal and true in a way that never fails to warm the cockles of my heart (though I have no idea what a cockle is). And I deeply appreciate the friendship of Eric Winterbauer and Bob Vanasse, who have had to endure my early celebrations as well.

I would also like to thank Melissa Derwart, to whom I will always be grateful for her day-to-day kindness, care, and support early in this project. She is one of those of whom I can say with certainty that this book would not be a reality but for her.

And, finally, my heart flows with gratitude to the Countess Valerija Kordic of Croatia, my delightful girlfriend, who brings me enormous joy and laughter. If I make her smile to herself when I'm not around half as often as she makes me, she's smiling her pretty, royal head off.

Among my colleagues, first and foremost I wish to thank my mentor, Clyde Wilcox, who taught me public opinion and voting behavior—and also how to survive graduate school. His advice, especially that I focus my efforts on turning every paper into a conference paper, then a journal article, then a book, transformed my academic career. That said, he needs to tell me that journal article part again, as I seem to have skipped it somehow.

Second, I want to genuflect a bit before Jim Lengle, who taught me about presidential primaries. The reader will see that Professor Lengle is mentioned throughout this study, as his work on primaries helped set the stage for the play of the literature today. He didn't just teach me the subject matter, he (probably unwittingly) served as an example of what can be accomplished in the academy.

And special thanks go to Mark Rom, who taught me statistics—and under whose tutelage I remember starkly realizing I was no longer a grad student, but an academic. Mark gave me tools I just couldn't wait to get home to use. I have a lot to learn on the quantitative side, to be sure, but somehow he managed to get me to see the ecstatic utility of statistical estimates to nail down the previously (to me) un-nailable.

I would also like to thank my fellow presidential primary scholars Barbara Norrander, Wayne Steger, Andrew Dowdle, Randall Adkins, Hans Noel, and William Mayer for their comments, suggestions, and data pointers at various stages of this research. All have been very forthcoming with ideas, time, and, well, data that helped shape this project. And, more than that, they have become colleagues and friends, which I value even more.

Finally, I would like to express my gratitude to the great Iowa scholar Hugh Winebrenner himself, whose direct help was kind—but who also blazed the trail on which *Grassroots Rules* could stroll. I may take issue with some of his conclusions in my book, but as the number of citations from his book amply demonstrates, my respect for his work knows no bounds.

Any mistakes that remain, as the expression goes, are my own.

Two more, to conclude.

Fervent, reverent thanks are due to my recently lost Grandma, Lucille Hull McIntyre, who supported my little school habit all along. She trickily engineered my interest in going to a good college as a teenager, inspiring me to actually work in high school, a new experience for me at the time. She underwrote my time at Harvard. She sent me to France to study abroad, twice since I didn't quite get it right the first time, an experience that transformed my life. Grandma Lucille changed me forever in ways I was lucky enough to express to her in person before she left us. Were she alive to see this book today, I'd get to hear her say once more that she was *thrilled, just thrilled.*

And finally, to my long-lost father, I would just like to say that I wish that he were here to see this day. He would have made a far better academic than I, had he not left us all so soon. This is my first book, but by now he would have written 10, and the gentle candle flame of this work would pale beside the piercing floodlight of his brilliance. The tragedy of his short life keeps my existence in perspective, and I yearn one day to be the father he wasn't able to be to me.

Thanks, to all of you.

GRASSROOTS RULES

The Cess Poll

Is the Iowa Caucus a Negative Force in Presidential Politics?

On January 21, 1980, KEMB-FM in Emmetsburg, Iowa, broadcast from the city water plant. With a pause between each, the announcer intoned the names of the two major candidates for the Democratic nomination that year, Carter and Kennedy, and then "undecided/don't care." After reading each one, he asked Emmetsburgers to flush their toilets to indicate their choice. The station measured how far the water level dropped for each. Undecided/don't care was the winner by a two-to-one margin, with Kennedy trailing Carter badly. The contest came to be known as the cess poll (Winebrenner 1998).

The main question this book addresses is whether the first-in-the-nation Iowa Presidential Caucus is a cess poll—and whether we should be flushing at "don't care" regardless. To answer that one question, it tackles a series of others whose answers ultimately (I hope) shed light on how presidential candidates win state nomination contests and even on the nomination itself.

But perhaps we should back up and define the book in a slightly more formal way. Its subject is the Iowa Precinct Caucus Presidential Straw Poll, known to most simply as the Iowa Caucus, which has for several decades been approximately the first contest in the American presidential primary process, usually occurring just before the New Hampshire Primary.

Caucuses, for those not familiar with them, are lengthy local party meetings used to conduct party business and select delegates to further regional conventions, which ultimately decide how the state's presidential delegates will be allocated. They are different from primaries, in which voters simply show up and vote as they would in a general election. Because of the time commitment that caucuses require, they tend to draw only the party's activists—and according to their folklore at least, caucuses as a result encourage primary candidates to rely more heavily on retail politics and grassroots organization[1] to win them.

To its critics, the Iowa Caucus in particular has some explaining to do, to put it mildly. Winebrenner, for instance, concludes his landmark work, *The Iowa Precinct Caucuses: The Making of a Media Event* (1998, 262), by saying, "The public interest is not well served when manipulated and distorted nominating events like the Iowa precinct caucuses determine the viability of presidential candidates." Manipulated? Distorted? Those are fighting words. To Winebrenner and his (numerous) fellow critics, the Iowa Caucus is *definitely* a cess poll.

Every time the snow flies the year before the U.S. presidential election, America notices again that a small, rural, overwhelmingly white state in the Midwest is helpfully eliminating a swath of candidates running for president. Accordingly, like clockwork, a quadrennial call to impose the death penalty on the first-in-the-nation Caucus rings through the media, the political science community, and especially the political superstructure of other states that would rather go first.

And they've got a point—or rather, several of them.

First, critics say, the press that comes out of the Caucus is crazily out of step with the technical importance of the contest. According to Brady (1989), for instance, Iowa receives about 243 times as much media coverage as one would otherwise expect given the number of delegates it allocates, even controlling for the date of the contest.

That said, there is a serious debate over whether Iowa actually has an impact on the nomination. Two recent studies (Adkins and Dowdle 2001;

Mayer 2004) contend strongly that what really matters is New Hampshire—and after it, Iowa is a bit of an afterthought. If that's true, and Iowa doesn't matter to the ultimate nomination, then critics' charge that it gets too much attention is a little moot. (Of course, this book would be a bit moot as well, so it is well worth exploring.)

Second, critics contend that the Iowa Caucus in particular has simply gotten away from what made it special: retail politics. Caucuses, according to their advocates, tend to encourage candidates to build, rather than to destroy—to rally supporters to them in elaborate, motivated organizations, not simply to run attack television ads as they do in primary states and the general election. But because of Iowa's prominence, critics charge, turnout there has soared, organization's importance has dwindled, and television has become a far more dominant force.

Not so fast, say Iowa's supporters—in this case, Iowans themselves. Political observers in the state acknowledge there is far more TV advertising than in years past, but they insist that "time on task" by the candidates themselves and powerful grassroots organizations still carry the day.

Third, critics point accusingly to Iowa's demography and ideology, saying both are totally unrepresentative of the party or of the country more generally. The state is racially homogeneous, they argue, and there can be no doubt that it is so.[2] According to data from the U.S. Census Bureau, as of 2005 Iowa was 95.79 percent white and 2.79 percent black, with 3.48 percent of whites identifying as Hispanics, while the country was 74.7 percent white and 12.1 percent black, with 14.5 percent identifying as Hispanics.[3]

In addition, goes this line of critique, caucusgoers in particular are philosophically more extreme than others of their party. The Democratic National Committee chair, Ron Brown, for instance, made the argument in 1992 that Iowa was nominating candidates too liberal to win the general election (Winebrenner 1998, 21).

Again, some have raised skeptical eyebrows. In a series of studies in the 1980s, Abramowitz, Stone, Rapoport, and others proposed a Moderation Hypothesis: in Iowa and elsewhere, ideologically extreme voters were strategically choosing candidates closer to the political center than they were, basing their choice on the candidate's ability to win the White House. If that Moderation Hypothesis is borne out in Iowa's actual outcomes, critics' charge on ideology is, again, moot.

By the same token, if in spite of Iowa caucusgoers' demographic unrepresentativeness, minority candidates are not losing out disproportionately, especially when controlling for other factors, it would take some edge off critics' charges on that front as well.

Fourth, a common concern about Iowa is its tendency to support midwestern candidates. Certainly in 1992, when Iowa senator Tom Harkin (D) ran for the presidency, the state gave little ground to other candidates. But more generally, regional favorites like Senator Bob Dole (R-Kan.) and Representative Dick Gephardt (D-Mo.) have overperformed in the Caucus.

Fifth and finally, there is Winebrenner's charge that the Iowa caucus results themselves are questionable. Overall, Winebrenner argues, "projections based on precinct caucuses are invalid and unreliable indicators of presidential candidate strength in Iowa." He cites three reasons. First, he says, no actual votes are taken. Second, the 15 percent "viability thresholds" mandated of caucuses by the national Democrats mean candidates' vote strengths include support from other candidates. Third, the "fluidity and duration" of Iowa's true delegate selection process undercut estimates made on caucus night (Winebrenner 1998, 50).

In 1976 on the Democratic side the result was "phony" and on the Republican side it was badly overblown, Winebrenner charges (pp. 71, 73, 75). In 1980 the process was improved somewhat, he reports (p. 101), but he says the real lesson was that "Iowa's political parties should be required to provide independently verified caucus results, or the media should ignore the state and its precinct caucuses" (p. 98). In 1984 the Democrats again struggled with how to report their results in a timely and accurate way, and the *Des Moines Register* called it "a botched caucus count" and a "pathetic performance" (pp. 124, 171). In 1996, says Winebrenner, "although only a straw poll, and unrelated to delegate selection, the results were 'votes' to the media and they were reported nationally and internationally" (p. 237). When constructing the Iowa caucus system and promoting it to the candidates and the national media, Winebrenner argues, "the promoters conveniently lost sight of the fact that caucus and convention systems do not produce outcomes in the way that primary elections do" (p. 254).

Winebrenner's argument leads to the single research question that undergirds this book: is the Iowa Caucus a negative force in presidential politics? While final judgment must be left to each reader, the following fundamental questions, were we to answer them, would certainly help us to better understand the Iowa Caucus's role and the presidential primary process more generally:

Does Iowa make any difference in who wins the nomination? If Mayer and Adkins and Dowdle are right and Iowa doesn't matter in its own right, why not write a book on New Hampshire? (Should we flush at "don't care"?) Or does the Caucus have an important impact on the outcome of the nomination, as it appeared to in both 1976, when Carter rode a win there to the White House, and 2004, when Kerry rode a win there to the nomination (and back to the Senate)?

Does retail politics really still matter in the Caucus? Is turnout now so high and TV now so dominant that the state has lost its claim on being a Lincolnian, social capital–rich, positive grassroots force in the presidential primary process? Or is pressing the flesh in person, persuading one thoughtful voter at a time, still the crucial tactic it supposedly once was?

Do Hawkeye State caucusgoers vote strategically or ideologically (or both)? That is, are they supporting those who can win or just choosing candidates based on who believes most like them? Are they crippling their parties by nominating candidates philosophically out of step with the American voting public? Or do they make allowances for candidates who are more likely to win the White House, letting them off the hook ideologically, as it were?

I set out to answer these questions. In the process, I hoped to illuminate issues broader than whether Iowa was a cess poll.

- I wanted to examine the early states' role in the primary more generally, measuring the impact of both Iowa and New Hampshire on the ultimate nomination.
- I wanted to test whether technology was changing the role of those early states, and of momentum more generally, by amplifying candidates' ability to capitalize on important events.
- I wanted to find ways of quantifying so-called retail politics, the oldest and most common tactic in all of politics and yet one so poorly understood.
- I wanted to find a measure of ideological crowding within a multi-candidate field, building on many past studies of how competitors'

philosophies interact with those of the electorate, to construct a useful tool that I (and others) could use in the future.

- Finally, I wanted to find out how presidential candidates win state nomination contests, and more specifically, I wanted to explore as completely as I could how candidates won in a single, crucially important state's contest—in fact, the most puzzling, mysterious state one could choose to predict in the presidential nomination process.

This study contains what I found out about all these issues, both inside and outside the Missouri River and Mississippi River borders of the Hawkeye State.

As I see it, the results fit within two separate but interlocking debates within the political science literature: what matters in winning the ultimate nomination, and what matters in winning an individual state's nominating contest.

First, the book is situated within the presidential primary literature's debate over the impact, nature, and desirability of variations on what thinkers like James I. Lengle (1981a) and Barbara Norrander (1996) have termed the "Rules of the Game." Those rules include the fallout from the Democratic Party reforms of the 1970s, the placement of the earliest states in the primary, the increasingly dominant role of front-loading, and the interplay of these forces with the "exhibition season" (or "invisible primary") of fund-raising, poll taking, and pundit opining during the year or so before the election.

Like the presidential general election literature, the primary literature includes elaborate and highly sophisticated efforts to predict which presidential candidate will ultimately triumph in the nomination battle. Those efforts, especially the early ones by Parent et al. (1987) and Bartels (1988), lay the foundation for understanding the role of substantive factors like the demographic and political lay of the land, as well as dynamic factors like candidate momentum and bandwagon effects.

In particular, theorists modeling multicandidate presidential primaries (Bartels 1988; Norrander 1993; Mayer and Busch 2004; Cohen et al. 2004) place a central emphasis on momentum. The models rely on success in preceding contests to proxy that momentum—but in the Caucus, there usually are no preceding contests. We need a better understanding of what predicts success in Iowa to calculate early-state candidate odds in future multi-candidate primary models.

If rules placing the Iowa Caucus first and emphasizing the momentum that Iowa generates are indeed exerting an important impact on nomination outcomes, as commonly held, then knowing what kinds of campaigns win in Iowa matters a great deal, and we need to understand the Caucus's nature better. If Iowa is not exerting a significant impact, to some extent the rules placing it first and the momentum it creates are less important.

Those examining Iowa's impact on the nomination in particular have focused on the intense media coverage it generates (Arterton 1978; Robinson 1981; Brady 1989; Mayer and Busch 2004) and the resulting devastation it brings to poorly performing candidates (Bartels 1989; Wolfinger 1989). But Adkins and Dowdle (2001) suggest the Caucus is of no predictive value in the nomination's outcome. Rather, they find, the preprimary exhibition season dominates who is nominated. This line of thought also explores how much state-to-state momentum matters in determining nomination outcomes (Lengle and Shafer 1976; Schier 1980; Polsby 1983; Stone and Abramowitz 1983; Norrander 1996; Hagen and Mayer 2000).

Thus the question, worth revisiting after Kerry captured Iowa and the nomination in 2004: how much does winning the Iowa Caucus really matter?

With respect to the Rules of the Game conversation, Chapters 3 and 4 are part of an active current inquiry by various researchers into the role of Iowa's first-in-the-nation Caucus and New Hampshire's first-in-the-nation Primary—including both the positive question of the degree to which they influence the ultimate nomination process, and the normative question of whether that degree of influence is a good or a bad thing.

With respect to the predictive literature, both chapters contend mostly with the dynamic side of the equation, estimating traditional and technological forms of momentum coming out of the early primary states.

In addition, Chapter 4 defies the long-standing premise reflected in several recent works that Iowa bows to New Hampshire in its ultimate impact on the nomination. In a sense, I see this result as supporting theorists who believe the Rules of the Game are crucial determinants of primary outcomes. The chapter also strongly challenges long-standing predictive assumptions about momentum's role, based on American politics' new wired world.

And most directly, Chapter 7 proposes a way to tackle forecasting outcomes in the Caucus—very likely the hardest nomination contest in the country to predict—which is intended to aid theorists like Mayer at Northeastern and Cohen and his colleagues at the University of California, Los Angeles, who are currently at work building and improving larger primary forecasting models that require some estimate of momentum going into Iowa.

Second, the study is part of the debate over what explains outcomes in electoral contests, including the degree to which American politics still fosters and draws upon Putnam's "social capital."[4] Within the primary literature, one line of this discussion centers on campaign effects—the impact on electoral outcomes of various tactics like television, in-person voter contact, and direct mail. Another line of discussion within that literature is the "vote choice" investigations of the interplay between ideology and electability—the "strategic voting" that rational choice theorists in particular contend is taking place.

Thus assuming Iowa is important, the next question to address is what factors influence which campaigns succeed in the state—that is, what explains Caucus outcomes. Many theorists have looked at vote choice and representativeness in the caucus and primary system (Lengle 1981b; Hutter and Schier 1984; Mayer 2000) and find that Iowa is demographically and ideologically deeply unrepresentative. However, as we have seen, one class of the vote-choice school qualifies that finding by positing that Iowa's ideological slant is mitigated by the caucusgoers' desire to pick a winner (Stone 1982; Abramowitz and Stone 1984; Stone, Rapoport, and Abramowitz 1989, 1992).

What this literature does not contain is a full exploration of what factors actually determine candidate outcomes in Iowa, as opposed to individual vote choice. Such an understanding could help determine whether the ideological and demographic unrepresentativeness of the state skews its actual outcomes and the degree to which those outcomes are mitigated by the previously observed individual caucusgoer's desire to favor electability. More generally, such a model could help answer the question raised by Winebrenner (1998): whether the Iowa Caucus structure still places a central emphasis on grassroots organizing and whether electronic media has passed grassroots by in terms of determining the state's outcomes.

In particular, Chapter 5 enters the melee over whether the Iowa Caucus—which may be the hardest primary contest in the country to explain—remains organization driven or is evolving into a kind of pseudo-primary. Chapter 5 lands heavily on the side of those who believe retail politics dominates the state.

Also, Chapter 6 participates in the literature's discussion over how caucusgoers' ideological and demographic skew interacts with their sophistication to produce strategic results, ultimately siding with the team of Abramowitz, Stone, Rapoport, and their colleagues, who have found caucus voters' political sophistication counterbalancing their staunch ideologies, finding that sophistication reflected in aggregate-level Caucus results.

A more specific summary of the questions asked and answered by each chapter follows.

Chapter 2: What Is a Caucus? This chapter asks, broadly and with a historical tone, How did the American presidential primary system evolve into its current form? Should we be concerned about that form at all? How did that system spawn the current role that Iowa plays, whatever that may be? And what candidates has the Caucus helped and halted since it gained its role at the forefront of the presidential primary process?

Chapter 3: Who Cares about Iowa? This chapter investigates whether the Iowa Caucus actually matters in how we pick our presidents. It adds new data on Kerry's 2004 win as well as Carter's 1976 win not included in past studies to help settle the score, relying exclusively on the current measures of momentum used in the literature, rather than taking technology into account as Chapter 4 does.

Chapter 3 finds as recent studies have that, measuring Iowa's momentum effects in the traditional way, the New Hampshire Primary results mediate the impact the Caucus has on the presidential nomination (Mayer 2004). However, it also finds that candidates' Iowa performance plays a modest role as a predictor of their New Hampshire vote share, controlling for pre-Iowa Granite State polls as well as performance in the exhibition season that precedes the election year on measures such as fund-raising and national polling. And the chapter identifies a potential explanation for the recent empirical finding that Iowa does not appear to matter to the ultimate nomination: New Hampshire may be filtering out Iowa's midwestern bias, at least with respect to Tom Harkin, the Hawkeye State's favorite son in 1992.

Chapter 4: From the "Big Mo" to "E-mentum." This chapter explores whether technological changes are amplifying the impact of momentum in presidential races. It asks, Do moments of increased momentum have bigger payoffs in a world of online fund-raising, Web-based organizing, and e-mail communication?

The question is important, the chapter argues, because the literature is rife with studies of momentum's impact on the state-by-state dynamics of primary election presidential politics. But the impact of that momentum appears to be changing. In 1980 George Bush the elder won the Iowa Caucus but could not capitalize on his "Big Mo." Yet in 2004, for the first time since Carter, Iowa momentum again carried a candidate to the nomination. The reason may be that the Internet finally allows cash-strapped, trailing candidates to jack into money and supporters online fast enough to catch up with front-runners, given a big-enough win. I term this technologically enhanced momentum *e-mentum*.

The chapter finds empirically that e-mentum is a quantifiable, statistically significant phenomenon, with respect to Iowa's impact on both the New Hampshire Primary and the ultimate nomination. It further estimates specific e-mentum bonuses from Iowa in both contests, as well as the amount by which current models seem to be underestimating Iowa's effects. That result also indicates that the Rules of the Game, with respect to early states and front-loading, matter more intensely than they have in the past—and that candidates should beware the trendy strategy of skipping Iowa.

Finally, the chapter seeks to provide a road map for others who wish to investigate e-mentum's effects, especially looking forward to 2008's crucial inflection points in the presidential campaign—Iowa and New Hampshire, for starters, but also South Carolina, Super Tuesday, the party conventions, and the presidential debates.

The chapter's results actually ratchet up critics' concerns about Iowa's distorted impact on the overall nomination. They also raise the stakes on the questions explored in the remainder of the book.

Chapter 5: The Ground War or the Air War? The literature on the first-in-the-nation Iowa Caucus includes overall qualitative research, national-level quantitative research on its impact, and individual (voter's-eye-view) state-level quantitative research. What it doesn't include is aggregate (candidate's-eye-view) state-level quantitative research, that is, a model to help explain success for a presidential campaign in Iowa.[5] This chapter unveils such a model, and examines its results with respect to which tactics matter most in boosting or busting presidential candidates in the Hawkeye State.

The results of this Explanatory Model indicate that candidates' days in Iowa relative to their opponents have the largest positive impact among the tactics tested. The model also supports the contention that the Democratic 15 percent viability threshold thwarts low-tier candidates on that side of the aisle. And it finds that greater television spending relative to competitors is actually associated with *lower* Caucus vote share, holding constant Iowa spending, and subject to important caveats about the quality of both television and Iowa spending data.

Those findings in turn strengthen arguments for Iowa's grassroots reputation. They also provide support for those who believe in the importance of the Rules of the Game, in this case on an internal, state-specific level. Finally, the findings undercut critics' charges that television has taken on a new dominance in the state, turning the Caucus into a glorified primary.

Chapter 6: Ideological Intrigue or Strategic Voting? This chapter uses the Explanatory Model to test the Moderation Hypothesis, the finding in individual-level studies that ideologically extreme Hawkeye State voters may strategically choose more electable candidates, sacrificing their own views to select winners.

The model finds that strategic voting dominates Iowa's aggregate outcomes, just as previous studies had found it dominates Iowa's individual vote choice. Specifically, it estimates that Ideological Crowding—a factor I developed to measure the concept in a multicandidate race—plays the largest role of any tactical or strategic factor in the model. However, it also finds that perceptions of electability matter significantly in determining Caucus outcomes, partially supporting the Moderation Hypothesis. The model's results also indicate that viability does not matter, holding Electability and Ideological Crowding constant. In other words, caucus attendees seem willing to compromise on philosophy when a candidate looks more likely to capture the White House, but *not* when the candidate looks more likely to capture the nomination.

The chapter also notes tentatively that minority candidates do not appear to suffer at the hands of the overwhelmingly white Iowa caucusgoer, and that in fact when controlling for philosophical placement and perceptions of electability, the estimate of minority candidates' differential performance is actually positive, though not statistically significant. However, it also takes pains to point out that those placements and perceptions might themselves be shaped by racial motivations.

Chapter 7: Predicting What Happens. Finally, Chapter 7 sketches the broad outlines of approaches to predicting Iowa Caucus results. It settles on a complex model made up of explanatory factors, Iowa polling, Gallup polling, and success in early straw polls, and demonstrates that approach's superiority to other approaches. I hope that it will also be clear, however, both that the approach is tentative at best and that the others all have their merits.

Given all that information, we should be able to draw some conclusions about whether the Iowa Caucus is a negative force in American presidential politics.

Is Iowa a cess poll?

What Is a Caucus?

Iowa and the Presidential Nomination System

The action begins in Iowa. It's where everything starts for everyone.

— G E O R G E H . W . B U S H

If "the action begins in Iowa," when did that action begin *for* Iowa? And since Iowa became "where everything starts for everyone," who has it started—and who has it stopped?

This chapter glances back at the evolution of the primary system and Iowa's role within that system. It reviews the history of caucuses and primaries in the presidential nomination system. Then it turns to a retelling of Iowa's tale specifically. Finally, it sketches out some of the questions raised by Iowa's part in U.S. presidential nomination history.

Two notes for the reader: For those familiar with the theory and history of the presidential primary system, this chapter will seem more like a long, lingering look back than a glance. Though it raises important issues directly relevant to the rest of the book, political scientists reviewing this chapter might cry "old hat" or, if French, "déjà vu," to paraphrase British humorist P. G. Wodehouse (p. 8). Accordingly, those not wishing to slog through Iowa Caucus 101 may skip this chapter with no harm done. Each chapter that follows contains a précis of the relevant studies that may seem skimpy to the layperson but will put those familiar with the nomination literature perfectly at ease with the debate in which the chapter is supposed to figure. Likewise, at each point where Iowa's history comes into play, it is briefly recounted in such a way that those familiar with presidential primaries over the last three decades will find perfectly sufficient.

Second, in the chapter's historical portions—in no way the focus of this book—I draw heavily from three works: the helpful summary of the primary system's evolution by Bass (1998), the essay on Iowa's role within that system by Squire (1989), and the definitive history of the Iowa Caucus by Winebrenner (1998). Anyone looking for a (far) richer analysis of any of these three topics can look to those works.

Caucuses, Primaries, and the Presidential Nomination System

To start at the beginning: What is a caucus?

A caucus is nothing more than a term for a political group or meeting. In the U.S. House of Representatives, for instance, the Congressional Black Caucus, Congressional Hispanic Caucus, the Out of Iraq Caucus, the Blue Dog Coalition, and the Republican Study Committee are all caucuses of like-minded members. In Congress and state legislatures,[1] there are Republican and Democratic caucuses, which either run the chamber or serve as the (more or less) loyal opposition. And in local party politics, a caucus is a meeting of the party faithful (Hull 2007).

Caucuses date to the hoary origins of the Republic. Since parties began to coalesce, they have met in caucuses to make decisions. In the early days of American parties, presidential nomination decisions were made by "king caucuses," gatherings of a party's most august members, centering on current elected leaders. So, not to put too fine a point on it, in presidential nomination politics, the caucus predates the primary by more than a century.

Candidate selection procedures evolved from legislative caucuses in the 1790s to the nominating conventions that continue to this day (Winebrenner 1998, 227). The concept of the caucus survived that transition; local parties would hold caucus meetings to discuss party business, select leadership, and designate delegates to go on to county, district, or state conventions. Ultimately, state conventions would select delegates to that party's national convention, held once every four years to select a president. This "caucus-to-convention" system survives in many states to this day—including, at least in part, in Iowa.

The caucus-to-convention system is increasingly rare relative to its modern competitor, the nominating primary election. The first nominating primary took place in 1842 in Crawford County, Pennsylvania, and was adopted swiftly by nearby counties but did not become widespread nationally until the progressive era, when reformers took to criticizing the closed system of nominations by party insiders, advocating the open primary instead.[2]

The Democratic South adopted these nominating primary elections most aggressively, likely because the one-party system there at the time already called into question the legitimacy of candidates. By contrast, Republicans were slow to adopt the system until after the Second World War, and even for Democrats, nonsouthern states in which the two-party system was most competitive held out longest against the reform. By 1946 primaries for selecting nonpresidential candidates had become almost universal—46 states had primary laws of one kind or another. Yet though Progressives had more than 20 states on board with presidential primaries as early as 1916, states actually began to fall away from the practice as midcentury approached. At the same time that nonpresidential primaries were sweeping through the states, the process of selecting the presidential nominee was kept separate. Instead, national nominating conventions emerged for both parties and continue to this day (Bass 1998, 228).

However, after the disastrous 1968 Democratic Convention in Chicago, where protesting antiwar supporters of Senator George McGovern were swept under a tide of police and tear gas as establishment candidate Hubert Humphrey was swept comfortably to the nomination, things changed. The Democratic Party established the McGovern-Frasier Commission to examine the presidential nomination system, seeking to expand the input of the party rank and file. From reforms out of that commission, and from aftershocks felt even today, rules forcing open caucuses led many states to abandon the older system for the more modern, plebiscitary system of primaries.

Thus in the 1948 election, presidential primaries had taken place in only 14 states with fewer than 5 million votes cast. By the time of the 1996 elections, 40 states held primaries and almost 25 million voters participated (Bass 1998, 245).

The caucus, then, has gone from the norm to an outlier, while the primary has all but taken over the nomination process. During this evolution, how has the Iowa Caucus resisted morphing and modification—or has it? What is its particular path through what has become a thicket of primaries?

A Brief History of the Iowa Caucuses

Jimmy Carter. Gary Hart. Dick Gephardt. George Herbert Walker Bush.
   Ever heard of them?

It's more than possible that if it hadn't been for the Iowa Caucus, the answer would be no. For more than three decades, the Hawkeye State has examined candidates up close and personal, and sometimes it selects someone America has essentially never heard of before. Its lore, part of it at least, held that the disarmingly honest Carter, the powerfully charismatic Hart, the intensely pro–little guy Gephardt, and the moderate, offbeat Bush could persuade Iowans that they would make good presidents. Given its caucus-to-convention structure, with a more-or-less formal process for determining support at the precinct level rather than statewide, Iowa is fabled for its ability to force candidates to campaign one on one, face to face, building support one potential caucus participant at a time.

Why? Well, in a primary, where voters must merely get to the polls once over the course of a day, the conventional wisdom holds that television ads and press coverage can swing support rapidly from one candidate to another. But in the Iowa Caucus, "voters" must show up at one designated time for their party's precinct caucus, or local party meeting, and stay for anywhere from an hour to three hours, conducting party business, selecting local party leadership and delegates to go on to the county convention a few weeks later, getting the opportunity to speak out in favor of their candidates in front of their neighbors, and finally participating in the presidential straw poll (on the Democratic side, often repeatedly, in one night). Attending a party caucus is a commitment—and it requires committed partisans, or at least committed supporters.

Thus, the mythic tale goes, candidates must build themselves up among caucus attendees in every precinct, rather than merely tearing other candidates down statewide. The saga plays out still today—and it's been going on a long, long time. Ever since it became a state in 1846, Iowa has relied on the caucus-to-convention system to select its presidential nomination delegates—except a single presidential primary in 1916, which was labeled a "farce" (see Hull 2007; Winebrenner 1998, 27). However, the first-in-the-nation Iowa Caucuses as an institution are more recent and in fact represent a historical accident.

In 1968 there had been no statewide reporting of results on either the Democratic or Republican side. On the Republican side, in Polk County, Rockefeller appeared to edge Nixon, with Reagan trailing far behind. The *Des Moines Register* had a sense that on the Democratic side President Johnson was in trouble and estimated a combined McCarthy-Kennedy showing of 40 percent. However, the state's delegates at the national convention broke 46–5 against McCarthy—more kindling in the fire that led to the McGovern-Frasier Commission (Winebrenner 1998, 41).

In 1972 Iowa Democrats pushed their Caucus back to January 24 because they needed more time between the Caucus and convention to meet the stringent requirements put upon them by their own rules and the national Democratic Party's decision to hold its convention early that year, on July 9 (Squire 1989, 1). The Republicans left their mid-April caucuses in place.

That year "a young campaign manager for an obscure presidential candidate"—future Colorado senator Gary Hart, running South Dakota senator George McGovern's campaign—grasped the potential lift he could achieve in Iowa. Under Hart's leadership, McGovern sent his "border runners" from South Dakota south and east into the Hawkeye State.[3] Senator Edmund Muskie received the endorsement of popular Iowa Democrat Harold Hughes on the eve of the contest, and the benefit of Hughes's powerful organization. Yet Hart's efforts paid off, giving McGovern a strong showing—he won 22.5 percent of the "state delegate equivalents" announced by Democratic Party officials against Muskie's 35.5 percent, with 35.8 percent uncommitted. Humphrey was a rounding error at 1.6 percent (Winebrenner 1998, 45).[4]

The following cycle, another dark horse grasped the potential of the first presidential contest. On the Democratic side, all-but-unknown peanut farmer and Georgia governor Jimmy Carter cultivated Iowa carefully, beginning long before other viable candidates. He was rewarded with a dramatic win in the 1976 Iowa Caucus that thrust him into national prominence, prominence that ultimately translated into the Democratic nomination and then the White House (Hull 2007). While Iowa cannot be said to have determined the outcome entirely, Carter himself "attributed some of his success to his favorable finish in Iowa."[5]

It was Carter's victory that thrust Iowa itself into the limelight, as well. "The Iowa caucuses really achieved national stature in that they were acknowledged by many participants and elite observers as being important *before they occurred*," reports noted Caucus scholar Peverill Squire. In fact, as Squire lays out, "while the state parties positioned the caucuses to be more consequential in the nomination process, it was Jimmy Carter's successful drive to the 1976 Democratic nomination that made them important" (1989, 3, emphasis in original).

In 1980 Iowa was to play a critical role once again. A virtually unknown former ambassador and CIA chief by the name of George Herbert Walker Bush adopted the Carter strategy. He set up camp in Iowa, worked the personalities one by one, and made clear that Iowa was a priority to him. Most important, with the help of leading Iowa moderates such as Cherokee (the Iowa town, not the Native American tribe) lawyer George Witgraff, who was to become his Iowa chairman, and Des Moines–area lawyer Ralph Brown, who served as executive director of the Republican Party of Iowa from 1975 to 1977, Bush built a strong organization in the state, lining up key supporters and prominent GOP Hawkeyes to turn Iowans out on his behalf.[6]

By contrast, Republican front-runner and standard-bearer California governor Ronald Reagan had given Iowa conspicuously short shrift, even going so far as to skip a crucial January Republican Party debate.

On Caucus night, the result was a deliciously narrow Bush win. The obscure figure won 33,350 votes in the GOP precinct straw poll, or 31.6 percent of the vote, with the mighty Reagan trailing just behind at 31,348 votes, or 29.5 percent (Winebrenner 1998, 94).[7]

Still, "with the New Hampshire primary election still five weeks away,

Reagan had time to recover from the Iowa loss, and he became a very active campaigner in that state" (Winebrenner 1998, 102). Bush fought on against Reagan but eventually succumbed to the latter's star power. Bush consented instead to be his vice presidential running mate to bring the conservative and moderate wings of the party together, and the ticket went on to best Carter in November 1980. Though Bush did not win the nomination, "Iowa was credited with giving Bush an early boost," according to the *Des Moines Register*'s longtime political analyst David Yepsen.[8] That boost was to put Bush in the position that allowed him to win the nomination, and eventually the presidency, in his own right.[9]

In 1984 President Reagan no longer had to battle for Iowa's attention—but a spirited contest took place on the Democratic side. Iowa and New Hampshire hammered out a deal in which the Hawkeye State would host the first-in-the-nation Caucus, and the Granite State would host the first-in-the-nation primary eight days later.[10] The result was to shake up the Democratic nomination battle considerably.

Carter's former vice president, Walter Mondale, had the advantage of national prominence—and as a former Minnesota U.S. senator, regional affinity. The field in addition contained Ohio senator John Glenn, a national hero as the first American to orbit the earth, as well as McGovern, the 1972 Democratic presidential nominee, though his time seemed to be long past.

However, the field also contained McGovern's former campaign manager, Gary Hart, who was now himself a senator. Hart took his own page from McGovern's playbook and finished a distant second to Mondale (who received a towering 48.9% of the vote)—which was second nonetheless, meaning Hart (at 16.5% of the vote) had edged his former boss (at 10.3%) and left Glenn nowhere (with only 3.5%).[11]

Hart's surprising finish catapulted the charismatic, brilliant young senator into the national media. Buzz around his bid exploded, and support poured in (Hull 2004). Before the Caucus, Hart, at 13 percent in New Hampshire polling support, had been trailing both Mondale and Glenn, at 37 percent and 20 percent, respectively.[12] Yet eight days later, Hart pulled off an extraordinary upset win, capturing 37.3 percent of the first-in-the-nation Primary's vote, besting Mondale at 27.9 percent and Glenn at only 12 percent.[13]

However, as hot as his campaign had become, Hart was unable to build up his finances and ground forces fast enough to overcome Mondale's political machine. Hart simply could not capitalize on his newfound fame and popularity quickly enough to best the prohibitive front-runner, who benefited from his past lavish fund-raising and his strong institutional base within the party, including the staunch support of U.S. labor unions. Ultimately, Mondale took the nomination. Hart's deputy finance director, then a 14-year-old wunderkind named Scott Berkowitz, states flatly that had the campaign had the technology to raise money faster, they would have beaten Mondale in 1984—but it was not to be.[14]

The next Caucus saw an active battle on both the Republican and Democratic sides of the ticket. In 1988 other states, including Michigan, Kansas, and Hawaii, jockeyed for early position. While Michigan justifiably attracted the view of the media, the contests in the other early states drew little of Iowa's spotlight, which, says Winebrenner, "was now viewed by the candidates and the press as the 'official' starting point of the presidential campaign." Of the eight Democrats who ran for the nomination in 1988, in fact, a "majority pinned their hopes on Iowa and New Hampshire" (Winebrenner 1998, 137).

In a precursor to 2008, Yepsen reports that the '88 politicking actually began "shortly after the 1984 election" and that "after the 1986 midterm election, a presidential candidate was a regular feature somewhere in Iowa during 1987."[15] The media converged on the state. In 1988 "with sixteen candidates active at some time during the Iowa campaign and very competitive races in both parties, there was more to cover than in any previous caucus contest" (Winebrenner 1998, 167). Winebrenner concludes that "Iowa withstood the challenge to its first-in-the-nation status by Michigan, Hawaii, and Kansas, and later by the Super Tuesday states, and emerged stronger than ever in 1988" (p. 177).

A decade of farm-state doldrums sharpened the debate in Iowa to a razorlike edge, Winebrenner says, and in his view that made Caucus participants more likely to support neighbors most likely to understand their plight. What's more, he notes, the 1988 cycle "saw the growth of conservative and evangelical strength inside the Iowa GOP."[16]

As a result, this time Iowa was not as kind to George H. W. Bush. The then vice president paid the price for his association with the Reagan administration during the farm crisis of the 1980s. He did not carry a single county in the 1988 Iowa contest and ended up in third place, behind Senator Bob Dole of Kansas and televangelist Pat Robertson (see Hull 2007; Winebrenner 1998, 173).

Both Dole's and Robertson's reigns lasted but a moment. Robertson faded from view quickly, and the Bush operation turned its guns on Dole, leveling him in the New Hampshire Primary that followed.

Also riding Iowa's wave of farm-state angst were two midwesterners, Representative Dick Gephardt (D-Mo.) and Senator Paul Simon (D-Ill.), who topped the charts on the Democratic side, defeating prominent Massachusetts governor Michael Dukakis, who had made himself an agricultural laughingstock by suggesting that the country's farmers plant alternative crops, specifically Belgian endive.[17]

A laughingstock! Strong words, you say? Well, *Saturday Night Live*'s Jon Lovitz spoofed Dukakis, saying,

> I don't think you can lead without a vision . . . and I have a vision for America. I see purple mountains over Decchio; I see wooded valleys over Rugala; I see Escarol from sea to shining . . . [timer sounds] . . . sea. I know I'm running out of time, so let me conclude that with direction, purpose, a little oil and vinegar, and maybe some feta cheese, there is nothing we cannot do. Thank you.[18]

Belgian endive notwithstanding, the impact of Gephardt's win was undercut by the magnitude of Bush's defeat and failed to translate into success beyond Iowa. Senator Ted Kennedy (D-Mass.) said of the results, "Only eight years ago I finished second in Iowa, and my presidential campaign was finished. This year Mike Dukakis finished third, and he's on the way to the White House" (Winebrenner 1998, 172).

Iowa senator Tom Harkin, a prominent Democrat, chose to run for the presidency in 1992. Harkin's announcement "effectively ended the national importance of the 1992 Iowa precinct caucuses" (Winebrenner 1998, 189). Television commentator Patrick J. Buchanan, who mounted a primary challenge to incumbent President Bush, also chose not to contest Iowa.

Says Winebrenner, "The unanswered question in Iowa was how the outcomes of the 1988 and 1992 caucuses would affect the 1996 event," considering that the winners had lost the nominations and the third-place finishers had won them (p. 203). However, he says, "the candidates and the media apparently accepted Iowa as the 'official' starting point for the 1996 campaign" (p. 245). Senator Dole again won the Republican nod in Iowa, but Buchanan's surge into second wounded Dole's quest for the nomination, an early indication of the Kansan's vulnerability.

In March 1999 Texas governor George W. Bush held a commanding lead in the polls of likely caucusgoers in Iowa. Pollster Craig Tufty commented in the media that "support for George W. Bush runs deep and wide."[19] However, Governor Bush's support appeared a little anemic in comparison to front-runners of other years. For instance, even late in the summer of 1979, Reagan led the next closest candidate by 25 points in Iowa. Trailing the rest of the field badly, with 1 percent, was an unlikely dark horse named George Herbert Walker Bush (Winebrenner 1998, 82). Having learned that lesson, Governor Bush's campaign in 1999 organized heavily and carried the 2000 Caucus. The runner-up, publisher Steve Forbes, had also learned a lesson from his defeat in 1996 and built a Caucus organization instead of relying solely on television advertising. However, the decision of Senator John McCain (R-Ariz.) to skip the festivities in Iowa and focus on New Hampshire undercut Forbes's potential bonus.

On the Democratic side, the race between Vice President Al Gore and Senator Bill Bradley (D-N.J.) at first seemed heavily competitive. However, Gore had 20 field operatives in Iowa whose toils helped him gradually leave Bradley behind and score a substantial victory, staving off any potential upset.

In 2004 Governor Howard Dean (D-Vt.) dominated the Iowa race from midway through the pre-election year. His surge of momentum carried with it supporters nationwide; those from inside and outside the state swarmed to his cause in the Caucus. However, in an early fall assessment, the campaign of struggling former front-runner Senator John Kerry (D-Mass.) concluded that he was trailing badly enough on his home turf of New Hampshire that an Iowa defeat would likely spell ultimate disaster. Kerry engaged top grassroots hand Michael Whouley to assess his Hawkeye State organization, and the conclusion was that it was strong enough to win, were the candidate himself to take up the cause in a more disciplined and focused way.

Kerry did renew his focus in Iowa, while a series of Dean national stumbles undermined Democrats' faith in the front-runner's chances of winning the general election. The combination proved toxic to Dean, who placed a distant third in Iowa to Kerry and upbeat upstart Senator John Edwards (D-N.C.). That Caucus night might ultimately have cost Dean the nomination and thrown it to Kerry—but that is a matter for debate and discussion.

And debate and discuss we shall. From this backward glance, we can now peer forward, analyzing with more precision the impact Iowa has on the contests that follow it and on who becomes the party's nominee.

But before we do, let us cover one more item of business.

Iowa: Good or Evil?

What have analysts concluded, based on their studies of Caucus history, with respect to this book's fundamental question: is Iowa's first-in-the-nation Caucus a positive or negative force in presidential politics?

We can break down the findings into five basic questions.

- First, does Iowa matter to the outcome of the nomination? That is, does any of this really make a difference?
- Second, to what extent is Iowa a good place to hold a high-profile event of any kind? Does it have merits, that is, that might make it a place we would choose to hold an early nominating contest if we didn't already have one there?
- Third, to what extent is Iowa's caucus system more "closed" than a primary, and what are the upsides and downsides if it is?
- Fourth, what harm does Iowa's unrepresentative nature do in the process? Do its demographic skew and ideological extremity on both the left and the right harm the process, by discriminating against either minority or moderate candidates, for instance?
- Finally, to what extent is Iowa's placement normatively wrong? Is it rooting out candidates in a way we would rather not have happen?

Let us tackle these one at a time.

In 1976 and 2004 Iowa seemed to make a big difference in the outcome of the nomination. Let us drill down and examine studies of three different ways Iowa affects how Americans elect presidents.

What effects can doing well in Iowa have on national support—on "momentum"? What kind of media coverage can it cause? Which candidates does it selectively boost—and bust?

There is little doubt about the remarkable surges of momentum enjoyed by Iowa's upset winners. For instance, as a result of Bush's win in the 1980 Iowa Caucus, his poll support spiked from 6 to 24 percent (Robinson 1981, 203, cited in Winebrenner 1998, 95). In 1984 as we saw earlier, Gary Hart's much-hyped (though distant) second-place showing behind Walter Mondale almost tripled his pre-Iowa New Hampshire poll support of only 13 percent to a crushing 37.3 percent Granite State win.[20]

How can early states possibly shift support so fast? In his explication of momentum on the heels of the Iowa Caucus, Bartels (1989) argues that "although consequential at every stage, expectations matter most in situations where information is scarce—especially for relatively unknown candidates early in the primary season" (Bartels 1989, 133–34). This suggestion makes sense for the insurgent candidates who were trailing before an Iowa win; most of the American public had not been exposed to them, after all. What's more, the American public had also not had the time to carefully study these fresh new faces for flaws. All they knew was that someone they hadn't heard of had bested the old bulls of the party.

Thus, Bartels argues, Iowa's immediate result is that "the next morning, if recent history is any guide, America has a new political star." Writing in 1989, he notes that "this pattern has been repeated, with minor variations, in three recent primary seasons. Jimmy Carter in 1976, George Bush in 1980, and Gary Hart in 1984 each managed to parlay a 'better than expected' showing in Iowa into media attention, recognition, and public support sufficient to make a serious run at his party's nomination" (p. 121).

During the 1988 contest, Bartels argues, "the fact that neither of the Iowa winners could parlay his post-caucus momentum into real success in the rest of the campaign has led some commentators to downplay the likely significance of the Iowa caucus. . . . But the actual course of the 1988 campaign, both on Super Tuesday and thereafter, seems to belie this reasoning," as polling from the southern states reflected a modest but clear 5-percentage-point bump from Iowa and New Hampshire for both Dole and Gephardt (p. 143).

Concludes Bartels, "The candidates' real political identities may not always matter from the start, in the first few weeks after an exciting new candidate like Carter, Bush or Hart emerges from Iowa with momentum; but they matter in the end. The danger, from an institutional standpoint, is that by then it may be too late" (p. 135).

Is it too late by the time Iowa takes place? Winebrenner thinks so. He notes that no one since Carter has popped up in Iowa and ridden the crest all the way to the White House. "The only dark horse candidate to parlay success in the caucuses to a presidential nomination was Carter himself. The presidential campaign has changed since Carter successfully employed the Iowa/New Hampshire strategy," he claims, including the addition of Super Tuesday, front-loading, and the dominance of paid TV (1998, 179).

However, in 2004 John Kerry's national poll support quadrupled, from 7 percent before his Caucus victory to 29 percent after it.[21] This shift in support is very like that seen by Bush the elder 24 years before.

It appears that the presidential campaign has now changed twice. First, early adopters like McGovern in 1972 and Carter in 1976 were able to capitalize on Iowa's cachet without other candidates contesting the Caucus. By the time of Bush in 1980 and Hart in 1984, the balance had begun to shift. Ever more candidates competed in the state. A front-runner already loomed over their prospect. With television's growing dominance, they could not raise money fast enough or gather supporters cheaply enough to compete.

Today, as I argue in detail in Chapter 4, the balance has shifted again. Today, a trailing candidate *can* raise money fast enough and gather supporters cheaply enough to overcome a front-runner. Kerry may have proved it in 2004—though mortgaging his house and loaning his campaign $7 million didn't hurt.

Suspend judgment while we turn to Iowa's role in generating media coverage.

Certainly, the literature is unanimous in its finding that Iowa stands out in terms of media quantity. In his musings on the Iowa Caucus's impact in a "front-loaded" primary system, Nelson W. Polsby recounts a compelling statistic: "In 1984, according to an actual count of news coverage appearing on all three television networks plus in the *New York Times*, Iowa, with 2.5 percent of the U.S. population, received 12.8 percent of the total news coverage accorded the presidential race from January to June" (Polsby 1989, 149, citing Adams 1987).

In another work, Polsby provides a comparison of Iowa to Tennessee—a state with the same number of delegates at stake, 87—in 1980. Not surprisingly, it shows that coverage was utterly inconsistent between the two. Polsby looks at the total percentage of news coverage of the presidential selection process given over to state primaries and caucuses that year. CBS allotted 14 percent of all of its coverage to Iowa and UPI allotted 13 percent. To Tennessee? Nothing (Polsby 1983, 70).

As we saw in Chapter 1, one compelling study along those lines is Brady's (1989) regression analysis of the amount of media coverage relative to other caucuses, which controls for the number of delegates the state controls and the date of the event. Brady finds that Iowa received 243 times as much coverage as one would otherwise expect.

Brady summarizes his results for media coverage in both primaries and caucuses this way: "Being first matters. Having delegates matters." But it is important to note that Brady's Caucus equation finds that neither of the variables that represent the date of the event or the number of delegates is statistically significant in predicting media coverage—only the Iowa dummy variable is (Brady 1989, 97). So among caucus states at least, Brady's conclusion might be better put as "being Iowa matters."

According to Winebrenner, his *The Iowa Precinct Caucuses: The Making of a Media Event* is based on the theories of Thomas E. Patterson and Michael J. Robinson, especially the latter's concept of "medialities"—events that the media generate as artifacts of their institutional biases, such as their desire for hard news and their tendency to cover elections like horse races as opposed to contests of ideas and philosophies (see Patterson 1980, cited in Winebrenner 1998, ix).

Robinson underscores Bush's 1980 win in Iowa as one of the clearest "medialities" of that presidential campaign (1981, 196). In Bush's win over Reagan in 1980, Winebrenner reports, the media agreed with the candidates that Iowa was important—perhaps more important than Bush's narrow win merited. "Although the closeness of the contest was widely reported," he says, "it was secondary to the fact that Bush won. The media trumpeted his victory around the nation" (Winebrenner 1998, 94). And, Winebrenner says, Thomas Patterson's analysis of the 1976 election "suggests that media distortion of the Iowa caucuses stems from a structural bias in the way presidential elections are covered" (p. 7).

As a result of the media's biases, Winebrenner says, "the caucuses have become a media event with an impact on presidential politics totally out of proportion to the reality of their purpose or procedural methods" (p. ix).

So yes, Iowa generates a lot of press—probably more than its due.

What candidates in particular does Iowa help and harm? Wolfinger poses the question, "Just why does a primary defeat knock a candidate out of the race?" (Wolfinger 1989, 166). Some answers he provides are, first, that "candidates need contributions and donors are discouraged by the prospect that they will be wasting their money." Therefore Iowa particularly endangers those who are running without a large cache of resources—"betting on the come," as the expression goes.

Second, Wolfinger says, in a more extreme example of betting on the come, some candidates run hoping not just money but popularity will come after an early win. Such candidates, running "on spec" as Wolfinger describes it, simply never catch on if they fail to achieve that early win.

Finally, argues Wolfinger, Iowa menaces those without "an identifiable and relatively enthusiastic constituency." Those with such a following are "a good deal more immune" to Iowa's winnowing effect than other candidates, Wolfinger says, citing the examples of Ronald Reagan, Jesse Jackson, and Pat Robertson (Wolfinger 1989, 166).

In sum, Wolfinger argues that Iowa does not so much shoo candidates into the nomination as it does shoo them out the door. "While the outcome of the Iowa caucuses will not anticipate either party's eventual nomination," he says, "those same results will certainly produce fairly convincing evidence that some candidates are no longer in the race" (1989, 164). In a crowning phrase, Wolfinger adds, "Iowa is not so much a king-maker as a peasant-maker" (p. 164). Winebrenner agrees. "One constant about Iowa's impact on the presidential nominating process is the elimination or mortal wounding of presidential hopefuls who do poorly or fail to meet the expectations of their role" (1998, 180).

Does Iowa only make peasants, or does it also make kings?

On one hand, analyst Charles Cook says, "If you look at the last seven presidential elections, [of] the last 14 Democratic and Republican nominations, 13 out of 14 have gone to a candidate who won either the Iowa caucuses or the New Hampshire primary or both."[22] And no American has become president since 1972 without finishing at least third in Iowa.

On the other hand, it may be just New Hampshire that is playing the role of king-maker, while Iowa only plays the role of peasant-maker. Or, as John H. Sununu, governor of New Hampshire, put it, "The people of Iowa pick corn, the people of New Hampshire pick presidents."[23]

Polsby notes the candidates seem to think it matters for a state to be early in the process, even as far back as 1976. He looks at the amount of money candidates receiving public financing spent per vote in selected states in 1976 and 1980, based on when the contest occurred. He finds that the candidates the year Carter won the nomination spent more than ten times as much per vote in Iowa as in California, at the end of the process. And in 1980 that ratio had climbed to 60 to 1 (1983, 61).

Brady makes the point that "New Hampshire has a much better record of choosing the nominee precisely because Iowa precedes it." As he puts it, "Iowa has been important in almost every quadrennium because its caucuses have defined the field of contenders either by catapulting newcomers like McGovern, Carter, and Hart to the forefront and dashing the hopes of other hopefuls or by providing a clear-cut sense of the vulnerabilities of incumbents such as Ford in 1976 and Carter in 1980" (1989, 91).

One study I'm particularly fond of (Adkins and Dowdle 2001) bears out his deprecation of Iowa. Adkins and Dowdle built a model of how candidates perform in the rest of the nomination fight; they based the model in part on performance in Iowa and New Hampshire. They determine that "the New Hampshire primary obviously holds a greater influence on nomination forecasting than do the Iowa caucuses" and find instead that "the reality is that momentum generated by these contests only seems to assist also-ran candidates in displacing other also-ran candidates" (2001, 440). Instead, they find, the front-runner in the preprimary exhibition season is almost invariably the one who has come home to win the nomination.

Mayer (2004) has explored this possibility in a compelling study. In it, he constructs a model to test Iowa's impact on the New Hampshire Primary—and includes in it pre-Iowa polling data from the Granite State, to control for the Caucus status quo ante. He finds that, holding pre-Iowa poll standings constant, winning the Caucus has no statistically significant impact on the New Hampshire Primary's results (though placing second may, he finds) (p. 111). He also demonstrates that first- and second-place finishes in Iowa are not statistically significant predictors of ultimate primary performance, controlling for first- and second-place finishes in New Hampshire (p. 106). On the basis of these results, Mayer argues that "Iowa does have an impact on many races, but that impact is mediated through New Hampshire" (p. 107).

Like Winebrenner, Mayer discounted the Carter strategy's effectiveness in the post-1976 world. "What is all too rarely mentioned about the 1976 campaign," he says, "is that Carter's efforts in Iowa had received a huge boost from one other special circumstance: through most of 1975, he was the only major candidate campaigning there" (1996c, 63). He goes on to argue, "The importance of momentum has probably been overstated" (p. 63). Though momentum is the only way to explain the bounce of support dark horses like Carter, Hart, and Bush received after the event, he says, "in five of the last six contested nomination races, the pre-Iowa front-runner ultimately won the nomination" (p. 65).

Whether—and why—these studies stand up to scrutiny and replication is a matter for further exploration.

So, does Iowa matter? Certainly, it can move national polls. And it does generate an enormous amount of press coverage. It seems to badly harm trailing candidates who do poorly. But it is not as clear that it can affect who actually wins the nomination. That gives us a good basis from which to build. And build we shall—in the next chapter, which estimates Iowa's impact on the nomination.

TO WHAT EXTENT IS THE IOWA CAUCUS A GOOD HIGH-PROFILE POLITICAL EVENT?

One question theorists have pored over is whether the Iowa Caucus is a "good" forum for a political event of the magnitude of the first-in-the-nation Caucus—that is, what claim might it have, based on its very unrepresentativeness.

The Caucus's supporters (not so much in the literature as in the state parties) point to these aspects of it:

1. Politics in Iowa are competitive, with no one party exerting control.
2. Politics in Iowa are clean, with a long tradition of rectitude and respect.
3. Turnout is strong in Iowa, both in elections and in the Caucus itself, demonstrating a significant interest in politics.
4. Organization, not advertising, rules Iowa politics.

Winebrenner concedes that Iowa's politics are in fact competitive and clean, as defenders of the Caucus argue. How competitive? He points out that 32.4 percent of those registered to vote in 1996 were independents; that the state has reelected both liberal Democratic senator Tom Harkin and conservative Republican senator Charles Grassley, and that in 1996 Iowans gave four of five House seats to Republicans as they were reelecting Harkin statewide and handing the state to Clinton (1998, 17).

As far as Iowa's cleanliness goes, he cites their strict gift ban—with a $3 de minimis provision—and the dire political fallout suffered by figures who crossed ethical lines. (Of course, those familiar with the Mingo scandal, involving former state senator Al Sorenson, a Democrat from Sioux City, and an exotic dancer in tiny Mingo, Iowa, might think otherwise, as Sorenson managed to win his next reelection campaign and remain in public life.)

Winebrenner also notes that participation is high, with a voter registration rate of 83 percent in 1996, compared with 74 percent nationwide, and a turnout rate of 59 percent in 1996, compared with 49 percent nationwide. "The high levels of voter registration and participation in presidential elections," Winebrenner concedes, "are evidence that Iowans have strong feelings of citizen duty" (1998, 16).

How about turnout in the Caucus itself? Mayer's data do reflect that Iowa turnout is far higher in the Iowa Caucus than in other caucuses across the nation. In fact, in 1988 Iowa's turnout rate among Democrats was 12 percent, higher than that for Rhode Island's primary that year. In the same year among Republicans the turnout rate was 11 percent, higher than GOP turnout in *five* states with primaries (Mayer 2000, 128). Stone,

Rapoport, and Abramowitz also find a high level of Iowa turnout relative to other caucus states (1992, 1080). But of course, Mayer acknowledges, "it is well-established that considerably fewer people participate in caucuses than in primaries" (1996c, 145).

Overall, then, there is some inkling that Iowa itself may not be all that bad a place to hold a high-profile political event. But on the matter of whether organization still matters, and how television figures into the equation, we will have to turn to the evidence. Chapter 5 addresses this question—which tactics matter most in the Iowa Caucus.

TO WHAT EXTENT IS IOWA'S SYSTEM "CLOSED"— AND IS THAT GOOD OR BAD?

What is the operative difference between the Iowa Caucus—at which a straw poll is conducted and announced that night—and a primary? In what sense is it reportable what a caucus does when it has a vague impact on the number of delegates selected by the state? Says Winebrenner, "For all intents and purposes the caucuses have been turned into primary elections without the openness and controls that go along with primaries" (1998, 257).

Andrew E. Busch agrees that the line between the two is blurred in the Hawkeye State. "The highly publicized Iowa caucuses," he says, "the first major delegate selection event in most recent nomination races, are often described as 'the functional equivalent of a primary'" (2000, 13).

Of course, on an operational level, such a conclusion stands in contrast to the finding of Mayer's study of caucuses more generally. For instance, in an informal analysis, Mayer notes that "the seven caucuses I attended lasted, on average, about an hour and forty-five minutes." In a more standard primary format in 1992, Mayer says, "I calculated that the average voter was able to leave the polling place about seven minutes after arriving there" (1996c, 124).

Supporters of the Caucus make the contention that it is organization and time on task, rather than demagoguery, money, or advertising, that carry the day in Iowa. For instance, in 1988 and 1996, in spite of Iowa's unrepresentativeness, Winebrenner acknowledges, "it is also likely that organizational ability rather than ideology played the decisive role in Iowa and other caucus states" (1998, 22).

That said, other factors like money and commercials may be playing an increasing role in the state, some speculate, which appears to raise an interesting theoretical tradeoff. To the extent that the Caucus has become "open" in a way that progressives originally hoped (and seminal pro-party theorist E. E. Schattschneider would cordially dislike, to use Tolk-ien's phrase [1994, xvii]), it would also lose much of its retail politicking cachet.

Regardless, it is an open question whether organization at the grass-roots level still holds the key to success in the Iowa Caucus. If it does, it is a test not just of polls, focus groups, and advertising but also of the ability to mobilize Americans at the grassroots toward a common goal. But that will require empirical verification. Again, Chapter 5 will attempt to quantify the answer to this question.

TO WHAT EXTENT IS IOWA "UNREPRESENTATIVE"—
AND WHAT HARM CAN THAT CAUSE?

Political scientists have divided on how unrepresentative Iowa Caucus vot-ers are of the nation and how much it matters. For instance, Mayer (2000) finds that Caucus participants in general are "distinctly unrepresentative" and that this is so "no matter which group one uses as a standard of com-parison." He also finds that more-ideological candidates in 1988 and 1996 (the Reverend Jesse Jackson, televangelist Pat Robertson, and commentator Patrick Buchanan) did better in caucus states, while more-moderate candi-dates (Governor Michael Dukakis, Vice President Bush, and Senator Bob Dole) did better in primaries (Mayer 1996c, 132, 143).

Winebrenner (1998, 11), for his part, argues that the small-town, ag-ricultural state is not representative "demographically or ideologically" and thus advantages some and disadvantages others. Iowa is, he says, "a small, homogeneous, midwestern farm state largely composed of small cit-ies and rural areas. . . . Although no state can legitimately claim to mirror the national electorate, Iowa is less representative than many." He asserts, "There is little disagreement that demographically Iowa is representative only of itself and perhaps a few other prairie states" (p. 21).

On the ideological front, Squire says, "some Democrats also criticize Iowa on the grounds that those who participate in the party's caucuses are too liberal, giving support to candidates who are too far to the left to be successful in the general election" (Squire 1989, 11).

Hutter and Schier find that "Iowa caucus attenders and state convention delegates were similar in their presidential preferences and political opinions and displayed patterns similar to those found in other studies of leaders and followers" (1984, 431).

Some more general thoughts on representativeness are important as well. Lengle argues most generally that caucuses "are probably less demographically representative of the party membership than primary electorates" (1981a, 112). And though it is not specific to Caucus attendees, Samuel Patterson described Iowa most generally as defined by its "middleness" (1984, 83).

Finally, Stone, Rapoport, and Abramowitz identify the effect of the unique character of Iowa. Simply put, "Iowa . . . does not have large urban centers, it has a small minority population, its culture and economy are more heavily dependent on agriculture than many states, it has a lower than average crime rate, a higher than average literacy rate, etc. Of course, any state is unique, but many critics suggest that Iowa is more atypical than most" (1989, 21). Such a statement would seem to provide an initial answer to the question of representativeness.

Stone, Rapoport, and Abramowitz set about unraveling the Gordian knot of Iowa's ideological representativeness. Overall, they find that "if caucus-attenders generally are higher status, more committed to their party, and more ideological than the average citizen, the Iowa caucus-attender is less so" (1989, 22). However, they find that this is because the timing and importance of the Caucus drives up Iowa's turnout, thus moderating the Caucus attendees' demographics.

Overall, demographically, they find that "for education and income, which are resources facilitating participation, Iowa caucus-attenders over-represent higher status groups and underrepresent lower status categories in the Iowa and national electorates" (1989, 25). And in earlier studies (Stone 1982; Stone and Abramowitz 1983; Abramowitz and Stone 1984; Stone and Rapoport 1994), these scholars sought to demonstrate that Iowa's activists "balance their personal preferences with their desire to support a winner, and that the latter outweighs the former" (Stone, Rapoport, and Abramowitz 1989, 41). This Moderation Hypothesis may lead an ideologically unrepresentative sample of voters to choose a relatively representative (or at least electable) candidate. Thus, they say, "the interests of individual nomination participants and party organizations may not be as disparate as many critics of the contemporary process believe" (Stone, Rapoport, and Abramowitz 1992, 1074).

Again, the debate is still open here. To understand the impact of Iowa's demographic and ideological skews, we will have to investigate their empirical impact on presidential candidates' Caucus outcomes. Chapter 6 will address this question of what Iowa's demographic profile means to candidates campaigning there.

TO WHAT EXTENT IS A SYSTEM WITH IOWA FIRST NORMATIVELY WRONG?

To cap off our theoretical review of Iowa-specific writings, let's examine the fundamental question of whether placing the Caucus first is simply a mistake.

Is the current system that flawed? Wolfinger isn't so sure. He refers us to the pre-reform system, noting that "the disinterested leaders whose peer review provided nominees like Warren G. Harding and John W. Davis may have been pursuing interests no less parochial than [today's] whale savers and abortion fighters" (Wolfinger 1989, 168).

What's more, he argues, with respect to the argument that Iowa is a "peasant-maker," "It would be a substantial mistake to attribute this particular consequence of the Iowa caucuses to the Democratic party reforms of the 1970s, events that are so frequently blamed for the salient features of the nomination process we study. The best evidence for this is pre-reform primaries that were pretty effective peasant-makers" (1989, 164). Wolfinger goes on to cite Harold Stassen in 1948's contest in Oregon, the 1960 Wisconsin primary's effect on Hubert Humphrey, and LBJ's "unimpressive performances" in New Hampshire and Wisconsin (1989, 164).

Bartels points out, "Obviously, one way to avoid getting nominees without track records would be to replace the sequential nominating process beginning in Iowa on Monday night with a national primary system." However, that would doom less prominent (or well-funded) candidates from the start (1989, 136).

Winebrenner's conclusion is that "perhaps the stage is too small," with only 1.3 percent of all delegates chosen being selected (1998, 258). What's more, his final analysis is that "the evidence presented is mixed" but "Iowa may well mislead the nation about the political appeal of presidential candidates" (1998, 23).

The king of the Caucus, as it were, goes on to argue that "Iowa has become a pawn in the national electoral process. The 'nationalization' of politics has led to the injection of outside money, outside issues, and simply outsiders into local politics" (1998, 257). He is concerned by the transmogrification of a local political act into a national Kabuki dominated by the pols and the polls.

Geer agrees that the opening salvo of the campaign has too much impact, saying, "There are additional problems with the current system not related to the capacity of voters in primaries to choose good candidates. Given the long series of primary battles, the initial contests, particularly in New Hampshire and Iowa, assume a great deal of influence in the process" (1989, 126).

Says Squire, "The current system has problems—too much power is given to Iowa and New Hampshire to narrow the field of candidates. Chances are, however, that little will be done to change the current rules under which both parties contest their nominations" (1989, 13). However, Squire concludes, "the main point to keep in mind is that there is no perfect system which is guaranteed to produce ideal candidates" (1989, 13).

Of course, Squire says, the presidency is the only national office on the ballot in all 50 states. Thus the first step toward selecting a president must necessarily be national, whether it is located in Iowa, in Ohio, or in Idaho. (Which in turn raises the question of whether any state should be first.) But Squire's conclusion on the normative question of whether Iowa should possess its marquee place over the door to the nominating process is that "if any state is to be given sole possession of the first spot on the election calendar, Iowa is as good a choice as any" (1989, 13).

But to conclude, Winebrenner believes flatly that "the Iowa results are neither valid nor reliable indicators of the presidential preferences of delegates selected to succeeding levels in the caucus and convention process" (1998, 254). He has identified a key criticism not fully explored—or challenged—by another political scientist. If the underlying basis of the Iowa Caucus is flawed, so might its conclusions be.

The political science literature has a healthy debate over the role of the Iowa Caucus in the presidential nominating process:

- Though many thinkers are united in their belief that losing Iowa can devastate a campaign, fewer are convinced that winning Iowa can help assure a campaign of victory.
- Though they are united in their belief that Iowa is unrepresentative, a few disagree that it is harmful or wonder if it matters.
- Though they are united in their belief that the media provide dramatically disproportionate coverage to the Caucus, some go further to describe a warping of the lens that provides that coverage.
- Though the principles seem to be in place for a firm playing field on which to hold such a colossal contest, still there are questions about the role of money and advertising in Iowa.

Most important, the academy comes to different conclusions about the Caucus itself. For some, it is a pernicious and baseless popularity contest, dominating the process on behalf of people it does not well represent. For others, the pernicious and baseless popularity contest may as well be held with a backdrop of cornfields and pigsties.

This analysis has raised legitimate questions to which we can now turn. We need to settle the question of whether Iowa's Caucus matters in the first place, at least as well as we can. Does it have any impact on the nomination? If not, the other questions are moot. Chapters 3 and 4 will undertake that task.

Next, we need to understand whether the myth of Iowa is just that: Is it truly organization heavy, or has it become "the functional equivalent of a primary"? Can the Hawkeye State defend its contest on the ground that it forces candidates to undertake retail politics, or do television ads dominate the results in a way that makes it no different from any other state's nomination test? Chapter 5 tackles this question.

We need to understand the extent to which Iowa harms centrist and minority candidates. Does its lack of representativeness drag its results toward white, extreme candidates on both sides of the aisle? Chapter 6 addresses this one.

Finally, given those findings, we will have a reasonable basis on which to pose the overarching question: Is Iowa harming how America elects its presidents? And that will be Chapter 8's job.

So, to kick off, does Iowa matter?

THREE

Who Cares about *Iowa*?

The Caucus's Impact on the Nomination

It would be fair to say that John Kerry and Howard Dean behaved *differently* the night of the 2004 Iowa Caucus. Kerry's was a sober speech, projecting gravitas and seasoned—if long-winded—intelligence. That stood in contrast to what rapidly became known as the Dean Scream, the good doctor's wild rebel yell of enthusiasm and defiance.

And the whole country watched.

Was it that night that swung the nomination to Kerry? More generally, does the Iowa Caucus matter in determining the outcome of the presidential primary process? Can it almost single-handedly set a candidate on the course to nomination, as it appeared to do in 2004 and arguably did for Jimmy Carter in 1976?

The question is a crucial one, for three audiences. The first is political scientists. In the literature, a decades-old debate still rages today over Iowa's impact. Theorists want to know what role Iowa plays because of concerns over the two earliest states' representativeness. They also want to know because of attempts to measure the impact of post-reform party nomination rules that have generally opened up state contests while increasingly front-loading the process, arguably bolstering the Caucus's clout. If it turns out Iowa does not actually matter to the outcome, as some have argued recently, those debates are partially moot. Thus the literature needs and is seeking (with considerable success) more definitive answers on what role Iowa plays.

The second audience to whom Iowa's role matters is the public. There is a quadrennial quarrel over the party nomination rules that place Iowa and New Hampshire first, with many saying the states play too big a role in the process. As the Caucus approaches, inevitably columnists and pundits weigh in with their critiques of and (rarely) compliments on the two states' roles. At every convention, a faction of states tries to either eliminate or circumvent Iowa's and New Hampshire's early positions. If in fact Iowa's early position is not as powerful as the popular wisdom would have it, perhaps that debate should be redirected, as well.

Finally, let's not forget the politicians. In practical politics, candidates must start plotting immediately after each presidential election how they should allocate their time and resources. Virtually without regard to when you read this, most would-be presidential candidates are making journeys to Iowa and New Hampshire. If the long, frosty nights shaking hands outside Polk County Central Committee meetings have little impact on the nomination's outcome, why not skip the state—and its disproportionate demands in terms of organization and candidate time? That was certainly the conclusion of Pat Buchanan in 1992, John McCain in 2000, and both Wesley Clark and Joe Lieberman in 2004. Regardless of the outcome of those races, was their basic strategy correct?

Kerry's upset win over Dean in 2004 would suggest that the Caucus still has a major impact on the nomination fight, as it did in 1976 when Carter was thrust into the national limelight with a win there.

Along those lines, thinkers examining the Caucus's impact have focused on the disproportionate level of national media coverage it generates as well as on the resulting devastation it brings to poorly performing candidates.

But many have contested the Caucus's ultimate influence on the nomination's outcome. Several studies suggest the Caucus is of minimal predictive value in determining nominees and, rather, that the preprimary exhibition season and New Hampshire Primary dominate who is selected. Who is right?

To find out, it is worth starting with another look at the literature on the question, to see what problems are still troubling leading theorists. Then we can compile and review some data tools with which we can work on these problems. Those tools in hand, we can construct models to estimate answers to each one. Finally, we can explore those answers and their implications for the literature, the public, and of course our friends the politicians.

And before we get started, it's crucial to foreshadow one thing: This chapter's entire analysis is predicated on "traditional" momentum measures, that is, using the percentage won in the last contest as the operationalization of momentum—the technique that I use and my colleagues have used stretching back to Bartels (1988), who is in many ways momentum's maven. By contrast, the next chapter explores the possibility that technology is increasingly amplifying the momentum of major events in presidential races, including the Iowa Caucus. Thus the exploration of traditional momentum that follows is by no means our last word on what Iowa means to the presidential nomination.

Four Questions on Iowa's Role in the Primary

The literature contains a long-running battle over the true impact of the Iowa Caucus on candidates and, more to the point, whether winning it still represents a legitimate step toward the White House, even for dark horses.

On one side are those who underscore the remarkable surges of media and momentum enjoyed by Iowa's upset winners and the disproportionate amount of money spent there (Patterson 1980; Robinson 1981; Bartels 1989; Brady 1989; Polsby 1989; Winebrenner 1998). And whether or not it is a king-maker, the Caucus is universally acknowledged as a "peasant-maker" (Wolfinger 1989; Winebrenner 1998).

On the other side are those who make the not-contradictory point that Iowa may never again generate a Carter-style wave sweeping to the White

House (Winebrenner 1998; Mayer 1996b). Likewise, many theorists point out that Iowa's role is mediated by performance in New Hampshire in some way (Mayer 2004, 107; see also Brady 1989; Adkins and Dowdle 2001).

However, recent studies on Iowa and New Hampshire focus mainly on who wins or places in Iowa, as opposed to a continuous measure of overall performance in the state. They don't include 1976 and 2004, which are crucial to understanding Iowa's role. And they have not yet nailed down in what way New Hampshire mediates Iowa's momentum.

This literature seems to leave four questions we should address to understand Iowa's role in the nomination:

- First, does New Hampshire swamp Iowa's explanatory power, even using Iowa performance rather than just winning or placing in Iowa as the predictor and adding in 1976 and 2004 to the calculus?
- Second, to what extent does Iowa influence New Hampshire, again using continuous variables rather than dummy variables for top finishes?
- Third, assuming it is true that Iowa's role is swamped by New Hampshire and that it plays only a modest role in predicting Granite State outcomes, what more can we say about how the first-in-the-nation Primary is mediating the first-in-the-nation Caucus?
- Finally, we should just check: is Iowa's role changing?

Gauges for Iowa's Role in the Primary

This book's models are built on the pooled cross-sectional and time-series[1] database of candidates' level of effort, performance on various fronts, and activist assessments, all from 1976 to 2004, which I built over the course of the last seven years.[2] To answer the questions in this chapter, that database was bolstered with measures of candidates' performance in Iowa, New Hampshire, and the presidential primary popular vote writ large, as well as measures of success in the pre-election-year exhibition season—also known as the invisible primary.

Those variables break down roughly into national-level and state-level measures. The national-level factors include how the candidate was faring in national polls against his opponents before Iowa, as well as how much money the candidate had raised relative to his competitors—both standard measures of exhibition season performance in the literature (see, e.g., Adkins and Dowdle 2001). The national factors also include the candidate's share of the popular vote over the entire course of the primary.

The state-level factors include the number of candidates in the Iowa field, pre-Iowa New Hampshire poll strength, and of course vote share in the Iowa Caucus and the first-in-the-nation New Hampshire Primary. Those factors are examined briefly one by one below.

PRIMARY POPULAR VOTE SHARE

Within my dataset, primary performance is measured simply using Primary Popular Vote Share, the percentage of the total votes cast in all states' primaries and caucuses that each candidate won. That information is derived from *America Votes*, the semiannual compendium of election statistics (Scammon, McGillivray, and Cook 1996, 2000).

Note that the total number of primary votes includes those cast in Iowa and New Hampshire, which would tend to inflate slightly the explanatory power of those two states. However, considering that they represent only 2 percent and 0.5 percent, respectively, of that vote, I preferred to use the official total rather than factor the two states out. A future study should examine the impact of pursuing that course, but I believe the impact on the results would be minimal.[3] For some further questions and caveats about those data, see Appendix A.

IOWA CAUCUS VOTE SHARE

Each candidate's Iowa performance is measured using Iowa Caucus Vote Share, simply the percentage of the vote won by each candidate in each given race. The results are drawn from publicly available sources, especially the *Des Moines Register*. The relationship between Iowa Caucus Vote Share and Primary Popular Vote Share is shown in Figure 3.1.

A candidate's performance in the Iowa Caucus is obviously not the

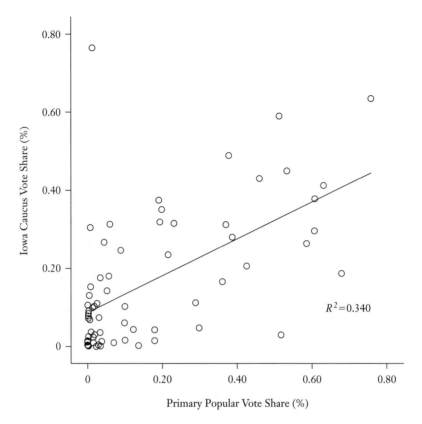

Figure 3.1. Relationship between Iowa Caucus Vote Share and Primary Popular Vote Share

sole determinant of his performance in the primary process. Information on Iowa performance alone allows us to explain about one-third of the variation in a candidate's primary performance (the bivariate regression R^2 is 0.340).

NEW HAMPSHIRE VOTE SHARE

By contrast, the linear relationship between New Hampshire and Primary results is very strong, as Figure 3.2 demonstrates. New Hampshire Vote Share, namely, the percentage of the Granite State primary vote also drawn

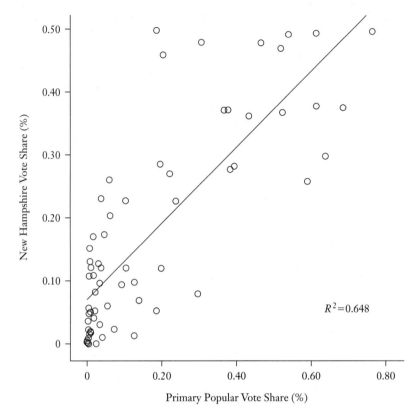

Figure 3.2.   Relationship between New Hampshire Vote Share and Primary Popular Vote Share

from publicly available sources, especially Gregg (1993),[4] explains two-thirds of the variation in candidate primary performance ($R^2 = 0.648$).

NATIONAL FUND-RAISING SHARE

For my database, the 1976–2004 national fund-raising data are drawn from Federal Election Commission reports and adjusted to 2004 dollars.[5] In all models, the basis of National Fund-Raising Share is the candidate's receipts for the third and fourth quarters of the pre-election year. The variable used is a candidate's percentage of the total dollars raised by all major candidates[6] of his party during that period. (For a discussion of why only half-year totals were used, see Appendix A.)

National fund-raising is commonly employed to gauge candidate performance during the exhibition season. Its relationship with a candidate's primary performance appears weaker than that with either Iowa or New Hampshire performance, but there still appears to be a correlation (Figure 3.3). As we will see, controlling for national polling strength and fund-raising produces an interesting empirical result when estimating primary performance.

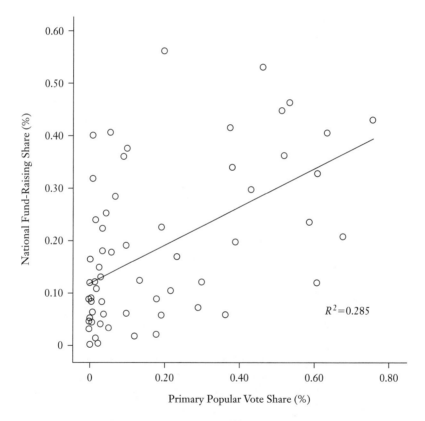

Figure 3.3. Relationship between National Fund-Raising Share and Primary Popular Vote Share

NOTE: National Fund-Raising Share is the candidate's share of active same-party candidates' total money raised during the second half of the pre-election year.

NATIONAL POLLING SUPPORT

I also gathered data on National Poll Support relative to the other candidates in the primary contest. Those data, drawn from the Gallup Poll closest to the Iowa Caucus, offer slightly less explanatory power over primary performance than New Hampshire performance but still a substantial amount, explaining 59.3 percent of Primary Popular Vote Share's variation, as Figure 3.4 shows.

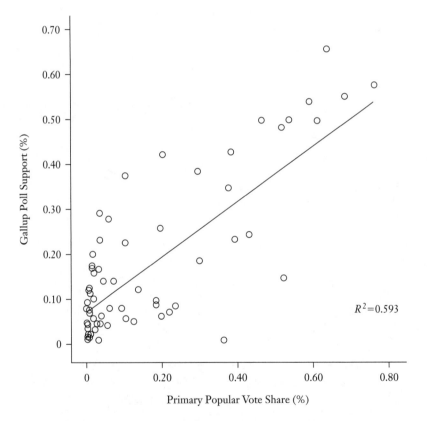

Figure 3.4.   Relationship between Gallup Poll Support and Primary Popular Vote Share

 NOTE: Gallup Poll Support is based on raw Gallup totals, scaled to include only candidates reaching the Caucus, then filled using Share of Field and National Fund-Raising Share.

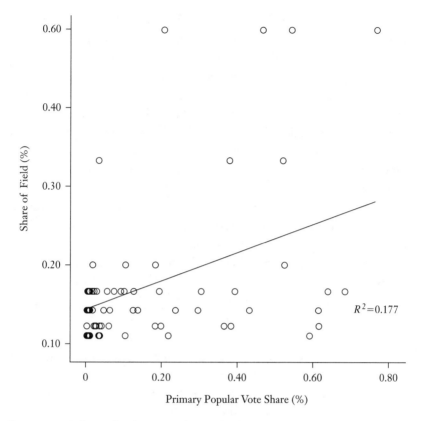

Figure 3.5.   Relationship between Share of Field and Primary Popular Vote Share

SHARE OF THE FIELD

Finally, the models include a theoretically important control for the Share of Field that the candidate represents at the beginning of the primary process (Figure 3.5). We would assume that a major factor in a candidate's primary vote total is the number of candidates he faces. In 2000 Al Gore and Bill Bradley faced off in a mano a mano duel for the Democratic nomination. By contrast, in 1996 Bob Dole was overrun with top-tier opponents—ten figured in the national polling before the primaries began—which would have a dramatic effect on his early vote totals and his final share of the vote. Yet those differences in primary performance have little to do with a candidate's strength.

To control for this artifact, we can include the percentage of the field that the candidate originally represented. It would be a factor more linearly related to percentage of the vote share than number of candidates in the field, while still capturing the same information. It has limited explanatory power ($R^2 = 0.177$), but regardless it is important theoretically and therefore will be included as a control in every model in this study.

Note that this model does not include a measure of endorsements or press coverage, two additional common metrics of success in the exhibition season. The model might also include a measure of front-loading, such as those used in the comprehensive study on the topic by Mayer and Busch (2004). After all, over the years, party leaders have explicitly acknowledged that they have tweaked primary rules to determine a winner more quickly and preserve their resources for the general election. That helps explain why nominees pile up larger and larger shares of the primary popular vote, which is not reflected in this chapter's models. The addition of any of those factors would strengthen future explorations.

Finally, it should be underscored that other, far more sophisticated models of primary vote performance can be found and come highly recommended (Bartels 1988; Norrander 1993; Adkins, Dowdle, and Steger 2002; Mayer 2004; Cohen, Noel, and Zaller 2004). The purpose of this study is not to compete with or replicate those models but merely to measure Iowa against the exhibition season and New Hampshire Primary. In fact, later chapters are explicitly predicated on bolstering those more thoroughgoing approaches to forecasting primary outcomes.

Measuring Iowa's Influence

With these tools in hand, let us turn to the four questions we should answer to determine the baseline role that Iowa and New Hampshire play in the outcome of the nomination fight, before we try to factor in technology's role in the next chapter:

1.   Does New Hampshire indeed mediate Iowa's influence on ultimate primary performance?

2. To what extent does Iowa influence New Hampshire, controlling for the effects of the pre-Caucus political landscape?
3. Granting that Iowa's role is swamped by New Hampshire, how can we describe how the latter mediates the former?
4. Is Iowa's role changing?

IOWA VERSUS NEW HAMPSHIRE: IT'S THE GRANITE STATE BY A LANDSLIDE

To address whether New Hampshire outperforms Iowa as a predictor of primary performance, we can build a basic model that includes both Iowa and New Hampshire performance for each candidate, using both to explain the proportion of the total primary vote a candidate wins, controlling for exhibition season performance and number of candidates in the field. Then using ordinary least squares (OLS) regression, we can estimate the independent impact of Iowa and New Hampshire performance on ultimate primary performance. (For details of the model, see Table B.1 in Appendix B).

The answer is stark. Controlling for New Hampshire results and measures of exhibition season performance, Iowa is not a statistically significant predictor of overall primary performance. That finding reinforces findings by both Adkins and Dowdle (2001) and Mayer (2004), even including 1976 and 2004 results and employing a continuous measure of Iowa performance rather than a dummy variable.

According to this model, then, controlling for New Hampshire's influence on the nomination, we cannot rule out the possibility that Iowa has none at all.

WHAT IS IOWA'S EFFECT ON NEW HAMPSHIRE?
SOME IMPACT, BUT HARD TO QUANTIFY

So New Hampshire appears to be standing between the Caucus and the final primary result. Win in Iowa and lose in New Hampshire, that is, and you risk losing every whit of momentum you gained, our 1976–2004 estimate seems to say.

If that is so, we should measure how much of a role Iowa's outcome plays in explaining New Hampshire Primary results, controlling for the impact of the exhibition season, as well as for pre–New Hampshire polling. That is, given the political landscape nationally and in the Granite State before the Caucus takes place, what effect does the Caucus have?

We can also build a straightforward model to address this question, using OLS regression to measure the independent impact of Iowa Caucus Vote Share on New Hampshire's results. Note once more that Iowa Caucus Vote Share is a continuous variable, a distinction from the Adkins and Dowdle and Mayer models that were (understandably) more focused on winning or placing in Iowa and New Hampshire than on overall impact. (For details of the model, see Table B.2 in Appendix B.)

The results here in terms of quantifying Iowa's impact are mixed. On one hand, Iowa is one of only two significant predictors of a candidate's New Hampshire performance and, along with New Hampshire polling, swamps the exhibition season measures of national fund-raising and Gallup polling, as well as the candidate's share of the field. In fact, none of those three controls are even significant, so we cannot reject the null hypothesis that they have no independent effect on New Hampshire Vote Share, controlling for Iowa and a candidate's standing in pre-Caucus New Hampshire polls.

On the other hand, looking closely at the model's results, we see that quantifying Iowa's impact is difficult. The model estimates that for every percentage point a candidate wins in Iowa, he gains about an eighth of a percentage point in New Hampshire, holding other factors constant. But the standard error is high; the confidence interval is such that we can say with only 95 percent confidence that a candidate would gain between a sixteenth and a quarter of a percentage point, all things equal. Such results could be decisive, but they are hardly overwhelming.

It is also important to qualify that this is by no means a fully specified model of New Hampshire performance. Were we to try to measure Iowa's actual impact more exactly, we might want to control for candidate level of effort in New Hampshire. For instance, a more fully specified model might include candidate choices such as television advertising, total spending in the state, and press coverage in the state. Campaigns matter, after all, and candidate choices in Iowa likely overlap with their choices in New Hampshire in ways that amplify the apparent impact of the Iowa Caucus Vote

Share variable in our model. Pre-Iowa New Hampshire polling captures most of these campaign effects but not the campaign effects of tactics like ads, (non-Iowa) earned media, and direct mail in the closing eight days of the campaign after the Caucus.

But that wasn't the question. The question was, controlling for the exhibition season and pre-Caucus New Hampshire polling, whether Iowa's results had a significant relationship with New Hampshire results. All qualifications aside, we can say with reasonable assurance that the answer to that question is yes. The first-in-the-nation Caucus matters to what happens in the first-in-the-nation Primary, even if how much is an open question.

HOW NEW HAMPSHIRE "MEDIATES" IOWA: FILTERING OUT GEOGRAPHIC BIAS

So Iowa has no impact on the nomination, controlling for New Hampshire, and has only a modest impact on New Hampshire itself. But why? What on-the-ground realities explain this empirical result?

To find out, I estimated a series of models to test the impact of each of Iowa's cycles on the primary. That is, I created a dummy variable for each presidential year from 1976 to 2004, and then I multiplied each by candidates' Iowa Caucus Vote Share to create eight interaction terms. Figure 3.6 shows the results.

Picture an enormous red flag waving before you. Only one of these standardized regression coefficients is in fact statistically significant at $p <$ 0.05. So we cannot reject the null hypothesis that Iowa had no impact on the nomination in any year other than 2004 ($p = 0.028$).

But granted, the results are instructive. They hint—and it is only a hint—that the Caucus initially had some modest impact on the nomination in 1976 and 1980, a result that by 1984 had faded almost entirely. They hint that in 1988 and especially in 1992 Iowa success was negatively correlated with primary success and may have somehow damaged those candidates who were successful in Iowa. Then, starting in 1996 and even more so in 2000, Iowa's impact may have begun to climb again.

We can say with reasonable certainty that in repeated sampling we would expect to randomly get an effect as large as the 2004 result in less than 3 percent of cases were its impact on the nomination zero. That is a hedging way of saying that in 2004 Iowa mattered to the outcome of

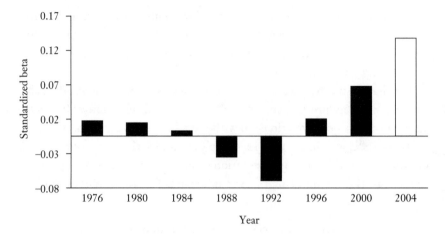

Figure 3.6. Impact of Iowa Caucus on candidate nomination performance by year, 1976–2004

NOTE: Standardized beta results for year–Iowa Caucus Vote Share interaction terms within Iowa versus New Hampshire Model. Only the 2004–Iowa Caucus Vote Share interaction is statistically significant.

the primary—controlling for the effects of New Hampshire. That is, in 2004 Hawkeye State results were no longer fully mediated by the Granite State.

Fair enough, these are mostly highly tentative results, and nothing on which we could base any conclusions. So let's reason through why the relatively spectacular pattern in Figure 3.6 might exist and test *that* proposition.

First of all, Carter in 1976 and then Bush in 1980 took advantage of Iowa's relative obscurity when no one else was trying there. By 1984 Hart was dogging Mondale hard in the state, competing for the Carter-Bush surge—and it paid off for him, at least in the short term. So by 1984 Iowa was fully competitive.

The more important mysteries, it seems, are 1988 and 1992. How could doing well in Iowa harm a candidate, controlling for New Hampshire? Any student of the Caucus will tell you the likely answer: The 1988 and 1992 results were badly skewed by home-state geography. In 1988 Dick Gephardt won the Caucus from his home base across the southern border in Missouri, and Bob Dole won it from nearby Kansas. Both went on to be badly beaten in New Hampshire and to lose the nomination. And in 1992 Iowa senator

Tom Harkin made moot the entire contest, dominating the outcome in Iowa but going nowhere in New Hampshire and the rest of the country.

In 1996 Dole won the Caucus again. Buchanan then edged him in New Hampshire, but Dole went on to capture the nomination anyway. In 2000 both front-runners, Bush and Gore, beat their competitors in Iowa. Bush then lost New Hampshire to McCain—but went on to capture the nomination anyway. And in 2004, of course, Kerry badly upset Dean in Iowa, beat him again in New Hampshire—along with Lieberman and Clark, who had both skipped Iowa—and ran away with the nomination.

So here's a theory: could it be that what New Hampshire is really doing is filtering out Iowa's geographic bias? That is, when the first caucus selects a candidate more because of midwestern affinity than anything else, the first primary promptly trounces him and restores order to the race. This we can test.

Entering a dummy variable just for Tom Harkin, the results are clear. (For details of the model, see Table B.3 in Appendix B.)

Controlling just for the anomalous result of Senator Harkin's 1992 bid, Iowa has a significant, positive impact on the nomination ($p = 0.035$), even controlling for New Hampshire. The Harkin variable is likewise significant, and in the expected negative direction ($p = 0.032$). According to this estimate, every additional percentage point a candidate wins in Iowa adds about a quarter of a percentage point to his final Primary Popular Vote Share, controlling for the Iowa Favorite Son and other factors in the model. Note also the substantial boost to the model when controlling for the Harkin anomaly. The model's R^2 rises from 0.729 to 0.793; the adjusted R^2 rises from 0.708 to 0.773; and the F-statistic rises from 33.960 to 38.961, both of which are highly significant ($p < 0.001$).

So here's the answer. New Hampshire has mediated Iowa in at least one important way: it knocked Tom Harkin end over end, eliminating Iowa's most significant deviation from its responsibility to select quality national candidates. Put another way, New Hampshire filtered out Iowa's favorite-son error in 1992.

Taking this analysis one step further, we should check to see whether New Hampshire is filtering out *both* the favorite-son lapse and other geographic bias more generally. To do so, we can add to our model a variable for home-state geography, Home State Near Iowa, that is, candidates hailing from states near Iowa—including all border states and Kansas, which is a few miles away from being a border state. (For details of this model, see Table B.4 in Appendix B.)

It appears as though home-state geography alone is not a significant predictor of primary vote share ($p = 0.547$), and it has virtually no impact on the other estimates within the model. But perhaps this should not be too surprising. As we will see in later chapters, home-state geography is not a statistically significant predictor of Iowa Caucus Vote Share, either. As a result, there may be little actual geographic bias to filter out.

And a less naïve way to understand the result is that some candidates have managed to parlay their midwestern credentials into Iowa success and some have not. In fact some, like Bob Dole and Dick Gephardt, have at times successfully leveraged those credentials (1996 and 1988, respectively) and have at other times failed to (1980 and 2004, respectively). The picture of midwestern candidates is cloudy enough that we cannot see it clearly through the filter of New Hampshire we have placed on this model.

REGARDLESS OF HOME-STATE GEOGRAPHY,
IOWA'S IMPACT SEEMS TO BE INCREASING

We have already seen that without controlling for home-state geography 2004's Iowa impact on the nomination was significant and positive. Running this analysis again, we can see that controlling for home-state geography has no impact on 2004's impact or significance. The implication here is that, regardless of Iowa's home-state bias, the state's results appear to matter more every presidential year (Figure 3.7).

Why is that? What could be causing the Iowa Caucus's impact to swell such that in 2004 it finally emerged from behind the New Hampshire Primary? Well, that of course raises the initial question of the chapter again. . . .

Who Cares about Iowa?

Back to Des Moines, 2004. Kerry has just dealt Dean a crushing blow in the Caucus. The media has klieg lights focused on both, highlighting Kerry's confident verbosity and Dean's never-say-die raving. On that night, America was a snapshot of 1976, when Carter was suffused in the glow

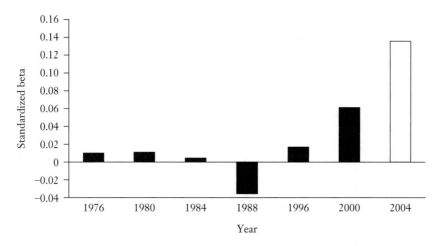

Figure 3.7. Impact of Iowa Caucus on candidate nomination performance by year when controlled for Favorite Son and Home State Near Iowa, 1976–2004

NOTE: Standardized beta estimates for year–Iowa Caucus Vote Share interaction terms, with Favorite Son and Home State Near Iowa variables. Only the 2004–Iowa result interaction is significant. The year 1992 was not included because, when controlling for Favorite Son, its results are actually highly negative and Favorite Son highly positive, though neither is statistically significant.

of his Iowa win, casting a long shadow over his bested competitors. Both Carter and Kerry went on to capture the nomination. And in the decades between, candidate after candidate has wrestled with the role the Hawkeye State plays in the presidential primary process. After all these years, what can we say about the traditional impact of carrying the Iowa Caucus?

For one, we have found that, statistically at least, New Hampshire does ring more true than Iowa as a bellwether, even factoring in 1976 and 2004. Controlling for the first-in-the-nation Primary's results, the first-in-the-nation Caucus's results are not statistically significant in predicting a candidate's performance in the overall primary vote, holding exhibition season performance and the size of the field constant.

We have also found that Iowa is to some extent a bellwether of New Hampshire. Our results show that the Caucus leaves some imprint on Granite State decisions: Iowa results are stronger predictors of New Hampshire results than exhibition season measures and size of the field. However, controlling for pre-Iowa New Hampshire polling, the Caucus is statistically significant but has an impact of only between a sixteenth and a quarter of a percentage point for every percentage point won.

Here's where it gets more interesting. A year-by-year analysis of Iowa's impact on the nomination gave us a hint both that home-state geography might be playing a role and that Iowa's role itself may be changing.

Accordingly, it seems that all by himself Tom Harkin obscures Iowa's role in nomination outcomes. Controlling for this favorite son, using a continuous measure of Iowa performance, and including 1976 and 2004 in the model, Iowa Caucus Vote Share is statistically significant and positive over the entire 1976–2004 period. The model's estimate is that for every percentage point a candidate wins in Iowa, he gains about a quarter of a percentage point of final primary vote share, but only when holding constant the impact of the one favorite son who has run for the nomination from Iowa (a calculus that may have helped persuade Iowa governor Tom Vilsack, who was briefly a 2008 candidate for president but actually trailed in Iowa polls, to step aside).

Finally, we saw that controlling for both Favorite Son and Home State Near Iowa, Iowa's impact still appears to be increasing. What is more, in 2004, for the first time, its impact was statistically significant without controlling for home-state geography. That raises snarled questions—questions the next chapter aims to untangle.

The bottom line is that, empirically, traditional momentum from doing well in the Hawkeye State has a small, clear impact on a presidential campaign's ultimate performance—but an impact that is filtered by performance in the Granite State.

But what about nontraditional momentum? After all, in 1976 Carter surprised the field. With candidates more prepared for a shock in Iowa, his feat was never replicated—until 2004. Is it possible that the reason is that political technology is increasing the importance of all major momentum inflection points of the campaign, including Iowa? Today candidates have geometrically increasing access to the fabulously fast fund-raising available online, the ability to accept swarms of supporters through websites, and the cheap communication line e-mail opens with those supporters. Would that not explain Kerry's tectonic shift after the Caucus? Would it not explain why Iowa's impact was statistically significant for the first time in 2004?

To coin a phrase, is momentum evolving into "e-mentum"?

The next chapter explores that possibility.

From the "Big Mo" to "E-mentum"

Technology and Early States' Emerging Impact

The morning after his victory over Ronald Reagan in the 1980 Iowa Caucus, George Bush the elder was chatting with Bob Schieffer on the CBS *Morning* show about his prospects in New Hampshire and he let drop one of his many cultured pearls of wisdom. "What we'll have, you see," Bush said, "is momentum. We will have forward 'Big Mo' on our side, as they say in athletics."

Schieffer asked, "'Big Mo?'"

A cordial Bush responded, "Yeah, 'Mo,' momentum" (Bartels 1988, 123).

Or, described more simply—and ironically, in the longer term—by Gary Hart in 1984 after doing modestly well in Iowa and seeing attention on him explode, "You can get awful famous in this country in seven days" (Bartels 1988, 123).

Awful famous is right, in his case. And until 2004, the open question was whether a presidential candidate could ever again get awful famous enough fast enough to pull off what Jimmy Carter did in 1976: riding a win in Iowa all the way to the nomination.[1] John Kerry started out a more formidable candidate, who held the front-runner title for months, granted. Also, he had a crucial advantage: personal wealth. Just before the Caucus, with every campaign scraping nickels together, Kerry mortgaged his home and dumped $7 million into his campaign coffers—a critical doubling down that must have contributed to his victory both in Iowa and in the nomination.[2]

Another key factor in Kerry's victory was the appearance of Jim Rassmann,[3] the (Republican) soldier whose life Kerry saved on March 13, 1969, in Vietnam.[4] And his mid-2003 engagement of Michael Whouley, the organization whiz who served Clinton and Gore as well, was the last, and perhaps decisive, one.

Nevertheless, in Dean he also toppled a front-runner far more formidable than Carter's competitors. And regardless of how Kerry reached victory, the impact of the early key events in 2004—Iowa and New Hampshire—seemed to have an important effect on the race, one worth verifying empirically.

But the argument of this chapter is that John Kerry did not ride the same Big Mo that swept Jimmy Carter to the White House, George Bush to the vice presidency, and Gary Hart into peaceful intellectual obscurity. He rode a different kind of momentum altogether: a microchip-driven, high-tech tidal wave that carried him farther faster than it was possible for a candidate to travel in 1976, 1980, or 1984. This new kind of momentum, I argue, amplifies key events in presidential races by flowing dollars and supporters into the campaign faster than it was ever possible to in the past, using Web-based, e-mail-linked, blog[5]-boosted online sign-up and fundraising tools.

Call it "e-mentum."

To test this hypothesis empirically, this chapter adds two models to those in the previous chapter. These are based on the same original database stretching back to 1976 and include new 2004 results as well. It updates the last chapter's traditional-momentum models to add a measure of e-mentum to the mix, in an attempt to identify, based on the technological tools a candidate employs, any statistically significant increase in Iowa's impact on either the nomination or New Hampshire. It then uses those revised models to estimate quantitatively what additional impact e-mentum may be giving to Iowa.

A peek at the results up front: as we saw in the last chapter, controlling for exhibition season factors and New Hampshire results, Iowa is not a significant predictor of ultimate primary performance and has a limited impact on New Hampshire. But adding *any of three* e-mentum factors—Internet metrics based on candidates' e-mail communication, online sign-up, or website traffic—makes Iowa highly significant and a powerful influence in both contests over the entire 1976–2004 time period. (Likewise, with its e-mentum factored in, New Hampshire's already obvious impact on the nomination becomes even more stark.)

Put another way, you cannot understand Iowa's changing impact on the nomination over that time period *without* taking e-mentum into account.

Momentum Dominates Our Understanding of the Nomination—and History

The overall question of whether e-mentum is on the rise is important because past studies are crammed with exquisitely accurate estimates of the impact of momentum on the state-by-state dynamics of both primary and general election presidential politics (see for instance Bartels 1988, 1989; Brady 1989; Norrander 1993; Mayer 2004; Cohen et al. 2004). If momentum's nature is in fact changing, we should begin to understand that change.

We should reexamine the history of this specific aspect of the Caucus, just briefly. As we have seen, in 1980 George Bush the elder won the Iowa Caucus but could not capitalize on his Big Mo, and the same is true of Gary Hart. In 1988 Dick Gephardt suffered the same fate, as did Bob Dole the same year.

In 1992 Pat Buchanan posed a significant challenge to incumbent president George H. W. Bush in New Hampshire but failed to mount more than an insurgent campaign. By 2000 John McCain could demonstrate that the Internet allowed candidates to ride momentum to enormous fund-raising totals, though he also was not quite able to translate a New Hampshire win into the GOP nomination.

In 2004 the Internet played a crucial role in helping Howard Dean raise upwards of $50 million during his meteoric rise and fall. In Iowa, as the race shifted, e-mentum based just on early primary state wins may have for the first time allowed cash-strapped candidates like Kerry and Edwards to siphon off enough resources quickly enough from the online community to fight another day. Kerry galloped up the same online money trail Dean blazed. In the wake of Kerry's Iowa Caucus victory, the ultimate nominee was able to raise $26 million in just two months—powered by $18 million flowing in over the Internet, $2.6 million of it on a single day following his Super Tuesday victories.

That's a lot of money.

Dean took to the stage in Des Moines on January 19, 2004, defeated after having reportedly led into battle the largest Internet army ever assembled in politics. If the howl he let out was any indication, the Internet's perceived potential to transform American politics took a lashing in the 2004 Iowa Caucus. But perhaps the opposite was true. Perhaps the Internet's real impact in 2004 was in amplifying Dean's momentum before the Caucus, and then amplifying that of whatever candidate happened to be riding the crest of the Big Mo afterward.

If that is the case, since momentum pervades the literature of presidential politics, our thinking about its role might need to change, especially when looking forward to 2008. All the crucial inflection points in the presidential campaign—the Iowa Caucus, the New Hampshire Primary, Super Tuesday, the party conventions, the presidential debates—may need to be reevaluated, taking into account this new technology-driven factor, e-mentum.

Measuring Internet Activity and Iowa E-mentum

To find out what role the Internet is playing in amplifying early primary states, especially Iowa, I turned back to data from a survey I conducted in Iowa just before the 2004 Caucus, which asked active Iowa Republicans and Democrats (former caucusgoers and those voting in the last two primary elections, respectively), for each 1996, 2000, and 2004 candidate, the following:

- Had they signed up online as a supporter of the candidate?
- Had they received an e-mail from the candidate?
- Had they visited the candidate's website?
- Had they read an Internet news story or commentary on the candidate?

While measuring Internet activity from 1996 and 2000 using a 2004 survey is admittedly suspect, recall data are better than no data at all. Likewise, while using a survey of Iowans to project the impact of Iowa on New Hampshire and the primary writ large may seem fruitless, I argue that the measures are metrics only—and their success bears that out. Theorists will simply have to judge the results while keeping those two caveats in mind and come to their own conclusions. I would strongly encourage others to test my results with other data that stretch both further back in time and beyond the banks of the Missouri and Mississippi rivers that form Iowa's borders.

Regardless, using those data, I constructed three metrics of a candidate's Internet activity for those years, which include four competitive fields in Iowa—the 1996 Republican race, the 2000 Republican and Democratic races, and the 2004 Democratic race. The metrics were built on three of the four questions mentioned above: Online Support, E-mail Contact, and Website Visits.[6]

The Online Support metric was the percentage of those surveyed from the candidate's party ("surveyed partisans") who reported that they had signed up online as supporters of the candidate. The E-mail Contact metric was the percentage of surveyed partisans who reported that they had received e-mails from the candidate's campaign. The Website Visits metric was the percentage of surveyed partisans who reported that they had visited the candidate's website.

Recall that in the last chapter we used the percentage each candidate won in Iowa—the Iowa Caucus Vote Share[7]—to model the Caucus's traditional-momentum impact, as the primary modeling literature suggests as a proxy for momentum (see Bartels 1988).

For this chapter, we can rely instead on three Iowa e-mentum factors, tapping the combined explanatory power of Iowa Caucus Vote Share and each of the Internet metrics.[8] The Internet metric used to create the e-mentum factors in the models presented below is Online Support, that is, the percentage of surveyed members who had signed up as online supporters for the candidate.[9]

Based on these Iowa e-mentum factors, coupled with the factors laid out in the last chapter, I was able to construct models addressing the question of how technology may be changing early-state momentum's role in the presidential primary system.

Does E-mentum Make a Difference?

From the discussion in the last chapter, we can say that, overall, New Hampshire appears to swamp Iowa's traditional-momentum impact on the primary race, though Iowa appears to have some impact on New Hampshire. That would tend to support Mayer's contention that New Hampshire "mediates" Iowa's results. On this foundation we can build an exploration of whether Iowa's or New Hampshire's impact on the nomination is on the rise proportional to the increase in candidates' use of Internet tools.

To that end, let's revisit the first two models from the last chapter, gauging Iowa's impact on the nomination and on New Hampshire, but factoring in each candidate's use of Internet tools.

IOWA E-MENTUM AND PRIMARY RESULTS:

A CRUCIAL MEASURE OF THE CAUCUS'S IMPACT

Does Iowa matter more in a world of nearly instantaneous fund-raising and supporter sign-up, even holding New Hampshire's results constant? To find out, I modified the Iowa versus New Hampshire Primary Vote Model by including an Iowa e-mentum factor. Note that, though all the results presented here and in Appendix B were those from the Iowa Online Support E-mentum factor, the results using the e-mentum factors from all three Internet metrics—Online Support, E-mail Contact, and Website

Visits—were virtually identical in both the primary and the New Hampshire models.

Moreover, for those with questions about the construction of the e-mentum factor itself, it is important to note that the result is the same not only across the three factors but across alternative specifications of the model. For example, a simple interactive term between Online Support and Iowa Caucus Vote Share is also statistically significant and at about the same level as the Online Support e-mentum factor, and the same is true for the other Internet factors, both percentage of supporters and percentage of all surveyed, and whether including the Caucus as a separate variable or not (with perhaps one or two exceptions among the 12 models).

Both to measure e-mentum's impact coming out of Iowa and to control for the Internet factors themselves, however, I felt that the specifications in this model were the most appropriate ones, though they are certainly open to question. (For details of the model, see Table B.5 in Appendix B.)

Before we turn to specific estimates, let's compare the Iowa e-mentum model itself to the traditional-momentum model in Chapter 3. First, recall that the traditional-momentum model explained about 77 percent of the variation in Primary Popular Vote Share ($R^2 = 0.777$; adj. $R^2 = 0.759$); the substitution of the Iowa e-mentum factor for Iowa Caucus Vote Share boosts that explanatory power up toward 83 percent ($R^2 = 0.842$, adj. $R^2 = 0.825$). The model's F-statistic also rises from 43.158 to 49.585 with that simple change.

More telling is the radical change in the significance of the model's factors. Suddenly, fund-raising screams from a nonfactor to become statistically significant ($p = 0.001$). New Hampshire Vote Share and Gallup Poll Support remain highly statistically significant ($p < 0.001$). And crucially, Iowa e-mentum itself is now statistically significant, even controlling for New Hampshire's results ($p = 0.018$).

Every indication is that this model is without doubt better specified than the traditional-momentum model. Now that 2004 has passed, it appears that leaving out e-mentum could misrepresent how Iowa and New Hampshire interact in the primary process. If this is a specification error, it will get only worse as time passes if we do not begin to accurately measure technology's effects on momentum.

The implications of the shift of Iowa e-mentum to statistically significant, even controlling for New Hampshire, are crucial. We have learned that the first-in-the-nation Caucus results themselves are not a significant predictor of primary outcomes, holding the first-in-the-nation Primary results constant. But after adding the explanatory power of a candidate's Internet capabilities, the factor explains a significant amount of the variation in primary performance. So while raw Iowa performance may not matter relative to New Hampshire, in 1996, 2000, and especially 2004 it has come to mean increasingly more.

Let's quickly quantify how much this individual Internet tool—which, remember, is only a metric of the candidate's overall technological edge—matters to boosting a candidate's momentum coming out of Iowa, holding Iowa results constant. In the model used to generate the Iowa e-mentum factor, the percentage of online supporters had a regression coefficient of 0.717. In other words, for every percentage-point increase in activists saying they had signed up online for a supporter, we would expect about a 0.7-point increase in the Iowa e-mentum factor. In the model above, the e-mentum factor has a regression coefficient of 0.316, meaning that a 0.7-point increase would translate into about a 0.2-point increase in final primary vote share. So every 1-point increase in supporters signed up online translates into a 0.2-point increase in final primary vote share, based on constant results in Iowa.

Note this impact occurs when holding not just the Iowa Caucus Vote Share but the Internet metric itself constant. That is, because the model controls for online sign-up generally, the 0.2-point increase in final primary vote share for every percentage-point increase in online sign-up is exclusively due to the interaction between the candidate's online sign-up and Iowa performance. The 0.2-point primary vote share increase is the Iowa e-mentum bonus to the candidate for every 1 point of supporters he is capable of signing up online. Were the candidate to win New Hampshire, another e-mentum bonus would be waiting for the candidate. (Note that rerunning the model with a New Hampshire e-mentum factor leaves Iowa e-mentum significant while sharpening the Granite State variable's power as well.)

Put another way, mere success in getting supporters signed up online, driving traffic to one's website, or disseminating information by e-mail is not what appears to directly affect primary success. Instead, it is the degree to which the candidate is using these Internet tools, coupled with momentum from a key event that the tools can amplify.

We should also quantify how much Iowa matters to the nomination, holding Internet tools constant, since the Primary Popular Vote Share Model without e-mentum was unable to identify any Iowa impact at all. In the model used to estimate the Iowa e-mentum factor, Iowa's regression coefficient was 0.886, meaning that for every 1 percentage point in Iowa performance, we would expect the Iowa e-mentum factor to increase by about 0.9 point. Given the e-mentum Primary Popular Vote Share Model's 0.316 regression coefficient on the Iowa e-mentum factor, that 0.9-point increase in the Iowa e-mentum factor would mean an increase in primary vote share of 0.3 percent.

So according to these two models, every 1-percentage-point increase in Iowa vote share for a candidate translates into a 0.3-point increase in the final primary vote share, holding the Internet metric and the other factors in the model constant.

The implication of these two estimates taken together is startling: Not including some measure of e-mentum in a primary election model leaves out a full half percentage point (0.2% and 0.3%, for a total of 0.5%) of primary vote impact for every 1 percentage point a candidate wins in Iowa and 1 percentage point of activists the candidate has signed up online, just based on Caucus-generated e-mentum. What more it leaves out depends on how many other critical junctures like Iowa there are in the race. It goes without saying that there could be many. And as the percentage of activists signing up online, getting contacted by e-mail, and visiting websites increases, the unmeasured effects of e-mentum will continue to grow.

Two caveats. First, the regression index technique I used to create the e-mentum factor is very much open to question. It may be that the combination of the two factors is amplifying the e-mentum factor's *t*-score, even though one of the two has virtually no correlation with Iowa Caucus Vote Share. I frown on interactive terms in this case because the Internet variables set all values before 1996 (or 2000) to zero, badly skewing the model toward the present, and I therefore prefer the regression index. But I likewise encourage other theorists to put the e-mentum concept to the test in other ways and with other formulations, to see if my contention is correct. I will certainly be doing so myself.

Second, it may be that Iowa and New Hampshire are capturing more of the impact of e-mentum than they generate themselves. Though I control for the Internet metric in the model, I do not control for South Carolina e-mentum, Super Tuesday e-mentum, debate e-mentum, and so forth. I would be glad to be corrected on Iowa's e-mentum effect in particular— but the technological impact itself appears to exist, and should be acknowledged and controlled for.

Accordingly, theorists may want to at least test for e-mentum at any point in a primary model where they currently measure momentum.

One final interesting result of this model: while both fund-raising and national polling strength are significant, the former has a negative sign. This result is common in models that include national polling: holding that crucial measure of party support constant, candidates who raise and spend more money tend to be those who lose. So while, as we have seen, fund-raising has a positive bivariate relationship with primary performance, when holding polling support (and the other factors in the model) constant that relationship is actually inverse. The more you raise *per point in the Gallup*, the worse you do in the primary. This counterintuitive result is worthy of further exploration.

WHAT IMPACT DOES IOWA HAVE ON NEW HAMPSHIRE? A WILD, WIRED ONE

Next, does Iowa affect New Hampshire more, with all the money and supporters to be had online that could never have been gathered in the sprint from one to the other before the Internet? To answer that question, I modified the New Hampshire Prediction Model by adding an Iowa e-mentum factor in place of Iowa Caucus Vote Share.[10] (For details of the model, see Table B.6 in Appendix B.)

In the first model of New Hampshire performance, the reader will recall, the Iowa Caucus Vote Share factor was statistically significant ($p = 0.04$), but the impact the first caucus had on the first primary was hard to quantify—somewhere between one-sixteenth and one-quarter of a percentage point. In this model of New Hampshire performance, by contrast, the Iowa e-mentum factor is highly statistically significant ($p < 0.001$); that is, the standard error is nowhere near the size of the regression coefficient.

As a result, it is straightforward to quantify how much Iowa matters to the New Hampshire results, holding Internet tools constant. As we noted above, in the Iowa e-mentum factor model, Iowa Caucus Vote Share's regression coefficient was 0.886, meaning that for every 1 percentage point in Iowa performance, the Iowa e-mentum factor would increase by about 0.9. Since the e-mentum New Hampshire Vote Share Model above includes an estimate of a 0.395 regression coefficient on the Iowa e-mentum factor, that 0.9-point increase in the Iowa e-mentum factor would mean an increase in New Hampshire Vote Share of about 0.4 point.

Thus these models indicate that for every 1-point increase in a candidate's Iowa Caucus Vote Share, the candidate would see a 0.4-point increase in New Hampshire Vote Share, even controlling for pre-Iowa New Hampshire polling. Given the New Hampshire model without e-mentum, that figure would have been about 0.16 point. So even though the model had a statistically significant Iowa factor, leaving e-mentum out of it understated Iowa's New Hampshire impact by about 0.24 point for every 1 point the candidate won in the Caucus.

Next, how much of an e-mentum bonus, based on their Iowa performance, are candidates getting in New Hampshire? Once more, in the model used to generate the Iowa e-mentum factor, the percentage of online supporters had a regression coefficient of 0.717. In the New Hampshire model above, again, the e-mentum factor has a regression coefficient of 0.395, meaning that a 0.7-point increase in the factor would translate into about a 0.3-point increase in final primary vote share. So every 1-point increase in supporters signed up online translates into a 0.3-point increase in New Hampshire Vote Share, based on constant results in Iowa.

That is, we can estimate that the Iowa e-mentum bonus in New Hampshire is about a third of a percentage point for every 1 point of activists candidates have signed up online.

Getting where this is going? Taken together, these estimates mean that leaving an e-mentum measure out of a New Hampshire model drops out more than a half percentage point (0.24% and 0.3%, for a total of 0.54%) in the state for every 1 point a candidate wins in Iowa and 1 point of activists the candidate has signed up, just because of Caucus-generated e-mentum.

Accordingly, once again, theorists may want to include some e-mentum measurement in New Hampshire models where they currently measure momentum, from Iowa or elsewhere.

With New Technology, Iowa Matters More and More

Is technological e-mentum amplifying key events in presidential races, including Iowa? On the basis of this analysis of Iowa's role vis-à-vis New Hampshire in the primary race, the answer appears to be yes.

In terms of Iowa's impact on the New Hampshire Primary, use of the Internet appears to give candidates about a 0.3-point e-mentum bonus coming out of Iowa for every 1 point of activists signed up online, controlling for other factors, including the percentage of activists signed up online itself. Also, factoring in e-mentum allows us to estimate that Iowa is having a 0.24-point additional impact in New Hampshire Vote Share for every 1 point the candidate wins in the Caucus relative to a model without e-mentum included. We may be badly understating Iowa's impact on New Hampshire by ignoring the budding effects of technology.

In terms of Iowa's impact on a candidate's final Primary Popular Vote Share, technological tools seem to be awarding candidates a 0.2-point e-mentum bonus just from the Caucus for every 1 point of activists signed up online, again controlling for the percentage of activists signed up online itself and other factors. And building e-mentum into a Primary Popular Vote Share Model allows us to estimate that Iowa is having a 0.3-point impact for every 1 point the candidate wins in the Caucus relative to a model without e-mentum included. In fact, primary models without e-mentum included, the one in the last chapter included, consistently find that the Caucus has no impact at all on primary results, controlling for New Hampshire and other factors. So we may actually be fundamentally misunderstanding Iowa's impact on the nomination by leaving out this new form of online momentum.

The most important finding here may be not so much how much Iowa matters, but the fact that e-mentum matters. Preliminary tests show that multiple Internet metrics generate virtually identical results and that e-mentum effects coming out of New Hampshire are just as strong as those coming out of Iowa, if not stronger. So we would do well to explore where else this phenomenon is occurring in presidential races: After Super Tuesday wins? After a successful convention? After winning a major debate? After winning a general election itself?

One further thought on technology's role: I would contend that e-mentum, which may have been the central reason Kerry in 2004 was able to successfully replicate Carter's 1976 Iowa strategy, may also lead to more candidates following McCain and Clark around Iowa to New Hampshire and even beyond. Why? Because potential future candidates have seen the massive jolt of energy that online technology gave McCain in 2000 and Kerry, Clark, and especially Dean in 2004 after gaining the momentum in the race. If e-mail, fund-raising websites, and blogs raise by orders of magnitude candidates' ability to capitalize on high-profile positive events in their favor, they will realize that they can once again translate a significant, surprising early-state win, not just into a few weeks of positive press, but into the devastation of their other competitors, just as it did in Kerry's case. That realization may lead them to skip Iowa with more confidence, knowing a shocking New Hampshire upset—or one in any of the other states flooding into earlier positions for 2008—can overpower a front-runner with a flood of online resources and shock troops. On the other hand, e-mentum may also lead candidates to seek a high-tech version of Carter's win as Kerry did, upsetting an exhibition season winner in Iowa and surfing the Internet tide to the nomination.

Will all this denigrate Iowa relative to New Hampshire, boost Iowa's role, or put them both at risk to later-state ambushes by candidates knowing they can raise $50 million in a weekend if they just surprise the public enough with a decisive upset? It's worth thinking about.

By way of both conclusion and transition, there appear to be three important sets of implications for this finding, one for each of three audiences who care about Iowa's role in the nomination identified in the last chapter.

First, the finding dramatically raises the stakes in the literature's decades-old debate about the nature of the Caucus, Iowa's electorate, and party primary rules more generally. Since over the entire 1976–2004 period, Iowa has had a large and (recently) exponentially increasing impact on the nomination, it matters a great deal going forward whether the state rewards honest grassroots politicking as Caucus supporters claim; whether the state is a demographically unrepresentative venue and if as such it trends toward or away from minority candidates; whether the Caucus picks candidates in or out of the ideological mainstream; and especially what the implications are of what parties choose to do with the Rules of the Game.

Second and following from the first, it also dramatically raises the stakes on those rules themselves. Specifically, it gives new immediacy to the debate among the parties, the pundits, and the press about the rules that place the Caucus and the New Hampshire Primary first in the process and front-load the remainder of the states to force a nomination decision faster, increasing the early-states' combined clout. After all, this analysis suggests that those like Sununu who pooh-pooh Iowa's nomination impact appear increasingly, empirically wrong. That means it is even more important to decide what kind of system best serves the interests of the country.

Third, there are the politicians to consider. Somewhere, right now, a dozen or so presidential candidates are implementing their strategy for their primary White House bid. Realistically, they have made up their minds whether to follow Jimmy Carter and John Kerry into Iowa or follow John McCain and Wesley Clark in the circuitous route that avoids it. This analysis suggests that given the current set of rules, ratified by both parties in their 2004 conventions, the latter course would be risky indeed.

Given those conclusions, it is time to turn to debates over what matters in winning Iowa. Is it organization, television, or something else? Is it ideology or strategic voting? It is to those questions that we can now devote our attention.

FIVE

Explaining What Matters

The Ground War or the Air War?

David Den Herder, organization director for Iowa Bush 2000, remembers fondly the day that presidential candidate Steve Forbes walked into the Des Moines Convention Center for a Farm Bureau gathering and was swarmed by a sea of bright green Bush Farm Team hats—"literally thousands of them," he beams.

Bush had been there before Forbes, and his organization had plastered the crowd in the gaudy hats in anticipation of other candidates' arrival. Forbes had a few pictures taken with small groups of farmers, most sporting the Bush Farm Team hats, of course. Then Forbes unceremoniously walked out.

"That's grassroots organization," Den Herder smiles. "That's the Iowa Caucus."[1]

Caucus advocates' central contention is that organization, retail politics, and "time on task," rather than demagoguery, money, or advertising, carry the day in Iowa.[2] But its detractors point to an increasing role for television advertising, saying the Caucus is becoming merely another primary, losing a central argument for its first-in-the-nation status (Winebrenner 1998, 177–78).

This chapter explores this central question: What tactics matter most to a presidential candidate in Iowa? More specifically, it asks, does social capital–rich retail politics still matter in the Caucus, as popular lore would have us believe? Does contact from the campaign dominate other factors? Does the amount of press a candidate gets matter more than organizing, the claim of one Iowa operative? Finally, does television advertising play a dominant role, a minor one—or a negative one, as some go so far as to claim?

What Tactics Matter Most?

To probe those questions more thoroughly, we can look over not only the set of past studies of what tactics matter in Iowa—which is sparse—but the views of political professionals who make their living trying to win campaigns there. Specifically, we should focus on retail politics (including spending time in the state pressing the flesh, driving activists to rallies, and contact with voters by the candidate's campaign), generating press coverage, and television advertising, with notes on the structure of Democratic Caucuses in particular and on overall Iowa spending.

However, before we begin, there is a crucial and central caveat to both this chapter and the next. Past studies have repeatedly demonstrated that the single most important factor in how well any given candidate does during the nomination process is that candidate's support *before* the voting begins. National polling support, which the last two chapters included, is *not* included in the investigation below of what matters in determining Iowa's outcomes.

That raises a number of troubling questions. First, it must be true that a candidate's national stature, perhaps best measured by national polling, would have a dramatic impact on the success of that candidate's success in retail politics. For instance, in the 2000 race, then governor George W. Bush (R-Tex.) spent less time in Iowa than Governor Lamar Alexander (R-Tenn.). But when he did arrive, Bush's star power outshone Alexander's.

According to former Republican Party of Iowa (RPI) executive director Keith Fortmann, Bush "very carefully crafted the inevitability and expectation of success" that became a self-fulfilling prophecy in the Caucus.[3] If Bush's national prominence increased the impact of the time Bush did spend in Iowa relative to the time Alexander spent, it would skew our analysis of time in Iowa.

Brian Kennedy, a former chairman of RPI and GOP candidate for Congress from the Hawkeye State's northeast district, also observes that the capacity of an organization to "make something happen" in Iowa is based on the overall campaign environment. If the candidate has a bad message or is not appealing to voters, "there is no organization in the world that will save him," Kennedy says. Polling strength, both within Iowa and nationally, leads to a perception of viability on the part of a campaign. National polls especially, Kennedy said, can be driving results in Iowa. In the summer and fall of 1999, Bush's Iowa team could point to national polls showing that he was beating then vice president Al Gore and leading other Republican candidates to demoralize and demobilize other campaigns.[4]

Likewise, the candidate's record on fund-raising and whether the candidate is perceived as the front-runner also both matter in Iowa assessments, Kennedy believes. And viability also flows from the proportion of positive or negative content of the media attention a candidate receives, both nationally and locally. Of course, national fund-raising, candidate rankings, and polling strength against primary competitors and potential general election opponents all have an impact on that coverage, as well, Kennedy says.[5]

To get at this dynamic, the study reported in this chapter and the next includes controls for national fund-raising (overall resources but also the perceptions of strength they engender); perceptions of both electability (ability to win the general election) and viability (ability to win the nomination); and ideological crowding (perceptions of the extent to which the candidate's beliefs are hemmed in by other candidates in the field). Those three factors should capture a major portion of what national poll support reflects. However, including those factors *and* national poll support makes it impossible to tell what portion of a candidate's Iowa success is due to fund-raising, what to perceptions of electability, what to perceptions of viability, and what to mere popularity and name identification.

The problem is compounded because each of these factors interrelates with the others, and with other factors that might matter to who wins in Iowa. As nominations scholar Wayne Steger puts it,

> Who raises money (and who therefore can spend money)? In part, it is the people who are popular (known to be popular in a prior poll). Who gets on TV? The people raising money and who are higher in the polls. Who is higher in the polls? People who are on TV and spending money.[6]

Admittedly, we are about to wade into deep waters. To tease out the independent impact of each factor, including fund-raising, electability, ideology, and viability—which are examined in the next chapter—the following exploration leaves out national polling strength. In a sense, the analysis includes the popularity that polling measures but splits it up into its component parts. But both casual readers and scholars familiar with the topic should keep in mind that this decision could skew the results in one way or another.

RETAIL POLITICS

In the first chapter, we saw that a candidate's days in Iowa and grassroots strength have traditionally been associated with wins in the state. However, while a review of the literature turned up acknowledgments of the importance of organization in winning the Caucus, it found few explorations of that importance.

Whether retail politics dominates the Iowa Caucus or has been superseded matters beyond the borders of the Hawkeye State. Putnam's *Bowling Alone* (2000) makes a compelling case that what he terms "social capital" has declined precipitously in America.[7] As part of that trend, the in-person contact of canvassing and turnout efforts of the past have faded throughout much of the country, especially with respect to presidential politics. Gerber and Green (2000, 653) note that "whereas 6% of the public reported working for a political party in the early 1970s, just 3% did so in the mid-1990s." In turn, they argue, declining in-person political contact has tended to diminish turnout.[8] With politics generally moving toward the impersonal, if Iowa in fact still exhibits the personal touch of caucus politics, the state is both a happy counterfactual for social capital advocates and potentially even an example to be emulated.

That said, whether grassroots politics is still prime in Iowa is a matter of some contention. Money and commercials may be playing an increasing role in Iowa. Beginning in 1988, argues Republican strategist Ed Rollins, a new emphasis on paid media began to alter the nature of the campaign throughout the country. "If the use of paid radio and television increased in Iowa as it had nationally," Winebrenner (1998) says, "the retail nature of the Iowa campaign might be lost and with it the rationale for beginning the presidential campaign in a small state" (pp. 177–78).

Indeed, in 1996 publisher Steve Forbes's infusion of advertising seemed to alter the fundamentally organizational dynamic of the Iowa campaign. Republicans spent about ten times as much on television advertising in 1996 as they did in 1988, and "pundits wondered whether it was possible to 'buy' the caucuses" (p. 227). Of course, it turned out that Forbes finished a dismal fourth, notwithstanding his powerful poll ratings on the eve of the contest.

"Rather," Winebrenner argues, "the [1996 Iowa] campaign was a hybrid of 'retail' and 'wholesale' politics" (p. 243). In spite of Forbes's 1996 TV spending surge, Winebrenner concludes, "it is likely that the traditional Iowa campaign will continue in some form since the successful Dole, Buchanan, and Alexander campaigns each built significant organizations in Iowa and invested heavy amounts of personal campaign time in the state" (p. 243). That is true, he says, because Forbes failed in his bid to dominate the Caucus relying exclusively on an air war. Winebrenner's argument is borne out by the fact that Forbes himself turned to organization in addition to advertising in the 2000 cycle, and was rewarded with a strong second-place finish (losing to Bush, who constructed an elaborate organization as well).

That poses the crucial question of whether retail politics at the grassroots level holds the key to success in the Iowa caucus, such that it is a test not just of polls, focus groups, and advertising, but also of the ability to mobilize Americans toward a common goal. If that is no longer the case, caucus supporters lose a critical buttress to their argument for keeping the contest first in the nation.

There is less of a debate among Iowa political operatives than within the literature. Virtually all the political operatives I spoke with still believe retail politics counts most in Iowa, including former White House Political Director Sara Taylor, who says that grassroots in the Iowa Bush 2000 campaign, on which she served as coalition director, was "absolutely essential."[9]

Let's drill down into retail politics a bit, exploring a few specific kinds of retail politicking that may matter, according to the literature and Iowa political professionals.

PERSONAL CONTACT WITH THE CANDIDATE

Winebrenner (1998) reports that over the two years before the 1988 Caucus Gephardt spent 148 days in Iowa. That means that the candidate needed to meet or personally influence just over 200 people a day to reach the 31,000 supporters he needed to win the contest—which, with a series of medium-sized rallies and meetings, was certainly possible. Gephardt did triumph that year, giving an indication that days in Iowa—"time on task," as *Des Moines Register* pundit David Yepsen puts it—was an important factor in a candidate's success. According to Iowa pols, there's nothing like personal contact with the candidate when trying to win the Caucus (assuming one is not as abrasive as Texas governor John Connally, they stipulate).[10] Accordingly, as part of our investigation of retail politics, we should measure the impact of a candidate's personal time in the state, whether at rallies or campaigning one on one.

CONTACT FROM THE CAMPAIGN

We also saw in the first chapter that contact by the campaign was an important part of a candidate's organization. According to Winebrenner (1998), in the *Des Moines Register*'s December 1980 Iowa Poll, twice as many people said that they had been contacted by George Bush as by any other candidate. By contrast, Ronald Reagan in 1980 and Bush himself in 1988 both tried to wait and appear as though they were not running in Iowa until the last moment. Those strategies failed.

Accordingly, political operatives I spoke to were mixed in their views on the importance of different kinds of campaign contact, but they were united in believing that campaigns needed to reach out aggressively to caucusgoers to succeed.[11] Measuring the importance of candidate contact, it appears, is important as well.

That gives us three components of retail politicking to measure: days in Iowa, rally attendance, and campaign contact.

THE DEMOCRATIC 15 PERCENT VIABILITY THRESHOLD

There is a further wrinkle in retail politics' role: whether it matters differently to different candidates. Specifically, the Democratic political operatives with whom I spoke raised the possibility that organization mattered differently in the Republican and Democratic Caucuses.[12] For instance, prominent Iowa Democratic campaign operative Jeff Link states emphatically that Caucus organizational strength is more important to Democratic candidates than to Republicans in Iowa. "On the Republican side it's a head count," Link argues, "on the Democratic side it requires training."[13] The reason, Democratic operatives agreed, is their party's 15 percent viability threshold, which throws a heavy wrench into calculations of support.[14]

That structural difference makes it important for a Caucus-support model to test empirically for a difference in Democratic performance for candidates at or below 15 percent in support.

PRESS COVERAGE

There's an old saw that Fortmann repeats: An Iowa farmer is leaning up against a fence post and is approached by a national reporter. After exchanging greetings, the reporter asks, "Who are you supporting in the Caucus?" The farmer responds, "Is this on background?"[15]

Iowans are heavily exposed to press coverage during the Caucus, both from inside and outside the state. Link gives an example of the potential bone-powdering intensity of earned media in determining the outcome of the Caucus (and the primary more generally): During the plagiarism scandal that ultimately forced Biden from the 1988 race, Link says that there was a "disconnect" between his experience on the ground in Iowa and "what we were hearing on the news." As the Polk County field representative on the Biden staff, he said, he was "out running phone banks," and from his perspective the campaign was filling those phone banks and picking up supporters. So from an Iowa grassroots perspective, the campaign did not appear badly wounded, but from a national media point of view the plagiarism scandal was fatal.

Informed by that experience, Link believes that, in terms of effect on winning the Caucus, earned media and paid media rank "neck and neck," and he would put *both* ahead of organization.[16]

Granted, the Biden example did not demonstrate media's impact on the Iowa electorate. To some extent, it demonstrated the contrary: that the press could have an impact on the candidate's campaign, "forcing" him from the race, while Iowa voters quietly continued to line up behind him.

Nevertheless, a full model of Iowa outcomes should assess whether earned media plays an independent role in determining Caucus success.

TELEVISION ADVERTISING

Though organization plays an important role in determining the outcome of the Iowa Caucus, television advertising must as well—right? That question is actually a matter of considerable debate among the interviewed political operatives. On one hand, with eight or nine candidates tramping all over the state, and with retail politics at a premium, "having good staff humping around the state is more important" than television, senior Democratic legislative staffer Eric Bakker told me. "Otherwise people say, 'Oh, he's just trying to buy the Caucus.'"[17] By contrast, Den Herder argues that television is "important because it's the norm." Not doing television advertising gives the impression of being a nonviable candidate, he says.[18]

Whether television advertising is more important now than it used to be is a hard one to answer, given the data available. However, whether television is more important than organization over the entire time period studied is easier to answer, at least given the caveats on television advertising and Iowa spending data below and in Appendix A.

SPENDING IN IOWA GENERALLY

What is the independent impact of spending more money in the state? Among political professionals, the responses were mixed. Operatives identified limited resources to spend in Iowa as a major obstacle for struggling candidates—although one operative opined that a heavy emphasis on organization might overcome being outgunned financially.[19] Also, some operatives noted that Iowa spending interacted heavily with national credibility and organization power, to such an extent that it was hard to separate them.[20]

However, of course, one can empirically test the independent impact of national credibility, national fund-raising, Iowa spending, organization building, and such organizational efforts as phone contacts and direct mail. Empirically teasing out those factors from each other is challenging but possible.

Unfortunately, the data are such that conclusions about Iowa spending itself are highly suspect, as we will see in the next section and in great detail in Appendix A, so for the time being we will have to suspend judgment on the role of overall Iowa spending, while controlling for it in the model.

SEVEN TACTIC QUESTIONS

There appear to be seven campaign-tactic questions we should address to get a full view of what matters in winning Iowa. First, does the amount of time candidates spend in Iowa matter in how they fare in the Caucus? Second, does rally attendance matter in Caucus performance? Third, does campaign contact with voters matter in Iowa? Fourth, does the Democratic Caucus's 15 percent viability threshold create fundamental differences between the two parties' contests? Fifth, does press coverage make a difference in who wins or loses in Iowa? Sixth, what role does television advertising play in the Caucus—does it dominate organization, is it merely a norm that must be adhered to, or is it a potential negative when overdone? And seventh, is retail politics still of primary importance in the Iowa Caucus?

What Iowa Campaign Tactics Can We Measure?

To answer these seven questions, we will need to operationalize not only the concepts in question but a number of important controls. After all, we cannot build models that merely compare the tactics in isolation from other campaign effects. To be sure that we are teasing out the independent effects of the tactics themselves, we need to control for other factors we believe may be important to Caucus success.

Thus this chapter's models include factors to proxy the campaign effects we want to measure, as well as a set of other factors to hold constant candidate stature, resources, and ideology. But we delay the discussion of those controls until the next chapter, since it is there that their role is explored in detail. Specifically, we will put off until the next chapter a discussion of the candidate's "ideological crowding" relative to activists in his party, as well as the proportions of surveyed activists reporting a candidate was either viable in his party's primary or electable in the general election.

Nevertheless, in this discussion, we will lay out the operationalization of the majority of the study's Explanatory Model's variables. We will explore data on the number of days a candidate spends in Iowa, attendance at the candidates' rallies, and campaign contacts reported by surveyed partisans; the relative amount of money a candidate spends in Iowa; an approximation of the relative amount the candidate spends on television advertising in the state; a proxy for the amount of press coverage the candidate generates in Iowa; and whether the candidate is from a nearby state.

The candidate "level of effort" information (number of days spent in Iowa, Iowa spending overall, and television advertising, for instance) was drawn from Winebrenner's landmark study of the Caucus and dozens of other primary and secondary sources, mostly providing only small pieces of the puzzle at once.

The historical voter-level data (reported contact by candidates' organization, rally attendance, ideology scores, viability, and electability survey data) are a composite for each campaign taken from the voluminous time-series and panel survey data of Iowa and other state delegates, activists, and caucusgoers spanning 1980 to 1996 compiled by Abramowitz et al. (2001). The newest layer of voter-level data (1996–2004) come from my survey of politically active Iowa partisans conducted before the 2004 Iowa Caucus itself. Finally, the data on candidates facing the Democratic 15 percent viability threshold come from the Iowa Poll conducted by the *Des Moines Register* before each Caucus. The factors explored in this chapter's models are laid out in more detail below.

RETAIL POLITICS MEASURES

Quantifying the grassroots nature of the Iowa Caucus is as tricky as predicting corn harvests. As we saw above, a model attempting to do so should include "time on task" by the candidate himself; efforts by the campaign to reach out to Iowans where they live and work; and the extent to which the candidate literally rallied supporters at events in the state.

Accordingly, I gathered data on the candidates' days in Iowa relative to his opponents, the percentage of those surveyed reporting that the candidates' campaigns contacted them, and the percentage reporting that they attended rallies on the candidates' behalf.

Days in Iowa. The first factor in the Explanatory Model's attempt to measure retail politics is built around the number of days a candidate spent in Iowa during the election cycle leading up to the Iowa caucus. Most of the data for Days in Iowa come from Winebrenner (1998).[21] Republican and Democratic 2000 data come from an unpublished dataset provided to me by Winebrenner.[22] Republican 1976 and Democratic 1988 data come from Squire (1989, 5). For all years, Days in Iowa is counted through Caucus day.[23]

The actual operationalization of time in Iowa used in the Explanatory Model is the percentage of total Days in Iowa the candidate represented. This relative variable was arrived at by dividing each candidate's number of days in Iowa by the sum of the number of days in Iowa by all candidates of the candidate's party during the same period. Its purpose is to capture not only the overall level of effort that each candidate expended in Iowa grassroots politicking but also how that effort ranked relative to the candidate's opponents.

In the 2002–2004 election cycle, two candidates spent the most time in Iowa (Figure 5.1): Dean, at 76 days in Iowa, and Kerry, at 73. Gephardt invested 67 days in the state, perhaps surprisingly few since he explicitly banked his primary run on winning the Caucus. Edwards nearly matched Gephardt's effort, at 64 days in Iowa, and Representative Dennis Kucinich (D-Ohio) was close behind at 54.

From there the other candidates trailed badly, with Senator Joe Lieberman (D-Conn.) at 16, Reverend Al Sharpton at 7, and retired general Wesley Clark at 3. Clark had entered the race late and, like Lieberman, who eventually announced he would bypass Iowa, focused on New Hampshire.

No resource is more precious in a campaign than the candidate's time. Kerry's stress on Iowa is evident in these figures, and it was ultimately to pay off, big time. Dean's time, however, was not.

Contact by Candidate's Campaign and Rally Attendance. The second and third factors used to proxy retail politics were contact of activists by the candidate's campaign and proportion of activists having attended rallies. For 1996, 2000, and 2004 the Campaign Contact and Rally Attendance data all came from my own survey of Iowa active partisans. For pre-1996 data Campaign Contact and Rally Attendance were measured by the percentage of all partisans surveyed saying they were contacted by the candidate, taken from the database of Abramowitz et al. (2001). For some caveats and thoughts on these two factors, see Appendix A.

During the 2004 cycle, Dean, Kerry, Gephardt, and Edwards made the most contact with activists, according to my survey data (Figure 5.2). Approximately four-fifths of activists surveyed reported being contacted by those campaigns: 85 percent by Dean, 80 percent by Kerry, 79 percent by Gephardt, and 74 percent by Edwards. Kucinich trailed badly behind those four, with only 33 percent of activists reporting contact, and the rest of the field tapered off from there. An active effort to reach out to grassroots-level voters one by one is the mark of an aggressive Iowa campaign, and those in the top tier clearly made such an effort.

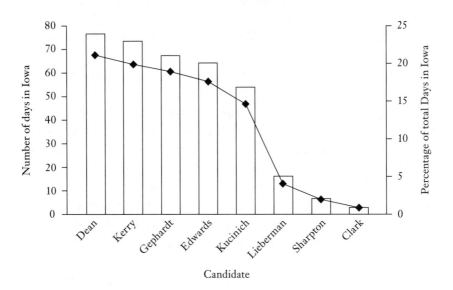

Figure 5.1.   Days in Iowa, 2004
 NOTE: Total number of days each candidate spent in Iowa between election day 2002 and Caucus day 2004 (bars) and percentage of the total Days in Iowa by all candidates that each candidate's number of days represented (line).

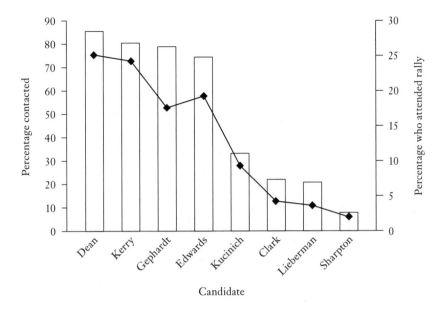

Figure 5.2. Campaign Contact and Rally Attendance, 2004
NOTE: Percentage of all partisans surveyed reporting that they were contacted by the candidate's campaign (bars) and that they attended a rally for the candidate (line).

The picture is slightly different with respect to rallies. Dean and Kerry were the candidates with the highest percentage of activists reporting that they attended a rally for each candidate, at 25 and 24 percent, respectively. Edwards and Gephardt were at the next tier at 19 and 18 percent, respectively. Again, Kucinich and especially the rest of the field lagged far behind.

Together, Campaign Contact and Rally Attendance give a snapshot of the 2004 campaigns' outreach to local potential caucusgoers, individually and in group settings. It remains to be seen whether these factors can help predict the outcome in 2004 and explain Caucus results more generally.

IOWA TELEVISION ADVERTISING

Data on spending on television advertising do not exist back to 1976 except in the rawest form, buried deep within Federal Election Commission (FEC) filings. Accordingly, the data on spending for television advertising used in this study are inconsistent. For instance, for 2000 and 2004 the data employed are for total TV spending; however, for all 1988 and 1996 Republicans, the data are for the combined spending at two of the largest and most important stations in the state (WHO-TV and KCCI-TV). The sources are widely varied.[24]

Because measurements of television spending are mostly consistent within cycles, percentages of total television spending were always used in estimating models for this study. In that form the factor represents an index of the share of television spending for a candidate, rather than a comprehensive dollar figure. Since each set of TV figures may be regarded as a (nonrandom) sample of overall television spending, those percentage figures are the least flawed form of the variable. However, clearly this is not an ideal dataset and should by all means be updated, potentially from a report-by-report reading of FEC data.

For 2004, fortunately, we have highly reliable data on candidates' television expenditures (Goldstein 2003). On TV advertising the four top-tier candidates dominated the field as in no other factor (Figure 5.3). Dean, flush with resources, outspent the rest of the field by more than a half-million dollars. Gephardt ($2.3 million) and Kerry ($2.1 million) spent similar amounts, while Edwards invested $1.5 million. The rest of the field combined for only $35,000 in television spending.

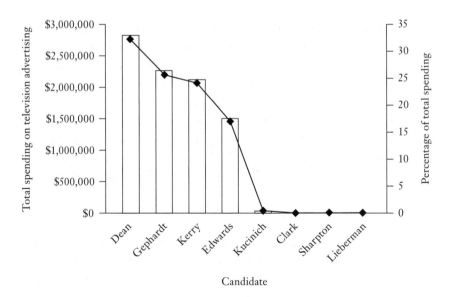

Figure 5.3. Television Advertising, 2004

NOTE: Iowa television spending totals from the beginning of the 2004 cycle (bars) and percentage of the sum of those totals (line), by candidate. No bar indicates little or no advertising.

The gap between the first and second tiers of candidates shows the concatenation of national resources and Iowa effort. That is, the gap points to two simple facts: Clark, Sharpton, and Lieberman did not contest the state, while Kucinich had precious little money. As a result, taking this variable into account should help us measure both wherewithal and where candidates went with resources.

But the gap also raises again the theoretical question about the role television plays in Iowa: How much does it matter relative to grassroots organizing? The Explanatory Model should be able to shed some light on that question, in spite of the overall weakness of the television data.

IOWA SPENDING

Data on spending in Iowa are reported on most candidates' FEC reports. However, FEC data on Iowa spending are suspect because spending limits encourage candidates to game the system by basing operations in other states (and potentially by outright deception). What's more, if reported Iowa spending is suspect, mixing non-FEC data—estimates usually from the media or an observing interest group—into a measure of Iowa Spending is suspect, as well. After all, not only are these other estimates little more than guesses but they do not take into account the fudge factor candidates use with their FEC filings. Thus the estimates available of the Bush and Forbes 2000 spending in Iowa are respectively two and three times the size of Edwards's and Gephardt's reported 2004 spending and five times the size of conservative activist and GOP candidate Gary Bauer's reported 2000 spending. Though it is likely that Bush and Forbes dramatically outspent Edwards, Gephardt, and Bauer, they may not have done so by such dramatic multiples.

Another challenge to gathering data is that non-FEC estimates of total Iowa spending are not particularly common. As a result, a researcher driven to find estimates often has to go to highly questionable non-FEC sources. For instance, I found a 1996 Forbes estimate in a Texans for Public Justice news release and, in a rich irony, a 2000 Forbes spending estimate on the World Socialist website.

Even so, national fund-raising, national polling figures, days in Iowa, and Iowa television-advertising spending together give considerable explanatory power over Iowa spending with non-FEC sources included, and

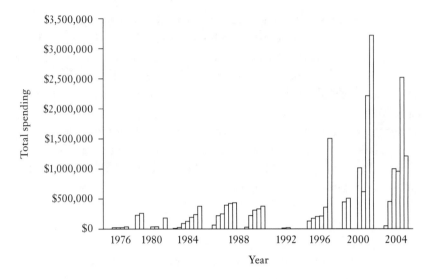

Figure 5.4.   Candidates' Iowa spending, 1976–2004

NOTE: Dollars spent in Iowa (2004 dollars) in the third and fourth quarters of the year before election year, by election year and candidate (each candidate shown as unmarked bar), including non-FEC sources and imputed values. Gaps indicate that a candidate either reported or was imputed as spending nothing in the state, or that data were missing.

thus by building a multiple-imputation ordinary least squares (OLS) model we can arrive at some reasonable approximation of what the percentages of the total spending in the state were, allowing us to successfully impute missing values. The Iowa Spending data, drawn from all sources and then filled in with multiple imputation, are shown in Figure 5.4.

The troublesome patterns in the data are readily apparent. In early cycles, Iowa spending data are badly underreported, as indicated by the few bars those years. Then, starting in 1996, we see a spike, which represents the Forbes imputed estimate—probably an accurate one, but certainly a startling departure from earlier data. In 2000 we see both a small spike, which is the Keyes imputed value—again, possibly accurate—and then two towering values, which are the Bush and Forbes estimates from non-FEC sources. In 2004 the two bars hovering around the $1 million mark, the Kerry imputed total, are the Gephardt and Edwards reported totals. But the $2.5 million bar for the Dean imputed total—though very possibly correct—lends a dramatic skew to the cycle's data. All in all, the considerable variation is mainly the result of imputation and non-FEC sources, which is somewhat problematic.

The picture improves when one considers the data in a theoretically preferable form, the candidate's percentage of the total spent in Iowa. This form has several advantages. First, as noted elsewhere we would expect the percentage of the total in this form to be more linearly related to the percentages of Iowa Caucus performance, the dependent variable (and empirically it is, for virtually all variables in this analysis).

Also, it allows one to measure candidates' level of effort relative to the other candidates against whom they are competing. After all, if Carter's spending in 1976 did not rival Bauer's in 2000, even in 2004 dollars, we still would not expect Carter to fare worse than Bauer. But even given the flawed data we have to work with, we know what to conclude given that Carter's spending was 35.6 percent of the spending in a six-man field while Bauer's was only 9.7 percent of spending in a same-size field.

Using the admittedly flawed FEC and non-FEC data to calculate each candidate's spending as a percentage of total Iowa spending by candidates of his party in that cycle and then imputing the rest of the values yields the results shown in Figure 5.5.

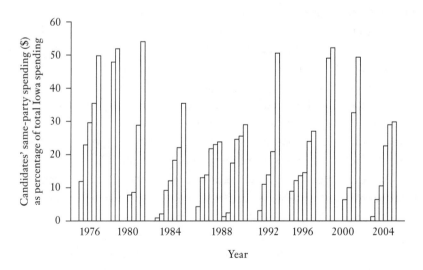

Figure 5.5.   Total Iowa spending, 1976–2004

NOTE: Candidates' percentage of same-party total 2004 dollars spent in Iowa in the third and fourth quarters of the year before election year, by election year and candidate (each candidate shown as unmarked bar), including non-FEC sources and imputed values. Both Republicans and Democrats are included in some cycles, so they may sum to 200 percent rather than 100 percent. Gaps indicate that a candidate either reported or was imputed as spending nothing in the state, or that data were missing.

Those results, each candidate's percentage of total spending in Iowa that cycle, are the variables included in the Explanatory Model. Granted, even within this more balanced variable, some unmistakable problems remain. After all, for 2000 the two tallest bars represent Forbes and Bush, still dominating spending in a way that may be systematically biased, and the underlying data are still heterogeneous. However, both eliminating (unique) non-FEC data and excluding Iowa Spending from the model altogether are even more problematic, as demonstrated in the discussion in Appendix A.

Overall, therefore, it seems important to report the Explanatory Model results including Iowa Spending and using both FEC and non-FEC sources, along with all the caveats associated with the data—but it is important to report also on what the model looks like without Iowa Spending, making clear that the variable's data challenges undermine the model's (interesting) conclusions on television spending. I have proceeded accordingly.

PRESS COVERAGE

The press coverage data for the models in this book came from a Lexis-Nexis search on the candidates' names, including common variants, for the period from the midterm election until mid-January of the Caucus year. It includes the total number of articles in four major papers that serve different regions of the state: The *Des Moines Register*, which serves the central part of the state and has the largest circulation; the *Iowa City Press-Citizen*, which serves the eastern and southeastern part of the state; the *Dubuque Herald*, which serves that major northeastern city; and the *Omaha World-Herald*, which serves the westernmost rim of the state. Those papers were the only Iowa-region papers carried by Lexis-Nexis. Press coverage data from before the Lexis-Nexis service began required multiple imputation. Note that no attempt was made to characterize the coverage as positive or negative, an important shortcoming of the variable.

The story was Howard Dean in the 2004 cycle. He captured nearly a quarter of all Democratic presidential candidate stories written in the sampled papers, about twice his share in an eight-candidate field (Figure 5.6). The Vermont doctor generated almost a thousand articles in just the four papers surveyed, an average closer to one a day than one every other day.

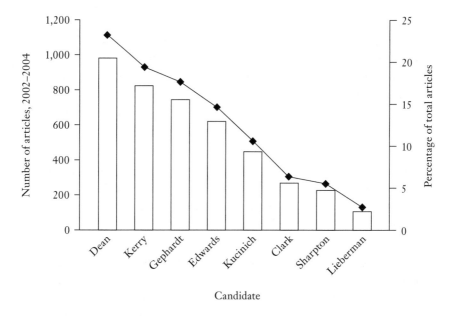

Figure 5.6. Press coverage in Iowa-region papers, 2004

NOTE: Number of print articles mentioning the candidate appearing in four major Iowa-region papers (bars) and percentages of the sum of those totals (line), by 2004 candidate.

And considering that Dean's candidacy did not catch fire right away, the concentration of those stories was likely close to the Caucus.

Though Dean garnered the most coverage, the drop to the rest of the field was not nearly as steep as with other factors, nor was there as much of a gap between first-tier and second-tier candidates. Kerry captured about a fifth of the total coverage, Gephardt and Edwards each about a sixth. Kucinich, though hardly a prominent national figure during this time, was included in almost 500 stories in the sampled papers. And the three candidates who did not contest the Caucus still got some measure of press coverage as well.

THE DEMOCRATIC VIABILITY THRESHOLD

The Explanatory Model also includes a dummy variable to account for the 15 percent Democratic viability threshold. We would expect that a candidate going into the Caucus with an average of less than 15 percent support would face a disproportionate challenge, as in precinct after precinct he would be eliminated from consideration entirely. On the flip side, Democratic candidates with *more than* 15 percent average support would benefit from the elimination of the rabble beneath them and fare disproportionately better. Since neither is the case for Republican candidates, we should control for the possibility that Caucus math significantly impedes lower-tier Democrats.

To generate the Under 15% Democratic Viability Threshold dummy variable, I used data from the Iowa Poll; each candidate was marked as 1 for having less than 15 percent or 0 for having more. Note that there is some concern in reading too much into the dummy variable itself, as it is based on polling data external to the Explanatory Model. Its significance should not necessarily be taken as proof positive of the ill effects of the viability threshold, as the dummy variable based on polling data might be capturing other reasons why trailing Democrats do poorly relative to other candidates with similar levels of performance. But it is important to at least control for the influence of the threshold, and the results of the significance tests require some analysis regardless of the fact that they reflect polling data.

INCUMBENT PRESIDENTS, FAVORITE SONS, AND HOME STATES NEAR IOWA

In the Caucus, it would be theoretically important to control for the effects both of being an incumbent president and of running against one, over and above other fund-raising, viability, electability, and ideological advantages the president might have, for which the model already controls. There are two reasons to do so.

First, presidents may be the only candidates Iowans don't expect to constantly visit the state, and for whom any visits would have dramatically disproportionate impact. Therefore, failing to control for the two incumbent presidents who got into competitive scrapes in Iowa (Ford in 1976 and Carter in 1980) would skew our understanding of candidate days in Iowa.

Second, it stands to reason that it would be disproportionately difficult to organize the state's party activists against their own president, in a way that it would not be difficult to launch a television attack in a primary. Granted, this assumes that one of the hypotheses of this study is correct, that organization matters more than television advertising in Iowa. But if that assumption is false, the dummy variable would have to have negative impact on the model. Therefore, a dummy variable is also included for candidates *opposing* an incumbent president, to control for this effect.

In addition, the literature and political professionals refer to the rule of thumb that midwestern, neighbor-state candidates do better in the Iowa Caucus than those from farther away. For instance, Winebrenner (1998) notes that "the tendency for Iowans to support midwesterners in the caucuses continued in 1996, even though Dole's support was somewhat modest" (p. 247). Likewise, former Iowa GOP official Tim Hyde relates that Pete DuPont's campaign believed his chances in the 1988 campaign were good in part because of the candidate's Illinois residence.[25]

Accordingly, the database also contains a dummy variable control for home-state geography. The factor is coded as 1 for candidates from a state that borders Iowa (namely, Minnesota, South Dakota, Nebraska, Missouri, Illinois, and Wisconsin) or from Kansas, which is a few dozen miles away from bordering Iowa, and as 0 for those from other states.

Finally, I include dummy variables to account for the 1992 race, in which Iowa senator Tom Harkin ran for president, both for him as a favorite son and for those who ran against him, considering the overwhelming advantage he enjoyed.

The incumbent-president and favorite-son factors are particularly helpful to include in the model instead of controlling for fixed effects for time. Theoretically, it makes no sense to include dummy variables for each cycle, after all. All cycles sum to 100 percent, so from cycle to cycle there cannot be theoretically significant positive or negative impact performance for candidates overall. So fixed effects for time, ultimately, have been excluded from this model.

Instead, it makes a great deal more sense to control for the theoretically valid skewing effects within a small number of cycles, where one candidate or another is disproportionately advantaged and the other disproportionately disadvantaged in ways the model does not more generally address.

Given that set of tools, let's turn to building models to address the questions about which tactics matter to presidential candidates in the Iowa Caucus.

Testing Campaign Effects in Iowa

The Explanatory Model built on the foundation of the data presented above aims to sharpen our view of the role that each factor plays in the outcome of the Caucus, rather than maximizing the model's overall power (in contrast to the Predictive Model presented in Chapter 7). It is not intended to be a forecasting tool and accordingly excludes virtually all polling, straw poll performance, and other estimates of a candidate's Iowa outcome.[26] Instead, it includes only tactics, evaluations, and factors that would matter in generating the outcomes themselves. That is, the factors in the Explanatory Model are presumed to be *causative*. The factors in the Predictive Model, by contrast, are presumed only to be *accurate*.

The Explanatory Model is presented in Table B.7 in Appendix B. Note that this Explanatory Model is identical to the one discussed in Chapter 6. The only difference is which factor is highlighted during each analysis and which is considered a control.

Before we estimate this model, let's revisit the seven campaign-tactic questions we laid out that are based on our review of the literature and conversations with Iowa political professionals.

1. Does the amount of time a candidate spends in Iowa matter in Caucus performance?
2. Does rally attendance matter in Caucus performance?
3. Does campaign contact with voters matter in Caucus performance?
4. Does the Democratic Caucus's 15 percent viability threshold create fundamental differences between the two parties' contests?
5. Does press coverage matter in Caucus performance?
6. What role does television advertising play in the Caucus?
7. Is retail politics still of primary importance in the Iowa Caucus?

For each of these research questions, and given the data available, I hypothesized the following:

1. Candidates' percentage difference from the average number of days spent in Iowa would have a significant, positive impact on their Caucus vote share.

2. Candidates' percentage of surveyed partisans contacted by their campaign would have a significant, positive impact on their Caucus vote share.

3. Candidates' percentage of surveyed partisans reporting that they attended a rally for them would have a significant, positive impact on their Caucus vote share.

4. Democratic candidates with less than 15 percent support in the Iowa Poll would fare statistically significantly worse on average than other candidates.

5. Candidates' percentage of total press coverage in the four major papers on which I gathered data would have a significant, positive impact on their Caucus vote share.

6. Candidates' estimated percentage of total television spending (and Iowa spending, with appropriate caveats) would *not* be statistically significant at $p < 0.05$ with respect to its impact on Caucus vote share.

7. Finally, the three retail politics factors in the model—Days in Iowa, Rally Attendance, and Campaign Contact—would be statistically significant and positive when taken together.

To test these hypotheses, I estimated the Explanatory Model using OLS regression. The results are presented in Table B.8 in Appendix B.

First note that the Explanatory Model forecasts Iowa Caucus performance less powerfully than later predictive models, explaining about 85 percent of the variance in Caucus performance, with an R^2 of 0.867 and an adjusted R^2 of 0.820, but that that explanatory power is still highly statistically significant ($F = 18.152, p < 0.001$). I performed the appropriate tests and found a troubling amount of multicollinearity in the model, but the factors most afflicted by it, Electability and Ideological Crowding, remained statistically significant, so I believe the model is still quite sound. I also visually examined the residuals for heteroscedasticity and found none to speak of.

The Explanatory Model presents a fairly clear picture of what tactics matter most in actually determining Iowa outcomes. Five factors emerged as statistically significant predictors of Caucus performance, controlling for everything else in the model: Days in Iowa, Television Advertising,

Under 15% Democratic Viability Threshold, Electability perceptions by surveyed activists, and Ideological Crowding. The latter two factors will be discussed in detail in the next chapter. The first three are each discussed in detail below. Those broad results reported, we can turn to a discussion of the results on individual hypotheses. At the beginning of the chapter, we raised a number of questions to be laid before a macro model of candidate performance in Iowa. We now have some interesting answers to those questions.

DAYS IN THE STATE MAKES A CRUCIAL DIFFERENCE IN CANDIDATE PERFORMANCE

My first hypothesis, that candidates' percentage difference from the average number of days in Iowa would have a significant, positive impact on their Caucus vote share, appears to be correct. The Days in Iowa factor is significant ($p = 0.034$), and the regression coefficient indicates that for every percentage point more than the average number of days a candidate spends in the Hawkeye State, he can expect to edge up 0.061 of a percentage point in his vote share in Iowa.

Considering that Kennedy was 131 percent above the average in 1980 and Reagan was 100 percent above the average in 1976, these can be major differences—an estimated 8.0 and 6.1 percentage points added to their totals, respectively. A more vivid example might be Gephardt in 1988, who clocked in at 82 percent above the average Days in Iowa that year. As we have seen, Gephardt's time in the state paid off, and he won the Caucus with 31 percent of the vote. According to the Explanatory Model's estimate, Gephardt's time in Iowa would have added about five percentage points to his vote total. Considering he beat Senator Paul Simon by only 4 percentage points—well, Gephardt's time in Iowa might have made history. After all, Dukakis came in a respectable third at 21 percent in Iowa, but had Simon won the state, not Gephardt, things might have been different in New Hampshire. We cannot know, but these examples give a sense for how important retail politicking in person appears to be in Iowa.

CONTACT BY CAMPAIGNS ALONE DOES NOT APPEAR TO MATTER

My second hypothesis was that candidates' percentage of surveyed partisans contacted by their campaigns would have a significant, positive impact on their Caucus vote share. That hypothesis was not borne out, according to this model ($p = 0.709$). In fact, the estimated regression coefficient in the model is negative, implying that were it significant, additional contact would actually hurt a candidate. That is beyond unlikely, but we cannot rule out that Campaign Contact has no impact on independent Caucus performance based on the results of this model alone.

RALLY ATTENDANCE ALONE ALSO DOES NOT APPEAR TO MATTER

My third hypothesis was that candidates' percentage of surveyed partisans reporting that they attended a rally for them would have a significant, positive impact on their Caucus vote share. That hypothesis was also not borne out. As with Campaign Contact, Rally Attendance is not statistically significant according to this model ($p = 0.258$). And also like Campaign Contact, the beta on the variable was negative, indicating that were it significant, higher Rally Attendance would in fact be associated with lower Caucus performance, all things equal. Rally Attendance can also be crossed off our list as an independent, positive factor in explaining Caucus vote share, at least given these data.

THE DEMOCRATIC VIABILITY THRESHOLD
APPEARS TO HARM THOSE BENEATH IT

My fourth hypothesis was that a Democratic candidate with less than 15 percent support in the Iowa Poll would fare statistically significantly worse on average than other candidates. That hypothesis appears to have been correct. The Under 15% Democratic Viability Threshold dummy variable was highly statistically significant ($p = 0.008$) as a determinant of Iowa Caucus Vote Share.

In fact, according to the model's estimate, being below that critical threshold of support costs a Democratic candidate a crippling 7.5 percentage points—at least half of his support, assuming that the Iowa Poll accurately reflects the candidate's standing.

That said, the results should be taken with a whole shaker of salt, rather than just a grain. After all, the Under 15% Democratic Viability Threshold factor is a derivative of polling data in a model with no other estimates of support. Accordingly, it may be a proxy for any number of other reasons

why Democratic candidates under that threshold perform more poorly—
or the explanatory power may come entirely from their having less than
15 percent support.

Regardless, to my knowledge this is the first time any statistical analysis
has identified this particular effect from the Rules of the Game in Iowa.
Thus the finding is worthy of further study.

PRESS COVERAGE ALONE DOES NOT APPEAR TO MATTER, ALL ELSE EQUAL

My fifth hypothesis was that candidates' percentage of the total press coverage in the four major papers on which I gathered data would have a significant, positive impact on their Caucus vote share, another hypothesis
that proved incorrect. In point of fact the Press Coverage variable was not
significant ($p = 0.553$), controlling for other factors. I would add a caveat
to this result: as Appendix A reports, my data on press coverage, while con-
servatively constructed, are relatively thin. Until we can gather more data
to look further back in time, we will have to look elsewhere for explanatory
power over the Caucus.

TELEVISION ACTUALLY HARMS CANDIDATES, CONTROLLING
FOR SUSPECT IOWA SPENDING DATA

My sixth hypothesis was that candidates' estimated percentage of total
television spending (and Iowa spending, with appropriate caveats) would
not be statistically significant at $p < 0.05$ with respect to its impact on Caucus vote share. This hypothesis was the most interesting one to be proved
wrong. In fact, television spending is significant in the Explanatory Model
($p = 0.039$)—and *negative*. Thus spending too much on television advertising relative to one's competitors may actually *harm* candidates in Iowa,
controlling for other factors, crucially including both the flawed data on
television advertising described above and the Iowa Spending factor with
serious objections against it. (See Appendix A for more detail on those
concerns.)

To address the legitimate objections about Iowa Spending's role in the
Explanatory Model, I ran it again without that factor and examined the results. All variables that were statistically significant remained so, and with

the same signs, except for one—the Television Advertising metric. It remained negative but was no longer statistically significant ($p = 0.135$).

This result stands to reason: If we believe the central contention of this chapter, spending on caucus-style organization and retail politics is the best investment for a candidate, because it influences Iowa's outcomes more than spending on television advertising or other more primary-like political tactics. Thus, holding spending on other (presumably more organization-oriented) tactics constant, investing more resources in TV advertising relative to one's competitors appears to be a mistake. So spending a dollar more than one's opponents on TV, holding total dollars spent constant, is a dollar closer to losing Iowa.

These results are highly questionable, given the low quality of the data for both Iowa Spending and the Television Advertising metric. However, they are certainly worth further investigation.

AMONG TACTICS, RETAIL POLITICS MATTERS MOST IN IOWA

My final hypothesis is that, taken together, the three retail politics factors in the model—Days in Iowa, Rally Attendance, and Campaign Contact—would be statistically significant and positive.

To determine whether this hypothesis is correct, we can perform an additional test, known as a block F-test, based on Fisher's F-statistic. (The process for conducting it and the actual results of this test are contained in Appendix A.) The results of the test indicate that the joint explanatory power of these three factors in the model is statistically significant at the $p < 0.05$ level ($F = 24.07$, which actually has a p-value much closer to 0.01 than to 0.05).

Those results indicate that in the Iowa Caucus, retail politics matters most among the tactics we tested, given that press coverage is not statistically significant—and especially given the (tentative) results indicating that television advertising may actually count against a candidate, controlling for other factors.

Thus among the tactics we tested, only a candidate's days in Iowa, specifically, and his grassroots heft, more generally, stand out as having a statistically significant, positive impact on the candidate's Iowa Caucus Vote Share.

Conclusion: Grassroots Rules

With those results in hand, we can turn to the overarching question of this chapter, namely, what tactics matter most to a presidential candidate in Iowa. The answer should now be clear: if nothing else, appealing to Caucus-going Iowans with one-on-one personal visits and more broadly with some mix of retail politics writ large is the tactic that rules the Caucus.

This leads us back to our discussion of the broader context, as laid out by Putnam (2000) and Gerber and Green (2000). Iowa appears to be one place where old-style, in-person, social capital–driven politics is still practiced and rewarded at the presidential level. The findings in this chapter support Iowans' answer to the Caucus's many critics: Iowa demands grassroots organization, and grassroots organizing is the healthiest form of politics in America.

With those conclusions about tactics in hand, we can turn to a somewhat more subtle topic: the elegant interplay of ideology and electability.

Explaining What Matters

Ideological Intrigue or Strategic Voting?

In 1988 Pete DuPont just "couldn't break in to Iowa," in spite of spending "every other dime" in the Hawkeye State, recounts former Iowa GOP official Tim Hyde, who served as volunteer national political director for the DuPont campaign that year.

The reason, says Hyde, was that DuPont simply "wasn't credible nationally." He tells the story of an Iowan receiving a personal phone call from DuPont but refusing to support him because she "didn't want to waste her vote." Vice President Bush was looming over the whole process, she said, and if she wasn't going to support him, she wanted to make certain she backed someone who could beat him.

So DuPont's time in Iowa—he spent 92 days in the state during that cycle, more than any other Republican candidate—was irrelevant.

By contrast, Hyde recalls that in 1976 he was sitting at the kitchen table of a local Democratic activist when the phone rang. She answered and whispered ecstatically to Hyde that it was "Governor Carter, calling from

Georgia." The fact is, Hyde says, "she was impressed," and likely backed Carter in the end. Says Hyde, "Iowans don't rubber-stamp the front-runner, but you have to be in the hunt nationally."[1] It was a precondition for success that Carter met and DuPont did not.

Then there is ideology to consider. An Iowa presidential campaign is like "a giant Velcro ball picking every possible piece of lint it can," says Bob Haus, the former Iowa Senate Republican Caucus staff director, head of the Iowa Gramm organization in 1996 and a senior Iowa advisor to Forbes in 2000. What's more, he says, the campaign "doesn't care what color the lint is."[2] Put another way, presidential campaigns in Iowa tend to think strategically about their ideology, trying to modulate their message to attract every stripe of voter they can—at least if they want to win, that is.

They'd better, because nearly three decades of research indicate that Iowa caucus voters are thinking strategically about their vote choice, as well. That literature finds that caucusgoers tend to weigh candidates not just by their proximity to the voter's ideology but by their ability to win in the fall.

This is a matter of debate, of course. Others point to the extreme ideological starting point of these voters, as well as their demographic differences from the broader electorate, and conclude that the Hawkeye State is just a bad place to have a first-in-the-nation Caucus.

How does this dynamic look from a candidate's-eye view? That is, how do ideological and strategic factors play out in terms of aggregate candidate performance in the state? This chapter aims to find out.

Of Unrepresentativeness and Electability

Accordingly, let's delve into the debate in past studies over ideology versus strategic voting, using as an additional intellectual trowel the thoughts of Iowa political professionals.

STRATEGIC VOTING

As we saw in Chapters 1 and 2, on one hand, many have documented and catalogued Iowa's ideological skew (see, for instance, Winebrenner 1998; Mayer 2000). On the other hand, some have noted that the Iowa Caucus in particular brings out more voters, lessening its characteristic ideological unrepresentativeness. It also brings out sophisticated voters, these thinkers find, voters who are often willing to sacrifice ideology on the altar of ultimate electoral success—a contention known as the Moderation Hypothesis (Stone 1982; Stone and Abramowitz 1983; Hutter and Schier 1984; Abramowitz and Stone 1984; Stone, Rapoport, and Abramowitz 1989).

The mechanism at work in that hypothesis is the Iowa voters' assessment of a candidate's viability (chances of surviving the primary process to win the party's nomination) or electability (chances of becoming president if nominated) (see Abramowitz et al. 2001). Empirically, past studies determined that the only significant effect was that of electability—that viability did not appear to be factored in to the voter-level Caucus decision (Abramowitz 1989; see also Stone, Rapoport, and Abramowitz 1989, 19–50). That raises the interesting question of whether we can find evidence of these individual (voter's-eye-view) mechanisms at work using an aggregate (candidate's-eye-view) model.

Most interview participants cited the perception of a candidate's perceived chances of winning as an important factor in determining vote share in Iowa, saying caucusgoers are more pragmatic on ideological factors than outsiders believe, regardless of their views.[3] They also point out the importance of perceptions of both national and local inevitability in shaping Caucus outcomes, the dynamic commonly termed the "bandwagon effect."[4]

The Explanatory Model of Iowa Caucus success may help shed light on whether the demographic and ideological skew of Iowa caucusgoers is indeed blurred by "strategic" voting of some kind. Some scholars find it at the individual level. Can we find it in the success of the campaigns themselves?

DEMOGRAPHIC SKEW AND MINORITY CANDIDATES

A final knock on Caucus voters is that they are not just ideologically unrepresentative but demographically unrepresentative both of the parties and of the nation as a whole. The same theorists who note Iowa's ideological skew (Winebrenner 1998; Mayer 2000) point this out, but some who defend Iowa ideologically grant its demographic unrepresentativeness (Stone, Rapoport, and Abramowitz 1989). Still others grant that caucuses generally are less representative than primaries (Lengle 1981b, 112). By contrast, a few thinkers argue that it's important to define what one is comparing the state to, because depending on that decision, one can arrive at the conclusion that "the state of Iowa is not so unrepresentative a place for the first major authoritative expressions of candidate preference" (Wolfinger 1989, 163).

Whether or not Iowa voters are unrepresentative is not central to determining who wins—unless, of course, it matters in selectively disadvantaging some candidates, for instan ce, those who are minorities. It seems worthwhile to investigate any significant average performance difference for the Jackson (1984 and 1988), Keyes (1996 and 2000), and Sharpton (2004) campaigns, controlling adequately for viability, electability, and ideology.

These three active minority candidates' relative liberalism and conservatism, respectively, as well as perceptions that they could not win, would have a great deal of explanatory power over their performance. And of course, perceptions of viability and electability might be partially a proxy for racial proclivities on the part of either national polling subjects or caucusgoers, so teasing out true assessments might be a challenge.

Those five Iowa campaigns run by three African American candidates, one on the Republican side and two on the Democratic side, may give us a test of whether the Iowa demographic skew matters in terms of minority performance.

So who's right? Does the Explanatory Model tend to support those theorists who see only ideological skew or those who see scheming based on viability or electability? Does it matter if a candidate is perceived to be struggling in the primary, or is it only those perceived to be at risk in the general election who suffer disproportionately? Do objective measures of viability like national fund-raising create perceptions of inevitability or futility that affect Caucus performance? Does caucusgoers' demographic unrepresentativeness warp the Caucus's ultimate candidate choices, perhaps harming the chances of minority candidates? Let us turn to the measures we'd need to answer such questions.

How Can We "See" Strategic Voting in Iowa?

The operationalization of issues as sticky as ideology, viability, and electability is, well, tricky. Below I have laid out in some detail my attempts at strategic voting measures. I believe the Ideological Crowding measure in particular would reward attention.

IDEOLOGY

I obtained original raw ideology scores for each candidate from the database of Abramowitz et al. (2001) for 1980 through 1992. For 1996, 2000, and 2004 the data come from my own survey of Iowa party activists, which was designed to mirror wordings from the database of Abramowitz et al.

Using those data, I calculated three factors I found most useful in characterizing ideological positioning among these bountiful Iowa fields of candidates. With so many factors at work in those fields, it is crucial to have properly tuned tools to distinguish between them, and I believe these three interrelated scalpels are useful in that regard.

The first measure is Ideological Proximity, the distance between the candidate and the survey respondent, according to the respondent's own placements. It can be found simply by subtracting one from the other and taking the absolute value of the result. In equation form, Ideological Proximity can be expressed as

$$IP_A = |I_A - I_r|$$

where IP_A is the respondent's reported Ideological Proximity to candidate A; I_A is the respondent's ideological placement of candidate A on a 5-point scale, from "Extremely (or Very) Liberal" (1) to "Extremely (or Very) Conservative" (5); and I_r is the respondent's placement of himself or herself on that same scale.

The second measure is Ideological Vote Share, which is the percentage of the candidate's party members surveyed to whom the candidate had the nearest (smallest) Ideological Proximity, with proportional percentages allocated to tied Ideological Proximity measures with other candidates.

The Ideological Vote Share calculation laid out in Appendix A parcels out voters to the candidates they say they most resemble ideologically. If two candidates fall at equal distances from a given voter, each is awarded half the voter; if three candidates tie, each gets a third of the voter. The variable is intended to provide a better measure of the space candidates have opened between themselves and their opponents ideologically, in the only currency that matters: proportion of voters.

Ideological Crowding, then, is only the proportion of voters other candidates have captured—every voter *not* in a candidate's Ideological Vote Share. Ideological Crowding represents the proportion of those surveyed who placed another candidate either equidistant from or nearer to them ideologically. Thus the factor is a useful measure of how ideologically hemmed in a candidate is by other candidates within the community surveyed. In the case of my survey, of course, that community is politically active Iowans. So Ideological Crowding within this study is a measure of the degree to which a candidate has been squeezed out by other candidates in terms of perceptions of his views. Appendix A contains a detailed description of how to calculate Ideological Crowding given survey data with liberal-conservative candidate placements and respondent self-placements.

The high concept of an Ideological Crowding variable for the Explanatory Model was suggested by Norrander, and this particular formulation was suggested by the technique used by Cohen, Noel, and Zaller (2004) of using coders and cross-sections of voter data. Their technique is an ingenious one for those without access to survey data and comes highly recommended. For those with the luxury of using survey data, on the other hand, using Ideological Proximity, Ideological Vote Share, and especially Ideological Crowding may be a more accessible technique and may take Cohen, Noel, and Zaller's idea of calculating proportion of the voting public to which a candidate is closest a step closer to empirical reality.

The 2004 cycle provides a good glimpse into why these ideological measures would be superior to ideological placement scores alone. Figure 6.1 maps the average ideological placement scores of the top Iowa contenders. Note that these are perceptions only—those familiar with Howard Dean's governorship in Vermont, for instance, would be astonished at how liberal Iowans finally decided he was.[5]

The question is where we go from here. It does not matter so much what a candidate's philosophy is perceived to be, after all, but how that interacts with the electorate's philosophy. It is only when we examine relative ideology that we get finer gradations between the candidates.

Ideological Proximity—again, the percentage of those surveyed placing

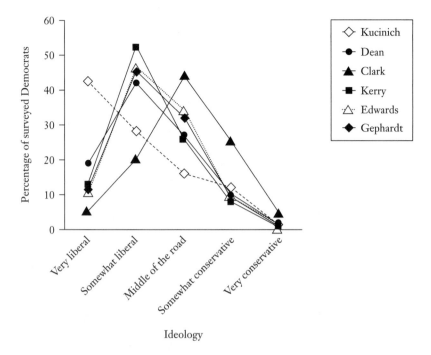

Figure 6.1. Ideological placement scores, 2004

N O T E : Percentages of surveyed Democrats placing each of the 2004 Democratic candidates at some ideological point.

themselves at the same ideological point as a given candidate—clarifies the view of the field somewhat (Figure 6.2). When we sort candidates by this factor, we see that Representative Dick Gephardt (D-Mo.) and Kerry rank highest, trailed closely by Senator John Edwards (D-N.C.) and a bit more distantly by Dean.

Ideological Vote Share provides an even sharper view both theoretically and empirically, though in 2004 it actually deviates further from the ultimate Caucus results. Both Dean's and Kucinich's Ideological Vote Share, notice, is higher than their Ideological Proximity, relative to other candidates. The implication of this finding is that, although fewer surveyed Democrats reported they were in synch with them ideologically, they had more elbow room among those who were. As we saw in Figure 6.1, Kucinich was considered more to the left than any other candidate, so one

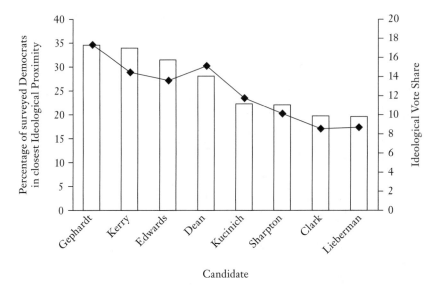

Figure 6.2.   Relative ideological position, 2004

NOTE: Percentages of surveyed Democrats placing each of the 2004 candidates at the same ideological point as themselves (left-hand axis, bars), and percentage of surveyed Democrats for whom a candidate is ranked ideologically closest, with ties allocated proportionally (Ideological Vote Share, right-hand axis, line).

imagines that many respondents on the far liberal fringe of the spectrum perceived that they had no closer alternative than him.

ELECTABILITY AND VIABILITY

Prior research has demonstrated that a candidate's electability (in the fall) and viability (in the nomination) influence candidate choice (Stone and Abramowitz 1983). As with ideology, the original 1980–1992 electability and viability data in the model are from the database of Abramowitz et al. (2001), and from 1996 on, the data all come from my own survey of Iowa party activists. The variables themselves come from questions about survey respondents' perceptions of the chances for each candidate to win the general election and gain the nomination, respectively.

Viability is the percentage of candidates' same-party respondents *not* saying they had no chance to win, that is, the percentage answering anything else but that the candidates were certain to lose or whatever the worst rank was in the survey (though all meant something similar, some surveys used different constructions than "certain to lose," such as "definitely would lose").

Electability is slightly different—it is the percentage *not* responding that the candidate would more likely lose the general election, again among same-party respondents. Like Viability, it is obtained by finding the percentage of those surveyed with electability concerns—but instead of including only those in the most pessimistic category, Electability uses all those who list any of the "lose" categories, including "probably would lose" or "definitely would lose."

The difference in modulation comes from existing literature, which has tended to discover that electability concerns, not viability concerns, matter most in dooming candidates (Stone and Abramowitz 1983). Thus Viability is intended to catalogue those with the strongest possible feelings that it is not worth supporting given candidates in the primary, that is, a sense of total futility in voting for them. Electability, by contrast, is intended to gauge all those with doubts about the ultimate success of a candidate in the fall.

In 2004, the difference between viability and electability was relatively stark. With respect to the nomination, Iowa caucusgoers generally felt that Dean was the most likely to be successful. In particular, doubts centered on Edwards's chances of being the nominee, with fully 20 percent reporting that they felt he "probably would lose." Still, those surveyed generally gave the top four candidates some chance to win. Virtually no one reported that Dean, Kerry, Edwards, or Gephardt would "definitely lose" (Figure 6.3).

Not so with respect to the general election. Whereas only a handful thought Dean would likely lose the nomination, a substantial proportion of surveyed Iowa Democrats felt that he would lose in November to President Bush (Figure 6.4). And where Dean stood out to surveyed Iowa Democrats before the Caucus as the candidate least likely to lose the nomination, Kerry stood out as the candidate least likely to lose to Bush.

Many media reports raised the question of whether the perception that Dean might be more vulnerable against Bush cost him Iowa. The question before us empirically is whether such perceptions more generally could help explain the 2004 Caucus, and whether Electability and Viability matter significantly in winning Iowa, not just in 2004 but since 1976.

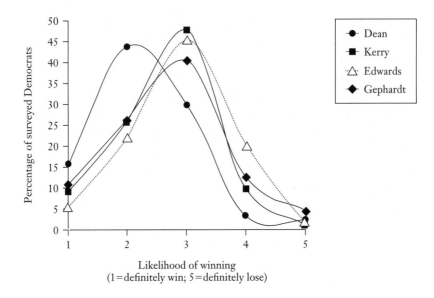

Figure 6.3. Likelihood of top candidates winning nomination, 2004

NOTE: Percentages of surveyed Democrats placing each of the top four 2004 candidates at a given likelihood of winning.

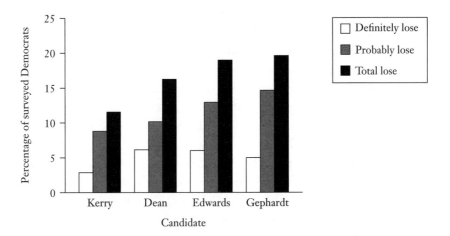

Figure 6.4. Likelihood of top candidates losing general election, 2004

NOTE: Percentages of surveyed Democrats placing each of the top four 2004 candidates at a given likelihood of losing.

NATIONAL FUND-RAISING SHARE

In Chapter 3, we reviewed the importance of national fund-raising in gauging a candidate's success in the Iowa Caucus. As mentioned at that time, national fund-raising can be measured by candidates' percentage of total dollars raised by all major candidates[6] in their party during the third and fourth quarters of the year before the election, or their National Fund-Raising Share. (For a discussion of why only half-year totals were used, see Appendix A.)

With respect to cash raised, at least, on Caucus day the 2004 Democratic Primary was no contest: Dean was winning (Figure 6.5). With more than $30 million raised in the second half of the pre-election year and a towering 41 percent of the total dollars raised by the field, he was virtually without second. Clark took in just less than $14 million, less than half what Dean raised. Kerry had less than $10 million for the period, Gephardt less than $7 million, Lieberman less than $6 million, and Edwards actually raised less than Kucinich, both coming in below $5 million. Sharpton brought up the rear with about a quarter of a million dollars raised.

Does the Iowa Caucus nurse on the mother's milk of politics? With Na-

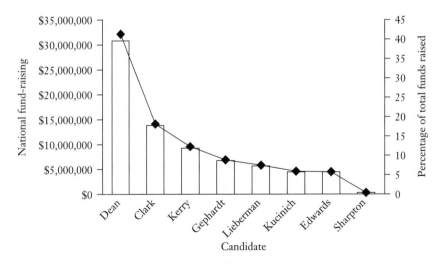

Figure 6.5. Candidates' national fund-raising, 2004 dollars, and percentage of total funds raised

NOTE: Fund-raising totals in the third and fourth quarters of 2003 (the pre-Caucus year) in 2004 dollars (bars) and percentages of the sum of those totals (line), by candidate.

tional Fund-Raising Share data and (admittedly suspect) Iowa Spending data in the Explanatory Model, we can move a step closer to finding out.

AFRICAN AMERICAN CANDIDATES

To control for a demographic bias, I added a dummy variable for the five minority candidacies to my dataset. Its results would be analogous to testing a demographic moderation hypothesis: Does the fact that Iowa caucusgoers are demographically unrepresentative translate into a proportionally worse performance for minority candidates or does the unrepresentative demography of Iowa not hamper minority candidates, ceteris paribus?

Teasing Out Strategy from Ideology in Iowa

The addition of Electability, Viability, and Ideological Crowding to the Explanatory Model sets up a crude duel that helps test the mettle of the Moderation Hypothesis. If Ideological Crowding is statistically significant (and negative) and neither Electability nor Viability rises to that level, we know that at any given level of electability and viability, ideological factors outweigh "strategic" voting factors, holding the other factors in the model constant.

By contrast, if either Electability or Viability is statistically significant (and positive) and Ideological Crowding is not significant, we know that at any given level of ideological infringement, candidates get extra elbow room if they seem to be poised to succeed, again holding other factors constant. If none of the three are significant, we can draw no firm conclusions; if all are significant, then each is playing a role, holding the other constant, and strategic voting of some kind is going on.

Granted, there is no "moderate" or "extreme" measure in the Explanatory Model. Merely pitting perceptions of potential success against ideology fails to take into account the direction of ideological distance. However, if Iowa voters choose strategically as some past accounts would have it, we may be able to find Electability or Viability remaining statistically significant, controlling for Ideological Crowding in the Explanatory Model.

With these thoughts in mind, I conducted an analysis related to the one in the last chapter to answer the questions we posed earlier in this chapter (see Table B.9 in Appendix B):

1. Does the Explanatory Model tend to support those theorists who see only ideological skew or those who see scheming based on viability or electability?
2. Does it matter whether a candidate is perceived to be struggling in the primary, or is it only those perceived to be at risk in the general election who suffer disproportionately?
3. Do objective measures of viability like national fund-raising create perceptions of inevitability or futility that affect Caucus performance?
4. Does caucusgoers' demographic unrepresentativeness warp the Caucus's ultimate candidate choices, perhaps harming the chances of minority candidates?

With the data and variables available, I hypothesized the following:

1. Both Ideological Crowding and Electability would be statistically significant, the former negative and the latter positive, supporting those who believe strategic voting is taking place.
2. Viability would not be statistically significant at $p = 0.05$ controlling for Electability, supporting prior findings that it is the latter, not the former, that matters in strategic voting.
3. National Fund-Raising Share would be statistically significant and positive, not only because it would point toward the resources to compete effectively in the primary but also because it would bolster perceptions of inevitability or futility, which would in turn affect candidates' Caucus performance.
4. The African American dummy variable would be significant and negative, indicating that Iowa's demographic unrepresentativeness was damaging minority candidates, even controlling for ideology, electability, and viability.

With those hypotheses in mind, let's revisit the estimation of the Explanatory Model, this time looking not at tactics, but at strategic voting factors. How did the hypotheses hold up? (See Table B.10 in Appendix B.)

My first hypothesis was that both Ideological Crowding and Electability would be statistically significant, the former negative and the latter positive. That hypothesis was correct, supporting theorists like Abramowitz, Rapoport, and Stone, who believe strategic voting is taking place. Specifically, Ideological Crowding was significant at $p = 0.025$, with an estimated regression coefficient of -0.849, meaning that, for every additional percentage point of those surveyed *not* listing the candidate at least tied in ideological proximity to themselves, we would expect a candidate's vote share in the Iowa Caucus to drop by about 0.85 percentage point.

This is no isolated, marginal effect. The model is estimating a constant of 77.5 percent in the Caucus, which is not statistically significant, though only by the slightest hair, with a p-value of 0.051. That is, in the nonsensical case where a candidate had zero ideological crowding, zero viability, no effects from television or Iowa spending or time in the state, a zero percentage of share of the field, and so forth, the model estimates that candidate would receive 77.5 percent of the Caucus vote (though technically we cannot reject the null hypothesis that the constant is in fact zero since it is not statistically significant).

Instead, of course, all those values are nonzero for each candidate, and according to the Explanatory Model, Ideological Crowding is the central mechanism pulling candidates down from that 77.5 percent share to what we would ordinarily expect a candidate to get. (The mean vote share in Iowa from 1976 to 2004 for all 69 candidates who reached the Caucus is just under 17.4%.)

To get some gauge of the size of Ideological Crowding's effect—and the damage it can wreak on a candidate—let's look at General Wesley Clark, the candidate with the highest degree of Ideological Crowding in the 2004 field, with 91 percent of those surveyed placing another candidate closer to themselves than him (as always, including a proportional share of ties).

According to these estimates, Clark would expect to lose a towering 77 percentage points of his vote share in Iowa just based on his Ideological Crowding. Before the reader immediately begins checking my math, remember this: given a constant of 77.5 percent, the predicted value of 0.5 percent in the Caucus (77.5% − 77%) is almost exactly what Clark actually got—which was virtually nothing. And that quick-and-dirty estimate ignores the entire remainder of the model.

That said, there is usually a fair amount of Ideological Crowding in a field as large as Iowa's. Thus the 2004 candidate with the least Ideological Crowding, House Majority Leader Dick Gephardt, had fully 83 percent of those surveyed report another candidate as closer to them than he was. According to the Explanatory Model, we would estimate that Gephardt would lose about 70 percentage points of his Caucus vote due to Ideological Crowding, putting him at 7.5 percent, about 3 percentage points lower than what he actually received.

Which brings us to the second factor in the mix here: Electability. The Electability factor also proved statistically significant in the model, at $p = 0.041$, with a regression coefficient of 0.248. That estimate implies that, for every additional percentage point of those surveyed *not* responding that the candidate would more likely than not lose the general election, we would expect the candidate's vote share in Iowa to rise by about a quarter of a percentage point.

To return to the example of the 2004 race, Clark was actually perceived as a mid-tier candidate with respect to Electability, with 61.4 percent of those surveyed on the positive side of the ledger on his chances of capturing the White House were he nominated. (Again, not 61.4% saying he would win; 61.4% *not* saying he would more likely lose.) According to the Explanatory Model's estimate, Clark would receive a boost of about 15 percentage points in the Caucus based on this high an Electability score, all else equal.

Once more, before the reader rushes to point out that he received nothing of the kind, let's quickly factor in the other significant variables in the model: First, he would lose 7.5 percentage points from being under the 15 percent Democratic viability threshold. Also, he would lose another 5.6 percentage points given that he was 91 percent below the average number of days in Iowa during the 2004 cycle. (Since he spent nothing on television, there would be no effect from the Television Advertising metric.) This puts our Clark estimate at about 2.4 percent in Iowa, not so very far off the mark for a model intended to explain rather than predict outcomes.

Gephardt's 80.4 percent Electability factor, we would estimate, would award him about 20 points in Iowa. Factoring in campaign effects, he too would lose 7.5 percentage points from being under the Democratic 15 percent viability threshold; he would gain about 3 points from his 49 percent above-the-average number of Days in Iowa; and he would lose about 11 percentage points from running too much television, given that he alone accounted for 26.3 percent of the total—giving him about 12 percent in Iowa, which is only 1.3 percentage points off his actual total of 10.7 percent.

Both from these estimates and from the examples we can see that Electability is playing a major counterbalancing role to Ideological Crowding. Though the broad outlines of candidates' outcomes are attributable to their ideological position, they can easily run up (or drop) a couple of dozen extra percentage points exclusively on the basis of the perception they will win (or lose) the White House.

To conclude, let us look at the two perhaps most interesting examples from 2004, rather than the extremes: Governor Howard Dean and Senator John Kerry. Dean's and Kerry's Ideological Crowding were identical at 85 percent, giving them both a base of support in Iowa of only about 5.5 percent to build on. Dean would have lost more by overloading the airwaves, given that he racked up 32.3 percent of the television spending in the 2004 cycle (−13 points), as opposed to Kerry's 24.2 percent (−10 points). But he would have gained more by spending more time in Iowa, given that his total was 69 percent above the average (+4 points) and Kerry's was only 62 percent above it (+3.5 points). That means, factoring in both Ideological Crowding and campaign effects, we are left with two candidates in the red: Dean's pre-Electability base of support, as it were, was −3.5 percent; Kerry's was −1 percent.

In a sense, then, it came down to Electability. Dean's 83.9 percent Electability rating, we can estimate, won him 20.8 percentage points in Iowa. Kerry's Electability rating of 88.6 percent won him almost 22 points— enough to put him another half-length ahead of Dean.

The Explanatory Model would therefore place Dean at about 17.3 percent, which is nearly exactly what he got—18 percent. However, note that the Explanatory Model would put Kerry at only 21 percent in Iowa, which is 16 points below his actual total, 37.6 percent. Though it may explain most of the variation in Caucus vote share, the model obviously is neither capturing all of Kerry's surge nor is it a reliable predictor of candidates' outcomes more generally (a shortcoming addressed in Chapter 7).

As a final caveat, recall that these results rely on suspect Iowa spending data. Though the factor is not statistically significant, it plays an important role in both the model and in the estimates for Dean and for Kerry in particular. Its inclusion makes television spending statistically significant, a result we must continue to regard as tentative until the data can be improved.

That aside, we can say with reasonable confidence that Ideological Vote Share and Electability are dominating forces in presidential candidate performance in Iowa. Strategic voting is apparent at the aggregate level of candidate performance.

VIABILITY DOES NOT MATTER, CONTROLLING FOR IDEOLOGY AND ELECTABILITY

My second hypothesis was that Viability would not be statistically significant, controlling for Electability. That hypothesis was also correct, supporting prior findings that it is the latter, not the former, that matters in strategic voting. The Viability factor is not significant at $p = 0.631$. It appears from this analysis that a candidate's likelihood of winning the primary is virtually absent from caucusgoers' strategic calculations. Instead, it is the candidate's likelihood of winning the general election that has a dramatic impact on their choices.

NATIONAL FUND-RAISING SHARE DOES NOT SIGNIFICANTLY AFFECT CAUCUS OUTCOMES

My third hypothesis was that National Fund-Raising Share would be statistically significant and positive. That hypothesis was not correct. The factor is not statistically significant ($p = 0.550$), controlling for the other variables in the Explanatory Model. Apparently, having the resources to compete effectively in the Caucus is already included in the model through Iowa Spending, the Television Advertising metric, and the retail politics factors, and viability and electability already reflected through the survey-based metrics of their perception.

MINORITY CANDIDATES MAY FACE NO DOWNSIDE, CONTROLLING FOR IDEOLOGY AND ELECTABILITY

My final hypothesis was that the African American dummy variable would be significant and negative. That hypothesis was also incorrect. The factor was not significant ($p = 0.514$) and was positive. The indication of this finding is that Iowa's demographic unrepresentativeness does not damage the prospects for minority candidates, controlling for their ideology, electability, and viability. A challenge could be raised that perceptions of ideology, electability, and viability may themselves be tainted by Iowans' racial attitudes, which bears further investigation.

IDEOLOGICAL CROWDING HAS LARGEST OVERALL IMPACT ON OUTCOMES

Moving beyond this chapter's hypotheses, let's examine the overall results of the Explanatory Model, including both campaign effects and strategic voting factors in our analysis. First, let's compare all the factors head to head, to see how they rank in terms of overall impact on Iowa outcomes. Figure 6.6 shows the results.

This diagram has a number of lessons. First, it appears that Ideological Crowding dwarfs the impact of other factors. Second, Ideological Crowding and Electability, the two significant strategic voting factors, both have a larger impact than any other variable. Third, according to our model with flawed television and Iowa spending data, Television Advertising actually has a larger impact than Days in Iowa on final Caucus outcomes—and, remember, in a negative direction. One hesitates to make too much of this finding without verifying it with improved data, but it is certainly worthy of additional exploration.

Fourth and finally, the most highly significant factor in the model, the Under 15% Democratic Viability Threshold dummy variable, has the

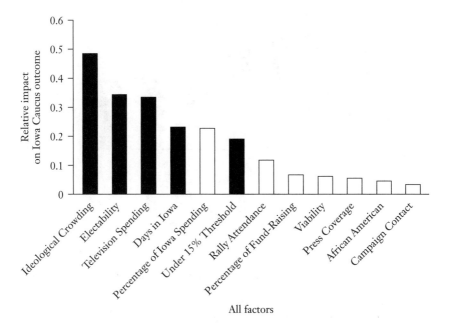

Figure 6.6. Impact of campaign effects and strategic voting factors on Iowa Caucus outcomes

NOTE: Absolute values of standardized betas for each variable of interest in the Explanatory Model, ranked by size, to capture overall scale of impact, with statistically significant factors highlighted in black.

smallest impact among significant factors, even smaller than one statistically insignificant variable (the nettlesome Iowa Spending).

Among just significant variables, one might ask, what are the relative impacts, and in which direction does each impact flow? The results of such an analysis are included in Figure 6.7.

What can we learn here? For starters, it appears that the most potent factor working in candidates' favor is their electability. That is, the largest force acting on candidates to draw them toward dramatic wins in the Caucus is the perception that they are capable of winning the general election. Next, spending time in Iowa pressing the flesh in retail politicking appears to be the only other statistically significant, positive force in the Caucus.

Starting from the other extreme, it seems that a lack of ideological elbow room is the factor doing the most damage to candidates seeking to be out-

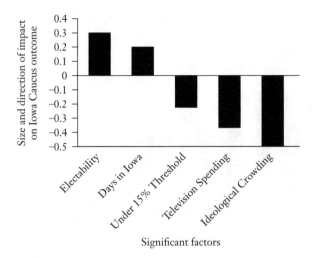

Figure 6.7. Size and direction of impact of campaign effects and strategic voting factors on Iowa outcomes

NOTE: Standardized betas for statistically significant variables in the Explanatory Model, ranked by actual value, to capture both scale and direction of impact.

standing in Iowa's field, as the old joke goes. Also—repeating full caveats for data problems in the model—running too much television in Iowa has a pretty astonishing negative impact, controlling for the problematic Iowa Spending variable, of course. Finally, the structural factor identified by political professionals has a modest but significant impact on final outcomes.

Among Strategic Factors, Ideology and Electability Rule

The main question of this chapter was whether we could find in candidates' Iowa Caucus performance the same "strategic" voting that has been identified in voter-level investigations. This analysis appears to have provided an answer. The Explanatory Model found that electability had an impact on candidate success in spite of ideology's tectonic role, at least in statistical terms.

Does that perception of electability necessarily flow from moderation? No. Additional investigations must take place to ascertain whether there are satisfying interactions between moderation, electability, and ideological vote share—and those investigations will take place.

But nonetheless, the Explanatory Model has discovered an engine that could drive a moderation hypothesis: strategic voting by the Caucus writ large for more-electable candidates holding their ideology constant. Further investigations will also be required to see whether candidates with higher perceptions of electability are generally more moderate. Yet the results seem to reinforce the findings of earlier scholars that caucusgoers choose candidates strategically (Stone 1982; Stone and Abramowitz 1983; Abramowitz and Stone 1984).

Another finding of interest was that Viability did not matter to Caucus outcomes, controlling for Electability and Ideological Crowding. The implication of this finding is that party activists seem to be reserving to themselves the decision of whether the candidate will win the primary. That is, it's up to the party who gets the nomination, so even if a candidate is struggling in the primary, activists still feel free to support that candidate—granted that he or she is close enough to them ideologically relative to other candidates and that the activist believes that, if nominated, the candidate would have a good shot at the White House.

Also, it appears that a candidate's National Fund-Raising Share does not significantly affect Caucus outcomes, controlling for other factors in the model. Apparently national fund-raising's impact on perceptions of inevitability or futility is captured directly through the Electability and Viability factors in the model, and the impact of additional resources is captured directly through Iowa Spending, Television Advertising, and retail politics factors.

Finally, the Explanatory Model also provides no evidence of systematic demographic bias. According to its findings, the overwhelmingly white populace of Iowa does not seem to slight African American candidates, all other factors being equal. Though this is far from proof, it raises the possibility of a demographic moderation hypothesis—that Iowa's white voters might be willing to gravitate toward a viable, well-organized minority candidacy. This finding may ameliorate one aspect of the criticism of Iowa's demographic unrepresentativeness, as found in Winebrenner (1998) and Mayer (2000).

Before reaching a final conclusion on that score, it would be crucial to measure the extent to which surveyed primary voters were building race into their assessments of viability, electability, and ideology. Perhaps the significance of race in the Explanatory Model is masked by holding these three perceptions constant—perceptions potentially colored by bias. In fact, my initial stab at exploring this question found that race had a significant correlation with perceptions of electability. If it can be shown in future research that surveyed Iowans merely discount the electability or viability, or both, of minority candidates or place them at greater ideological distance from themselves all things equal, then the Explanatory Model's initial finding on race might be moot.

In terms of final, overarching conclusions from the Explanatory Model, it seems that ideological maneuvering among the many candidates in the state is the strongest factor controlling the final outcome for Iowa presidential candidates. What's more, it seems that a candidate's perception of electability is the strongest factor working in favor of (or against) those candidates. The other variable working in candidates' favor in Iowa is the retail politicking the candidate does in person in the state. Finally, it is worth mentioning once more that political professionals pointing out the Iowa Caucus's structural differences between Republican and Democratic candidates have done us a service, as the 15 percent viability threshold in Democratic caucuses is the most highly significant factor in the Explanatory Model.

That is a raft and a half of results from a single model. Perhaps the reader will permit one more step: adding a whole new layer of data to attempt to predict Iowa's outcomes. It is to this that we now turn.

SEVEN

Predicting What Happens

Forecasting the Results of the Iowa Caucus

On Caucus day January 19, 2004, a panel of experts sat at a table in the rotunda of the Iowa Capitol, broadcast by Fox News. One by one, they were asked who would win that day. Each expressed more or less complete befuddlement. They concluded the questioning with David Yepsen, the veteran *Des Moines Register* dean of the Iowa press corps, who also sat at the table. Yepsen noted that Kerry and Edwards were clearly surging, that Gephardt had a tough, hardscrabble organization, and that he'd never seen anything like Dean's army. And then he, too, shrugged. He had no idea who would win, either.[1] The first-in-the-nation Iowa Caucus is not an open book.

Unlike primaries, caucuses do not "rhyme" with well-studied general elections, and the factors that influence them are therefore more difficult to spell out. Doing so is important, however, because for a generation, only candidates doing well in the Caucus have gone on to be president, and candidates faring poorly in Iowa have often found their campaigns ended shortly thereafter—or even beforehand. We saw in 2004 that Representative Dick Gephardt (D-Mo.) was forced out of the race after a fourth-place finish in Iowa—and that Governor Howard Dean (D-Vt.) lost his perch at the top of the Democratic field after his third-place finish and was ultimately defeated.

With those high stakes for candidates, as well as the heavy criticism historically leveled at the Caucus as unrepresentative demographically, ideologically, and geographically, it becomes especially crucial to grasp the mechanisms that drive success or failure in the contest. What's more, for forecasting of the whole primary to succeed, scholars frankly say they need a better starting place. With no contest before Iowa to gauge momentum going into the Caucus, they are left with what many believe is a relatively crude approximation: plugging in an Iowa momentum factor based on the size of the field.

For all these reasons, we must take the next step beyond explaining the results of past Caucuses. On the basis of that understanding, we must attempt to find out what *predicts* success in Iowa.

Iowa Is a Challenge in Forecasting the Whole Primary

The Caucus is important, not for the scant number of delegates it ultimately allocates, of course, but for its effects on the broader nomination battle. Thus political scientists have explored its impact on the rest of the race, including the amount of press coverage it generates, candidate attrition after its conclusion, and its role in determining nomination outcomes. Grappling with it has also concerned those focused on building models of overall nomination success.

Some of those nomination models explicitly or implicitly play down the Caucus's role. Grush (1980) excludes caucuses entirely from his analysis. Bartels's (1988) landmark study of the post-reform state-by-state primary process also excludes caucuses. In that work, Bartels builds a model of "substantive" and "dynamic" factors influencing each state's contest. Of Bartels's dynamic factors, one is an increase in voters' information on candidates as the contests take place and generate media coverage; the second is a "bandwagon" effect of voters supporting a candidate merely because that candidate appears to be winning based on recent contests. The first contest represents a challenge within this framework, because these dynamic effects are all but unmeasured. Bartels can estimate candidate chances only as $1/N$, where N is the number of candidates.[2] There must be a way to improve on that estimate.

Norrander (1993, 343) constructs a primary model that includes caucuses. That led her to an important finding: ideologically more-extreme candidates generally fared better in caucuses than they did in primaries. That finding followed logically from the Stone, Abramowitz, and Rapoport (1989) finding brought up in Chapter 6 that caucusgoers themselves were more ideological—but again, their study found Iowa Caucus attendees less ideological than those in other caucus states. Norrander's work again raises the question of whether Iowa boosts or busts ideologically extreme candidates—a dynamic that is controlled for in the model below, as we saw in Chapter 6.

Cohen, Noel, and Zaller (2004) are in the process of building out and updating Bartels's 1988 model. They improve it both by accounting for more than the top two major-party candidates in each contested primary and by measuring ideological positions, not just by proximity to states, but by proximity to other candidates ("crowding"). Still, statistically, Iowa poses a problem in their work because no prior votes are available to base their model on, so they must rely on Bartels's $1/N$ estimate of candidate chances in the Caucus.

On the basis of this literature, there is really only one question to answer with respect to Iowa: How can we best predict the Caucus's result?

Telescopes for Peering into the Caucus's Future

To go beyond explaining the results of the Caucus, we will need to add forecasting tools. Instead of relying on a model predicated on factors we believe would directly influence Caucus results, we need one predicated on factors that gauge various aspects of a candidate's *future* Iowa success.

To predict the Caucus, of course I gathered data on Iowa polling strength, the direct measure of potential candidate success. I also returned to the national polling data employed in Chapters 3 and 4 to proxy success in the pre-Iowa exhibition season. And I pulled together the results of early statewide straw polls, to tune the model, not just to public support but also to the power of candidates' organizations when push poll came to shove.

Using those data and an early version of the Explanatory Model, I attempted to predict the 2004 Caucus. The results of that 2004 Preliminary Predictive Model are included below.

Those preliminary results led me to revise the model into a more final form. With assistance and encouragement,[3] I tested data from the Iowa Electronic Market (IEM), an economic forecasting tool that works like a stock market of primary outcomes and pinpoints with exquisite accuracy a candidate's viability in the ultimate primary on any given day—but I found that, while the concept itself has virtually unlimited potential in forecasting outcomes, it was of no additional help in predicting outcomes over and above the other measures included below, since no IEM data are available for the Caucus itself.

Finally, of course, I refined the Explanatory Model to the point where I felt that it was accurately gauging both campaign effects and strategic voting, controlling for other theoretically important factors, and included that predictive power in the model as well.

These are the data that make up the Final Predictive Model presented in this chapter. More details on these data are provided below.

IOWA AND NATIONAL POLLING PERFORMANCE

The base of the Iowa polling data comes from the *Des Moines Register*'s Iowa Poll, the state's most looked-to survey on matters political. Since 1984 the *Register* has conducted the Iowa Poll directly preceding the Iowa Caucus. As a result, it creates an effective archaeological record of bygone Hawkeye State presidential campaigns.[4]

The national polling data used back when the 2004 Preliminary Predictive Model was run were poorly sourced, heterogeneous data. (Sadly, I had little control of when the 2004 Caucus was to be held, and had to use what was on hand at the time.) It was drawn from multiple sources, with an attempt to find the latest national poll that took place before the

Caucus—but with inadequate sourcing in some years.[5] By contrast, for the rest of the models in this study, I used highly reliable, homogeneous Gallup Poll data.[6]

To use Gallup, which of course did not test every candidate in the field and also included candidates who did not reach the Caucus, I took the survey data closest to the Iowa Caucus for every candidate with Gallup data who reached the Caucus and imputed data for missing candidates, in addition to normalizing the totals to 100 percent for each race both before and after imputation.[7] One note: polling data have long been suspect in the caucus process generally. Because turnout is so difficult to predict, and because so few voters actually show up (in Iowa, around 10% of those eligible to vote attended Caucuses during presidential years), pollsters have at times been off the mark with the results they put forward.

In 2004 the Iowa Poll was a success story. A glance at the Iowa Poll and the Gallup Poll data at the time can show they foreshadow the defeat that was to take place and the surprise with which the rest of the country might react to it (Figure 7.1).

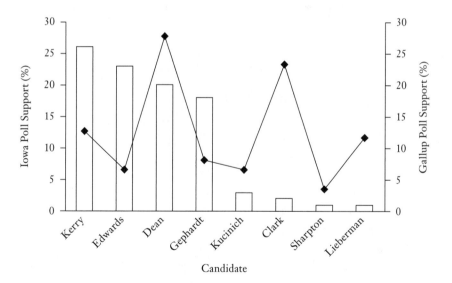

Figure 7.1.   2004 Iowa Poll Support versus Gallup Poll Support
NOTE: *Des Moines Register* Iowa Poll (bars) on the eve of the Caucus and national Gallup Poll (line) of the Democratic field conducted before the Caucus, scaled and normalized to 100 percent.

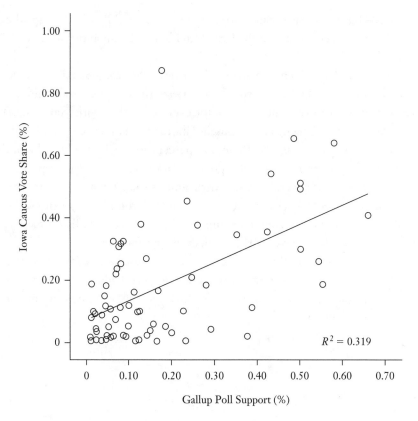

Figure 7.2. Gallup Poll Support versus Iowa Caucus Vote Share

NOTE: Iowa Caucus Vote Share is scaled, as reported by the *Des Moines Register* but proportionally factoring in undecided and uncommitted respondents. Gallup Poll Support is based on raw Gallup totals, scaled to include only candidates reaching the Caucus, filled using percentages of Share of Field and National Fund-Raising Share, then normalized back to 100 percent for each cycle.

Dean, the front-runner in the national polls, trailed Kerry and even Edwards, who was mired in single digits nationally.

An upset was brewing.

As you can see in Figure 7.2, Gallup polling has modest predictive power over the Caucus, with an R^2 of 0.319, meaning that the Gallup Poll can account for about 32 percent of the variation in Iowa Caucus Vote Share.

Perhaps it will come as no surprise that Iowa Poll Support has a much stronger predictive power over Iowa Caucus Vote Share, given that that is

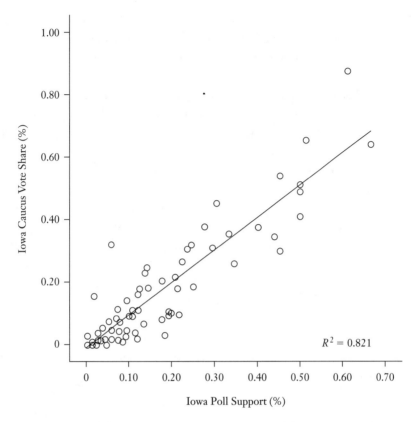

Figure 7.3. Iowa Poll Support versus Iowa Caucus Vote Share

NOTE: Iowa Poll Support is normalized to 100 percent for each cycle, filled using percentage of Iowa Spending (itself filled), Home State Near Iowa dummy variable, percentage of Share of Field, and Gallup Poll Support (itself filled), and scaled to factor out those undecided in the last *Des Moines Register* Iowa Poll.

its deliberate intent. Regardless, it does, with an R^2 of 0.821, meaning that Iowa Poll Support accounts for about 82 percent of the variation in Iowa Caucus Vote Share (Figure 7.3).

PRE-CAUCUS STRAW POLL RESULTS

Another factor built into the predictive models was success in early tests of grassroots support, as measured by the percentage of votes received by the candidate in the Ames Straw Poll (for Republicans) or Jefferson-Jackson Day Dinner straw poll (for Democrats) the summer before the Caucus. The base data were gathered from Winebrenner (1998), Squire (1989), and my own notes (for 1996 and 2000 Republicans).

Note that the Iowa Democratic Party does not always conduct a straw poll at the Jefferson-Jackson dinner, and thus data for Democrats on this measure are spotty. There was no statewide straw poll in 2004 of which I am aware, for instance. In all races without one of these two statewide party-sponsored straw polls, proxy "results" had to be estimated through multiple imputation.

Early straw polls capture a kind of predictive power different from Iowa polling: the power of the candidate's grassroots operation. The Iowa Poll measures a candidate's public support (though it has become increasingly sophisticated through the years at filtering out those not planning to attend the Caucus). The Ames Straw Poll and the Jefferson-Jackson Day Dinner, on the other hand, measure a candidate's ability to turn that public support into action.

As Figure 7.4 indicates, Pre-Caucus Straw Poll Support has a strong predictive relationship over a candidate's ultimate Iowa Caucus Vote Share ($R^2 = 0.626$).

THE EXPLANATORY MODEL FACTOR

Finally, I included in the model an estimate of Iowa Caucus performance from the Final Explanatory Model itself. To generate this factor, I merely regressed Iowa Caucus Vote Share on the Explanatory Model, including the four 2000–2004 Supporters' Internet metrics discussed in Chapter 4, and saved the unstandardized predicted values as another variable.

This regression method of indexing captures the explanatory power of all the factors used in the regression, combining that explanatory power into a single factor. Creating an index with a single factor, for instance, creates a variable with exactly the same t-score, p-value, and R^2 as the original factor, just expressed in units akin to the dependent variable.

The value of the Explanatory Model Factor is that it captures all the power of the campaign effects, strategic voting, and theoretically impor-

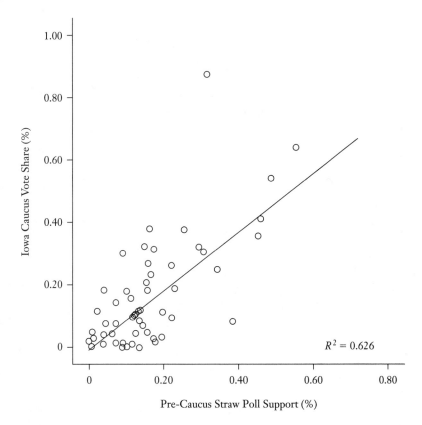

Figure 7.4.   Pre-Caucus Straw Poll Support versus Iowa Caucus Vote Share
    NOTE: Iowa Caucus Vote Share is a scaled percentage, as reported by the *Des Moines Register* but
proportionally factoring in undecided and uncommitted. Pre-Caucus Straw Poll Support is scaled, pre-
normalized, filled using Gallup Poll Support, Iowa Poll Support, percentage of National Fund-Raising,
percentage of total Days in Iowa, and percentage of Share of Field, and normalized back to 100 percent
for each cycle.

tant controls, thus allowing us to easily compare their predictive power to
the other predictive variables in the model. As Figure 7.5 demonstrates,
the Explanatory Model Factor is a very strong predictor of Caucus performance—unsurprisingly, since it has exactly the same R^2 as the Final
Explanatory Model itself.

Armed with these weapons, let's head into the arena of forecasting the
Caucus.

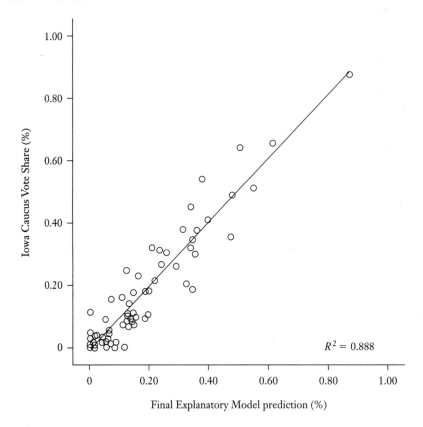

Figure 7.5. Final Explanatory Model predicted values for Iowa Caucus Vote Share versus actual Iowa Caucus vote share

NOTE: Final Explanatory Model prediction is an unscaled percentage found by regressing scaled Iowa Caucus Vote Share on the Explanatory Model with 2000 and 2004 Internet metrics included. Iowa Caucus Vote Share is a scaled percentage, as reported by the *Des Moines Register* but proportionally factoring in undecided and uncommitted respondents.

Preliminary and Final Predictive Models

The Preliminary Predictive Model, run the night before the 2004 Caucus, was premised on including the variables that explained the most variation of prior Caucuses. The most important difference from the preliminary Explanatory Model at the time was that it included national and Iowa polling data. The data used in the Preliminary Predictive Model are quite different from those of my more recent models. As a result, I have included details of imputation in notes for each factor in the model (see Table B.11 in Appendix B).

Note that there is an important theoretical reason to exclude polling data from the Explanatory Model. National polls and the Iowa Poll strive to capture what will happen in the primary or the Caucus, respectively. Including the polling data in a model of Caucus performance necessarily masks the performance of actual causative factors. Days in Iowa, press coverage, television spending, Iowa spending more generally, even ideological vote share—all these explain a candidate's popularity, which the Iowa Poll then measures.[8]

However, if the model's goal is to predict and not to estimate individual effects, the crucial question is its explanatory power, not the ability to tease out what role each tactic had in helping or hurting candidates. Both factors are excluded from the Explanatory Model for that reason but seem entirely valid for inclusion in the Preliminary Predictive Model, as long as we don't read any causation into their significance tests.

I theorized that the Preliminary Predictive Model would explain enough variation in Caucus results to help improve on $1/N$ estimates of candidates' first-state chances employed by some primary forecasting models (Bartels 1988; Cohen, Noel, and Zaller 2004). However, I also theorized that the presence of polling within the Preliminary Predictive Model would swamp other causative factors, obscuring most helpful significance estimates.

2004 PRELIMINARY PREDICTIVE MODEL RESULTS: IMPRECISE ESTIMATES FOR LOW-TIER CANDIDATES

The 2004 Preliminary Predictive Model powerfully predicted Iowa Caucus performance, though as theorized only a few of its components were individually statistically significant. The model explained about 90 percent of the variation in percentage vote support in the Iowa Caucus—the R^2 and adjusted R^2 were reported at 0.928 and 0.881, respectively. Not surprisingly, that explanatory power was highly statistically significant. (The estimation of the model is provided in Table B.12 in Appendix B.)

The 2004 prediction generated by the estimation of the model proved to be fairly accurate in rank order at least, considering how tangled the race had become by the time January 19 rolled around. The 2004 Caucus moved with extraordinary speed at the end and was considered a toss-up whose outcome the media took pains not to attempt to predict. The front-runner, Dean, was upset in a dramatic fashion that was to send his campaign into a terminal decline. Also, Gephardt's much-vaunted labor union organization was swamped by the sudden sky-high popularity of Kerry and Edwards, as well as the passion of the Deaniacs. Thus a prediction failing to call the rank order of only two candidates (plus a tie) might be regarded as a testament to the model's effectiveness at cutting through various competing factors to generate generally accurate results.

The scaled prediction is included in Figure 7.6. Note that the model correctly predicts the order of the first four finishers, though off by as many as 11 percentage points from their actual finishes (Kerry, 37.6%; Edwards, 31.9%; Dean, 18.0%; Gephardt, 10.6%). Though the model got much of the rank order correct, it did underpredict the highest finishers and overpredict the lowest finishers.

The Preliminary Predictive Model overestimated the performance of Lieberman, Clark, and Sharpton, none of whom seriously contested Iowa

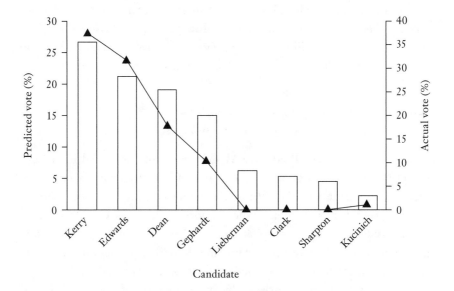

Figure 7.6. Results of 2004 Preliminary Predictive Model

NOTE: Actual 2004 Iowa Caucus Vote percentages (right-hand axis, line) and predicted vote percentages (left-hand axis, bars), scaled to sum to 100 percent for the pool of candidates.

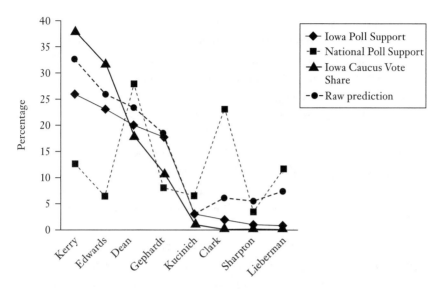

Figure 7.7. Results of 2004 Preliminary Predictive Model versus Iowa Poll Support, National Poll Support, and actual results
NOTE: The results of the Iowa Poll and Gallup Poll, the raw predictions of the Preliminary Predictive Model, and actual Iowa Caucus Vote Share, for 2004 Democratic candidates.

and who therefore received no delegates at all. Taken together, these low-tier-candidate errors certainly cry out for an Under 15% Democratic Viability Threshold control variable. These are lessons for the Explanatory Model and the Final Predictive Model—and the 2008 contests.

How do these early predictions compare with national and Iowa polling? As we see in Figure 7.7, at the top of the candidate spectrum, the predictions outperform Iowa polling. But at the bottom of the candidate spectrum, Iowa polling much more accurately forecast the ultimate defeat of Clark, Sharpton, and Lieberman.

Only three factors emerged as statistically significant predictors of Caucus performance, controlling for everything else in the model: Iowa Poll Support, Days in Iowa, and the control for a fixed effect in 1984. The Iowa Poll Support is no surprise—as mentioned above, since Iowa polling is endogenous to the model, it should muffle the other factors whose influence go into determining it.

Days in Iowa is more of a surprise as the estimate for its beta value is *negative*. This implies that controlling for the other factors in the model, including Iowa Poll Support, spending more time in the state is associated with worse Caucus-night results. From one point of view, this makes sense: if two candidates have the same level of popularity in Iowa but candidate A has spent twice as much time in the state as candidate B, it is a sign not of strength but weakness on the part of candidate A.

Finally, I have little to say about the anomalous 1984 result, except to retreat to the final defensive position that the Preliminary Predictive Model was not about identifying individual variables' impact. Perhaps others can opine on what specifically was different about 1984 that made its results lower on average than would be predicted—for *all* candidates. I view it as a spurious outcome rather than anything casting doubt on the Preliminary Predictive Model's other estimates.

Overall, though it failed to generate precisely accurate predictions, especially of second-tier candidates, the Preliminary Predictive Model did successfully call the rank order of five of the eight tightly locked crew of contestants, including the first four. And the predictions, while not laser-like, certainly improve on $1/N$ Iowa chance estimates employed by other theorists.

Finally, the lessons it taught were fodder for future investigation, including for refining the Explanatory Model and developing a Final Predictive Model—to which we now turn.

THE FINAL PREDICTIVE MODEL: CLOSING IN ON ESTIMATING IOWA CAUCUS PERFORMANCE

The Final Predictive Model contains a number of modifications from the Preliminary Predictive Model aimed at more accurately gauging individual effects. Those modifications include adding the power of the Final Explanatory Model, which factors in among other things a more proper measure of ideology, viability, and electability; a 15 percent Democratic viability threshold; and controls for Harkin's 1992 favorite-son dominance and incumbent presidents' disproportionate ability to project force in Iowa. The Final Predictive Model also includes a more standardized measure of national poll strength, based on Gallup polling. (The Final Predictive Model is presented in Table B.13 and its estimation in Table B.14 in Appendix B.)

This Final Predictive Model explains more than 90 percent of the variation in candidates' Iowa Caucus Vote Share (R^2 = 0.920; adj. R^2 = 0.915). The F-statistic is 183.116. We must take care in interpreting the F-statistic, which is badly inflated by the inclusion of the Explanatory Model Factor's 18 variables with a single degree of freedom, but regardless, 183.116 is plenty high. And all of the four predictive factors in the model are highly statistically significant.

In terms of individual factors, though we must not compare the Explanatory Model Factor's p-value to other factors as though it were a single variable, it is clear that the Final Explanatory Model itself provides additional predictive clout to our forecast, over and above the Iowa Poll and other variables. Iowa Poll Support holds its own, providing additional predictive power to the model, controlling for the other factors (p = 0.001). Perhaps more compelling is that Pre-Caucus Straw Poll Support also remains highly statistically significant (p = 0.006), controlling for the Iowa Poll, the Explanatory Model, and Gallup polling. The factor appears to measure something beyond campaign factors, Iowa public support, and national support.

Perhaps most interesting is the estimation of Gallup Poll Support, which indicates that its impact is highly significant (p = 0.003)—and negative. That is, holding constant Iowa public support; pre-Caucus straw poll success; and a fully specified model of campaign effects, strategic voting factors, and theoretically important controls, national standing is associated with highly statistically significant *lower* performance in Iowa. It appears the Hawkeye State has a rebellious side.

How does the Final Predictive Model do in forecasting? Putting it back in the same situation as the 2004 Preliminary Predictive Model, without Iowa Caucus Vote Share totals for the most recent Democratic field, we can reestimate 2004 results and compare them to the actual results, as well as to the Preliminary Predictive Model's estimates.

First, we find that reestimating the Final Predictive Model without 2004's Caucus results yields about the same performance (see Table B.15 in Appendix B). The overall predictive power is virtually identical (R^2 = 0.920; adj. R^2 = 0.914). The F-statistic, though again badly inflated, drops only slightly (to 161.024) with the loss of eight degrees of freedom, one for each 2004 candidate. And all the factors remain highly statistically significant and retain the same signs.

Now, how about the Final Predictive Model's estimates of the 2004 Iowa Caucus results?

First, we can say with some certainty that we are closing in. As Figure 7.8 demonstrates, the Final Predictive Model's results closely mirror the actual 2004 outcome of the Iowa Caucus. The Kerry and Gephardt estimates are 7 and 9 percentage points off, too low and too high, respectively, which are substantial errors. But the Dean and Edwards estimates are almost exactly correct, 1 percent and literally 0.1 percent off, respectively. Also, we can see that the lower-tier candidates are estimated with reasonable precision, indicating that incorporating the Under 15% Democratic Viability Threshold, if nothing else, has improved the overall predictive power of the model.

Though it's hardly fair, it seems important to quantify the improvement of this prediction over the $1/N$ estimate of candidate chances going into the Iowa Caucus traditionally used in the literature's macro models of can-

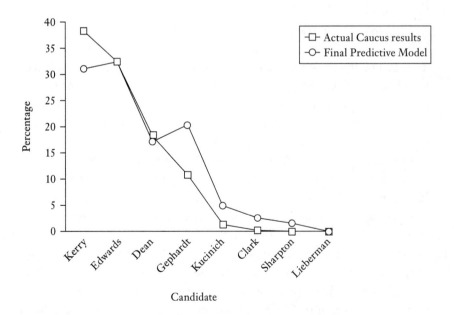

Figure 7.8. Closing in: Final Predictive Model estimates versus 2004 Caucus results

NOTE: Actual percentages of Iowa Caucus Vote Share and Final Predictive Model predicted vote for 2004 Democratic candidates.

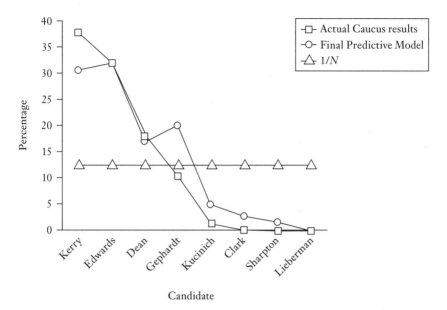

Figure 7.9. Literature's 1/N estimate of candidates' Iowa chances versus Final Predictive Model estimates

NOTE: Actual 2004 Iowa Caucus Vote percentage, Final Predictive Model predicted vote percentage for 2004 Democratic candidates, and 1/N for the race, in this case 1/8, or 0.125.

didate primary performance. That said, 1/N is actually *closer* than the Predictive Model for one candidate, namely Gephardt.

But getting Gephardt right is no argument in favor of the standard 1/N estimate. Net, the Final Predictive Model slashes more than 75 percentage points of error out of the 1/N estimate.

Graphically, we can see starkly how much more closely we can hew to Caucus results than 1/N: with the exception of Gephardt, there's just no contest (Figure 7.9).

It is no surprise that we can improve on 1/N estimates of candidate chances in Iowa. But did we improve relative to the Preliminary Predictive Model on which this analysis is based? That is, have we made progress in modeling Caucus outcomes since 3 a.m. the night before the 2004 Caucus? The answer is that the refined Final Predictive Model has eliminated fully 19.5 percentage points of error from that preliminary prediction.

First, the 2004 Preliminary Predictive Model under- and overestimated Kerry and Gephardt as well, so while those problems are actually slightly worse in the final model, the difference is slight. Second, the nailing of Edwards's and Dean's results alone cuts more than 10 percentage points out of the preliminary estimate's error. Third, recall that the Preliminary Predictive Model overestimated the performance of Lieberman, Clark, and Sharpton. With those substantial errors addressed in the model's specification, the estimates for those candidates are dramatically improved. Graphically, we can get some sense of these improvements, though it is much harder to pick out than in the case of $1/N$ (Figure 7.10).

If the revised estimates improve on my own original estimates, how do they fare against the *Des Moines Register*'s Iowa Poll, for which the intended purpose is to predict Caucus results? Before we answer, let's be clear: it is very easy after the Caucus to design a statistical model that outperforms a poll taken before it. To have a fair competition, we will have to wait for the 2008 presidential race. Also, of course, the Final Predictive Model *includes* Iowa Poll data. So the question really boils down to whether we can add anything over and above the Iowa Poll's predictive power. It appears from

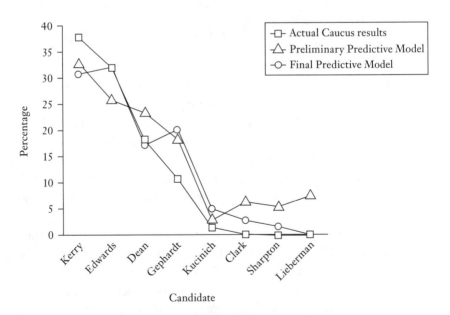

Figure 7.10. Predicted vote levels from 2004 Preliminary Predictive Model and Final Predictive Model versus actual Iowa Caucus results

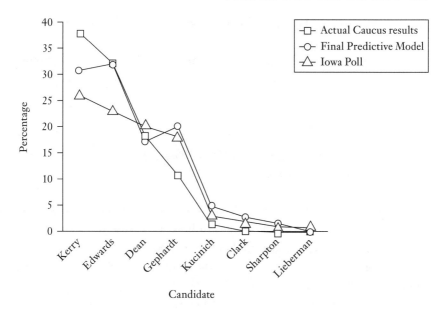

Figure 7.11. Beating the Iowa Poll: Final Predictive Model estimates versus *Des Moines Register* Iowa Poll results

N O T E : Predicted vote levels from Final Predictive Model and *Des Moines Register* Iowa Poll results, with actual Iowa Caucus results, for 2004 Democratic candidates.

our model fit and analysis of variance (ANOVA) estimates that we have, but what do the numbers show? The Final Predictive Model's estimates shave about 10 percentage points off the Iowa Poll's error in 2004.

Likewise, Figure 7.11 demonstrates visually that while most of the estimates are similar, for a couple of candidates the Predictive Model greatly outperforms Iowa Polling results. Though the Predictive Model seriously underestimates Kerry's performance, for instance, the Iowa Poll underestimated it by nearly 5 additional percentage points. And for Edwards, there is no contest: the Iowa Poll was 9 percentage points further away from his final total than the refined Predictive Model.

Once again, the Iowa Poll was both before the Caucus and included in the model, so this comparison is patently unfair. In fact, it makes little sense even to speak of it as a "predictive model" until the next presidential primary, when we can try it out again (for both Republicans and Democrats, by the way). Instead, we can merely state that the theoretically sound adjustments to both the Explanatory Model and the Predictive Model appear to have paid dividends.

Suffice it to say that it will be interesting to see if the Final Predictive Model can add precision to the Iowa Poll as the snow falls heavy on Caucus night in 2008.

We Can Predict Caucus Outcomes—Well Enough for Political Science Work, at Least

At the outset of the chapter, we raised a single question: How can we best predict the Caucus's result? We seem to have an answer, though we will have to wait until after 2008 to find out how good an answer it is.

That answer is that we can estimate the results very well, using the Iowa Poll, the Gallup Poll, the Explanatory Model including Internet metrics, and (often imputed) results of statewide pre-Caucus straw polls.

Estimates from this Final Predictive Model dramatically outperform the $1/N$ estimate of candidate chances commonly used in the literature to proxy momentum heading into Iowa, since no race precedes the Caucus from which to quantify that momentum. That is an indication that broad state-by-state models predicting and explaining primary performance may get a boost from a statistical approach to Iowa as a single case. It seems as though a model calculating Iowa candidate chances might bolster state-by-state primary models like those of Bartels (1988) and Cohen et al. (2004). However, incorporating these Iowa models into a broader primary predictive model to see what sort of benefit it yields requires empirical investigation—and is a project for another day.

The Final Predictive Model's estimates also mark an improvement over my original 2004 Preliminary Predictive Model, indicating that adjustments to the Explanatory Model based on interviews and theory have paid off and that the Explanatory Model can now add value to polling data in estimating a candidate's Iowa results. The clearest example of those adjustments' success is the revised model's refined ability to estimate candidate chances at the low end of the spectrum, which is likely based on the addition of an Under 15% Democratic Viability Threshold variable to the Explanatory Model.

Finally, the Final Predictive Model's estimates slightly outperform the *Des Moines Register* Iowa Poll overall, though again we will have to wait until after the next presidential race to test that proposition more fully.

We can also say that, in the case of 2004, the Preliminary Predictive Model demonstrated that a macro model of candidate performance can successfully *predict*—not just estimate—what campaigns stand a good chance of performing well in Iowa. Calling the top four finishers in order—Kerry, Edwards, Dean, Gephardt—in such a tough scrap indicates that candidate-view statistical modeling can indeed be helpful in showing which presidential campaigns are likely to succeed in the Hawkeye State. Granted, the predictions were imprecise, and the Predictive Model performed less successfully for candidates who had deliberately bypassed Iowa or fell under the 15 percent Democratic viability threshold. I hope the model has addressed some of those concerns, and we have a well-tuned model for the next election.

The Iowa Caucus plays an important role in selecting our president. Understanding which candidates will fare better or worse in the state is therefore important. On the basis of this analysis, we have a somewhat sharper view of how to tell who will win the Hawkeye State.

EIGHT

Is This Heaven?

Some Conclusions—and Some Beginnings

SHOELESS JOE JACKSON (RAY LIOTTA): Is this heaven?
RAY KINSELLA (KEVIN COSTNER): No, it's Iowa.

—Field of Dreams

What have we learned about the Iowa Caucus and its role within the presidential primary process? Let's run through the conclusions in the main structure of the book to see how they hang together. Then, in turn, we can build some beginnings atop them, especially about how presidential candidates win state nomination contests: the foundations for a dozen or so future research projects that this book has laid. Finally, let's come to some conclusions (and discuss a couple of beginnings) about whether the Caucus plays a positive or negative role in the primary process and, if negative, about what is to be done about it.

In the Nomination, Iowa Matters

An initial question posed in the study is whether Iowa matters to the nomination. The study's main two conclusions on this front are as follows.

IOWA'S (TRADITIONALLY MEASURED) MOMENTUM
IS FILTERED THROUGH NEW HAMPSHIRE

First, the study replicated the finding by Adkins and Dowdle (2001) and Mayer (2004) that New Hampshire dominates Iowa when measuring momentum in the traditional way. The study also found that Iowa has a modest impact on New Hampshire results, which again corresponds loosely with Mayer's finding on the subject.

However, in addition, we found that, when controlling for Iowa's favorite son Tom Harkin and home-state geography, Iowa appears to have had a significant impact on primary performance during the period studied, implying that New Hampshire was filtering out Iowa's midwestern biases—or at least its bias toward its own senator.

Finally, whether controlling for midwestern bias or not, Iowa's 2004 results seem to have been a statistically significant predictor of primary performance—implying that the Caucus's impact has *increased* somehow.

IOWA'S E-MENTUM IS *NOT* MERELY MEDIATED THROUGH NEW HAMPSHIRE

Second, the study explored the theoretical possibility that it is technology that is amplifying Iowa's impact, by giving candidates Internet tools to raise money, communicate with activists, and sign up supporters far faster than it was ever possible to do before. The preliminary finding was that this phenomenon appears to be very real and that leaving technology out of estimates of Iowa's impact on New Hampshire and the ultimate nomination badly understates that impact.

BECAUSE OF TECHNOLOGY, IOWA'S DISTORTED IMPACT
MAY BE GETTING MORE DISTORTED

Taken together, these first two conclusions lead to a third: the Iowa Caucus impact is distorted relative to the technical importance of the contest and getting more so as online politicking gets more intense. As we've seen, that raises the stakes on the debates within the literature, the press, and the political community about Iowa's future in the first-in-the-nation presidential contest slot.

In Iowa, Grassroots Organizing and Strategic Voting Matter

So, given that we have found that Iowa matters disproportionately, what can we say to explain Caucus results? That will tell us a great deal about what the implications are of Iowa's large and growing role in the nomination process. Specifically, we addressed two charges against Iowa: that healthy, social capital–rich grassroots organization mattered less and less (at least relative to television) in Iowa, and that ideologically extreme caucusgoers necessarily selected candidates less ready to compete in the fall.

OLD-FASHIONED RETAIL POLITICS REALLY DOES STILL MATTER IN THE CAUCUS

First, the study indicates that the amount of time candidates personally spend on retail politicking in the state relative to their opponents has a significant impact on their Caucus performance. Likewise, though rally attendance and campaign contact among activists do not appear to matter individually, holding other factors constant, these three retail politics factors taken together do matter significantly to how the candidate fares.

This provides the first empirical evidence of which I am aware to support Caucus supporters' most common refrain. Though Iowa political figures and commentators commonly assert the Caucus promotes the healthiest kinds of campaigning, the difficulty in measuring grassroots has left the question a theoretical one, until now: Grassroots rules.

THE 15 PERCENT DEMOCRATIC VIABILITY THRESHOLD
MEASURABLY SETS BACK LOW-TIER CANDIDATES

We also found an important difference between the GOP and Democratic contests: a 15 percent viability threshold in the latter tends to harm lower-tier candidates significantly in their results in the state. In fact, the specific estimate is that Democrats polling under that threshold going into the Caucus can expect to end up with 7.5 fewer percentage points than we would otherwise expect. For those polling under 15 percent, that's at least half their support.

That result may be anomalous because it introduces polling data into a model free from it. However, again, this is the first estimate of the threshold's actual impact of which I am aware. I hope that it will be of some use to others in the future.

MORE TV ADVERTISING MAY ACTUALLY HARM CANDIDATES, HOLDING IOWA SPENDING CONSTANT

Third, the explanatory portion of this study found that candidates spending more on television relative to their competitors may actually *harm* themselves, though only when holding other factors in the model constant, including suspect information on Iowa spending overall—a conclusion hemmed in by caveats. Assuming for the moment that the finding is correct, it implies that campaigns investing higher proportions of their Iowa spending on television may suffer because those resources did not end up devoted to caucus-style identification, organization, and mobilization of a candidate's supporters.

The finding that television spending may be toxic in too large a dose, controlling for overall levels of spending, though very likely confined to Iowa or caucus states more generally, would be highly controversial. I invite scrutiny of the finding and intend to scrutinize it myself.

IOWA IS STILL BUILDING SOCIAL CAPITAL IN PRESIDENTIAL POLITICS

This set of explanatory conclusions suggest a final one: Caucus supporters appear to be correct in lauding their contest for building rather than destroying. That is, it seems that candidates who do well in Iowa are those who focus on retail politics, something we ought to value in presidential politics, especially considering how rare it is. It also means more broadly that Putnam would be proud: here we have an example of a place in America where a vestige of social capital can be found in electoral politics. And as we've seen, it's a place that may be *gaining* influence over the process rather than losing it.

CAUCUS OUTCOMES REFLECT STRATEGIC VOTING, MITIGATING IOWA'S IDEOLOGICAL EXTREMITY

Our candidate-level explanatory investigation also turned up the "strategic" voting found in voter-level inquiries. Electability, it appears, matters to candidate success in Iowa, though ideological crowding is the main motor driving candidate outcomes. That tips the scales even further toward earlier findings by Stone, Abramowitz, Rapoport, and others that caucusgoers choose candidates strategically, lightening the load of their ideological baggage. It also tends to undercut critics like former Democratic Party chair Ron Brown who charge that the Caucus supports candidates too extreme to win in November.

VIABILITY DOESN'T SEEM TO MATTER IN THE CAUCUS, HOLDING ELECTABILITY CONSTANT

Another candidate-level result that echoed Stone and his colleagues was that viability (a candidate's perceived likelihood of capturing the nomination) does not appear to matter in the Caucus, holding constant electability (a candidate's perceived likelihood of capturing the White House). That would mean that caucusgoers are willing to forgive struggling in the primary if they believe the candidate would make a strong contender in the fall, but not vice versa.

DEMOGRAPHICS ASIDE, MINORITY CANDIDATES MAY NOT BE HARMED

Another explanatory finding: the study found no systematic anti–minority candidate bias in Iowa, in spite of its unrepresentative electorate. Had it found bias, that would have underlined a key implied criticism of the Hawkeye State's first-in-the-nation position; demographically unrepresentative as it is, if it had no downside to minority candidates, it might mitigate some concerns.

However, the study holds electability, viability, and ideology perceptions constant. It may be that those perceptions themselves are influenced by the race of a candidate. Beginning to sort that out will have to be the subject of a future investigation.

In Predicting Iowa, Explanatory Factors, the Iowa Poll, the Gallup Poll, and Straw Polls Matter

The study came to a number of conclusions with respect to the question of how best to estimate Iowa's outcomes.

PRELIMINARY 2004 PREDICTIONS DRAMATICALLY OUTPERFORMED $1/N$

The first stab at forecasting Iowa's results ranked the top four 2004 finishers in order. However, that preliminary prediction underperformed with respect to those who skip the Caucus and those under the 15 percent Democratic viability threshold. As a result, the Iowa Poll alone was in some senses a better predictor of the exact results than the prediction tool that included it. Regardless, either the Iowa Poll or the preliminary 2004 prediction would have dramatically outperformed the $1/N$ estimate commonly used to approximate candidate chances in Iowa in primary forecasting, since no race from which to quantify that momentum precedes the Caucus.

THE FINAL PREDICTIVE MODEL APPEARS TO OUTPERFORM THE IOWA POLL

Relying in part on lessons from 2004, I designed a Final Predictive Model using the Iowa Poll, the Gallup Poll, statewide pre-Caucus straw poll results, and explanatory factors like campaign effects and strategic voting measures. Though the model must be regarded as a work in progress until it can be tested in 2008, the reestimation of 2004 was promising on three fronts.

First, unsurprisingly, those estimates again outperformed the $1/N$ Iowa chances factor. Coupled with the preliminary predictions, we can say with some certainty that larger models of candidate primary performance like those of Bartels (1988) or Cohen, Noel, and Zaller (2004) would likely benefit by using virtually any variation of these predictive models—that is, using a standardized procedure to estimate chances in Iowa more accurately.

Second, theoretical and practical improvements to the Predictive Model improved its estimates over the 2004 Preliminary Predictive Model, indicating *only* that those improvements better fit our current data. Again, we cannot tell whether the Final Predictive Model will actually improve on the preliminary model's estimates until after the 2008 Caucus.

Third and most promising, the Final Predictive Model's estimates modestly outperform the *Des Moines Register*'s Iowa Poll itself, though again we will have to wait until the next presidential race to test that proposition more fully.

These results hint at a higher forecasting truth: building polling and straw polls on top of a fully specified campaign-effects model of candidate performance may be a promising—if time-intensive—formula for predicting other electoral contests.

From Conclusions to Beginnings

We now have a very clear snapshot of how presidential candidates win the Iowa Caucus. But those conclusions suggest a set of *potential* lessons for how they win state nomination contests more generally.

For one, it appears that, while Iowa's momentum is filtered through New Hampshire when momentum is measured traditionally, a portion of Iowa's extra jolt of technological momentum has an impact New Hampshire cannot stifle. A preliminary investigation also shows that New Hampshire has a similar additional e-mentum boost from candidates' Internet activity.

So if other high-profile events in the primary are likewise having technological momentum effects that carry through the next contest, political scientists should be both checking and correcting for them within their primary models. What's more, candidates should be factoring that new force into their machinations on how to win whatever states come after Iowa and New Hampshire. It may be that e-mentum is a new part of how presidential candidates win state nomination contests.

That conclusion thus leads to a beginning, as it were: it suggests a line of additional research to measure technological momentum bonuses in state-by-state primary models to see where the phenomenon is taking place and where it is not. It also suggests a line of research to those trying to model an individual state's outcome: better look beyond the last contest, to see whether the online resources and supporters poured into a campaign after a high-profile success several weeks before are having a significant impact on that state's results. And of course, it suggests a line of research to see e-mentum at work, tracking surges in online fund-raising and supporter sign-up after a high-profile win.

More new beginnings are suggested by the conclusion that retail politics is still hard at work in Iowa changing the course of the presidential campaign. Within Iowa, is that impact increasing or decreasing over time? Compared to Iowa, is retail politics significantly less of a factor in New

Hampshire and other primary states? How much of the importance of retail politics comes from Iowa's unique political culture and how much from the mere fact that it is a caucus state, not a primary state? How can we best measure retail politics and grassroots organization—through a single proxy, a set of proxies as in the current study, or an index that combines the explanatory power of a set of related factors? It would be a shame if the glimmerings of grassroots' true impact were snuffed out at the borders of Iowa-specific research.

Likewise, the conclusion that the 15 percent Democratic viability threshold seems to harm lower-tier candidates raises another way the Rules of the Game, as theorists like Lengle and Norrander have it, function not only within the primary. Extensive work has been done to understand how various styles of primary contests affect candidate strategy and electoral outcomes. Here is yet another tangle in that net to be combed out.

If the conclusion that TV spending can actually hurt candidates holds up, we are in for a wild ride of new research. Is that so, only controlling for overall spending in a state, as it appears in Iowa? Does the potential anti-television bias in midwestern states that researchers are exploring exist? Is it reflected in other parts of the country? Is TV advertising more effective in New Hampshire than in Iowa? More generally, is it more effective in primaries than in caucuses? And if it is, have candidates already responded by running proportionally fewer TV ads and focusing more on organization in caucuses than in primaries?

I concluded with an airy wave of the hand that the Iowa Caucus is still rich in Putnamesque social capital. But the implications that that would raise were it true are profound. How should we best operationalize the benefits that creates? Are the political parties more vibrant in Iowa and in caucus states than in other states? How about other forms of social capital: Lions Clubs, Rotary Clubs, bowling leagues? Is it possible that caucusing itself fosters some of the bygone Tocquevillian qualities of America to which Putnam yearns to return? And if so, shouldn't we shun the Democratic Primary reforms that fostered more openness by pushing states to move away from caucuses and toward primaries? Shouldn't we *correct* them?

The study concluded that electability, not just ideology, drives who wins and who loses the Caucus. The methodology behind that finding includes new operationalizations of both Electability and Ideological Crowding.

According to my estimations, Ideological Crowding especially, a theoretically transparent variable that nonetheless takes a bit of work to construct, turns out to be an astronomically powerful measure in explaining candidate outcomes in Iowa's multicandidate field.

This conclusion opens a methodological beginning: Is the Ideological Crowding statistic as powerful a tool in other states? Or is it merely an artifact of the philosophically extreme caucusgoer? It is my fervent hope that others will discover the joys of working with an ideological crowding variable, seeing the wonders it can perform statistically, especially in a crowded multicandidate primary field.

The conclusion also raises questions of comparability. Are Iowa outcomes more or less "strategic" than New Hampshire outcomes, for instance? More generally, are caucus outcomes more or less strategic than primaries? Can we find in the results of the contests (as opposed to surveys of the participants) evidence that the sophistication of caucus voters makes them more willing to entertain electability than primary voters?

Keeping to the strategic voting theme, we have not yet identified in the data the final link to the Moderation Hypothesis of Abramowitz, Stone, Rapoport, and others. Though our explanation of caucus results reveals the engine that would drive such a dynamic (the Caucus's tendency as a whole to reward candidates who are more electable), we have not yet traced that electability to more moderate ideologies. A new set of data might be required to complete such a task, since moderation cannot be imputed (and don't think I haven't tried). But given those data, the Moderation Hypothesis investigation based on candidate performance models like those in this study could and should roam from Iowa into New Hampshire and beyond.

The study concluded that minority candidates did not suffer at the hands of Iowa Caucus voters, controlling for ideology, viability, and electability. But that begins at least one crucial additional investigation: exploring the role that race plays in shaping perceptions of both ideological proximity and electability themselves. My initial prying into that grim reality indicates that both factors are heavily correlated with race, raising the possibility that surveyed Iowa activists were more likely to place minority candidates at a distance from themselves ideologically, as well as more likely to doubt those candidates' chances of gaining the White House. There is more to be said on this subject in the future, to be sure.

The conclusions of this study open the way for new beginnings. I, at the very least, will be happily puttering away, working to turn them into conclusions in their own right and hoping others will join in.

The Iowa Caucus Is a Positive Force in Presidential Politics

Now we come to the not-so-bitter end, and we are left with the question that opened this study: whether the Iowa Caucus is a cess poll—a negative force in presidential politics. Let's revisit the arguments, and apply what we've learned.

First, critics contend that media coverage of Iowa is wildly out of whack with its technical importance to the nomination. Yet recent studies argue that Iowa doesn't matter to the nomination, controlling for New Hampshire outcomes. We have learned that, measuring momentum traditionally, the latter view is correct. However, we have also learned that New Hampshire is filtering out Iowa's clear geographic bias, undercutting claims that Iowa skews the process toward the Midwest, to the extent that New Hampshire continues to follow it. Moreover, it appears that Iowa's impact is increasing, and e-mentum helps explain why Iowa's impact might be not only significant but growing.

Here I need to side with critics (and most others): because of media and technology, Iowa's impact is far greater than the technical significance of the straw poll taken at the precinct level of a several-month-long process. So the stakes of whether Iowa is a cess poll are high. That said, let's not lose sight of the implications of the Granite State's filtering of Hawkeye State results: the two contests appear to be working together to ensure that no overwhelming regional bias is introduced into the primary process. The concerns about Iowa favoring midwestern candidates do not appear well-founded statistically, but even in the one case where Iowa unquestionably did so, when Iowa senator Tom Harkin ran for president and won the Caucus, New Hampshire happily executed him. The same is true of 1988, when Missourian Dick Gephardt and Kansan Bob Dole triumphed in Iowa but perished in New Hampshire. That should give us some comfort.

Second, critics charge that the Caucus has become no better than a primary, with turnout high, television advertising dominant, and healthy retail politics taking a back seat. Iowa's supporters counter that though spending on television advertising has increased, time on task is still what wins the contest.

Here, I must side with supporters. Candidates' time in Iowa is the dominant determinant of their success, among tactics, just as supporters have long asserted. What's more, retail politics factors more generally do matter significantly in Caucus outcomes. And though the conclusion is tentative, our estimates point to TV spending actually harming candidates who overindulge in it. Iowa appears to remain a caucus driven by grassroots organization, perhaps the most warmly regarded tactic in American politics.

Third, critics accuse Iowa of being both demographically and ideologically unrepresentative. Advocates of "strategic voting" argue that Iowa's characteristics tend to partially mitigate ideological concerns, especially by harnessing the extreme ideologies of its participants to the hitching post of electability, and others say high turnout makes Iowa more demographically representative than most caucuses (which is still not saying much).

Here I side with supporters once again, on both counts—one firmly, one tentatively. This study found that Caucus outcomes themselves reflect the "strategic" assessments found among individual-level surveys of party activists, implying that Iowans are muting their ideologies in the service of getting a candidate into the White House. Likewise, the study found tentatively that at least minority candidates did not on the surface appear disadvantaged relative to their competitors, ceteris paribus. Thus the unrepresentativeness of caucusgoers both ideologically and demographically does not seem to translate directly into undesirable electoral outcomes.

Finally, we need to tackle Winebrenner's (1998) charge that the Iowa Caucus's results themselves are questionable. Recall that he cites three reasons why the Caucus is flawed: No actual votes are taken; the 15 percent viability thresholds mandated of caucuses by the national Democrats mean candidates' vote strengths include support from other candidates; and the "fluidity and duration" of Iowa's true delegate selection process makes results on caucus night moot by the time the state convention rolls around months later. Instead, Winebrenner urges, the Caucus needs an independently verified result.

Agreed, on all four counts. First, the voting process at the Iowa Precinct Caucus Presidential Straw Poll *should* be formalized and written into law.

Second, the Caucus *should* be funded like general elections or primaries are, with a standardized, independently verified process that makes it more credible both with Iowans and with partisans outside the state.

Third, according to this study, Winebrenner is empirically correct that the 15 percent viability threshold distorts outcomes, and Democrats *should* immediately eliminate this punitive and unfair rule, which militates against the very openness that drove the party reforms of the 1970s.

Finally, the delegate selection process *should* become binding, at least through the state convention, so that results on Caucus night are at least directly related to results at the convention.

But my staunch contention would be that the answer to each charge is these important but simple reforms, not to oust the Caucus from its first-in-the-nation position. Rather, the results of this study indicate that Iowa is doing exactly what it's supposed to be doing. On a high, prominent, well-lit stage, it is forcing presidential candidates to engage in a personal effort to meet and persuade voters to their candidacy. It is nurturing retail politics more generally, which Americans prefer to more nasty tactics in the election process, arguably kindling social capital whose dwindling we bemoan. It is selecting candidates with a blend of the party's true-blue ideology and an ability to win. And it may even be punishing candidates who rely too heavily on TV, which Americans generally believe to be among the lowest, meanest, and most intrusive of election tactics.

In short, the Iowa Caucus is a positive force in American presidential politics. (And it is most certainly *not* a cess poll.)

I would go further. I would suggest research into the cleanliness of politics in various states, to test empirically Winebrenner's observation that Iowa ranks relatively high. I would hypothesize that it does. And I would suggest delving into the content of primary television advertising with an eye toward testing empirically the idea that, because caucuses require candidates to build their organization up, not just tear their opponents' credibility down, they discourage negative advertising relative to primaries. I would hypothesize that they do.

If the results are as I hypothesize, both parties may want to consider moving *back* toward open, well-regulated caucuses and away from primaries, which have probably fostered exactly the kind of television-driven, sound-bite-heavy, attack-oriented presidential politics Americans deplore.

On this score, I side somewhere between Schattschneider (1942) and Fiorina (1980) and against those advocating maximum representativeness in primaries. If I am correct, the last three decades' drive toward more representativeness may be not only selecting worse candidates but harming the country's politics.

Finally, until an alternative comes along that provides the benefits the Caucus appears to, it has a claim on being first in the nation, not just based in tradition, but based on *utility*.

Is this heaven?

No, it's Iowa.

Notes on Data and Variables Used in the Study

Given the scope of the models used in this study, including a broad array of factors stretching back 30 years, it is important to list several technical notes and caveats that apply to the data that underlie them and to the models themselves. All of the conclusions reached in the study should be read in the light of these challenges, issues, and thoughts.

MULTIPLE IMPUTATION

First, most of the important variables used throughout this study required indexing or interpolation or both, since from 1976 to 2004 there were almost invariably candidates for whom no data were available. In each case, that interpolation was done using multiple-imputation ordinary least squares (OLS) regression models, that is, employing the predictive power of similar or related variables to estimate as nearly as possible what a candidate's missing value was likely to have been in reality.

King et al. (2001) lay out the challenge of such multiple imputation:

> When only one variable has missing data, one possibility is to run a regression (with listwise deletion) to estimate the relationship among the variables and then use the predicted values to impute the missing values. A more sophisticated version of this procedure can be used iteratively to fill in datasets with many variables missing. This procedure is not biased for certain quantities of interest. . . . Since the missing data are imputed along the regression line as if there were no error, however, the method produces standard errors that are too small and generates biased estimates of quantities of interest that require more than the conditional mean.

King et al. recommend a method of multiple imputation known as expectation maximization with importance sampling (or EMis) or at least some kind of formal multiple-imputation algorithm rather than the method described above. Those algorithms range from cumbersome to impossible when working within the limitations of SPSS, the statistics computer program I employed. Therefore, after experimenting extensively with them, I have chosen the imperfect but attainable technique of imputation through successive regression models. Readers are urged to take that into account when reviewing the models' results.

Because much of the older data—especially that from 1976—come from outside Iowa or are extrapolated back into the past from more recent data, any conclusions we might try to make about early Caucuses based on this analysis would be particularly suspect. Every effort was made to acquire data where available, but surveys of Iowa and reporting of state levels of activity simply do not exist in some cases. Though the models are designed to control for some of the cycles' particular circumstances, individual candidate data that are simply extrapolation cannot be relied on to the same extent as the actual numbers as they occurred.

On the following pages are tables (Tables A.1–A.8) for each of the three major sets of models in this study. The tables do not include dichotomous variables (for which there are data on all 85 candidates) and the Internet data for which 1996–2004 data are virtually complete (and data for other years are assumed to be zero). Note that for preimputation values of all three models, the listwise N tends to be relatively low, especially for the Explanatory Model. This is the main rationale behind the imputation: Though the database contains a great deal of data on a large number of candidates, with 18 variables in a single model and 69 candidates who reached the Caucus, the raw data invariably bring the listwise N down below a threshold of credibility for any results.

It is important to point out also that the postimputation tables include detailed descriptions of the multiple-imputation models used to "fill" each of the variables. This is to show as clear a path as possible to replication of my dataset. The order of imputation is based on the preimputation charts themselves: Imputation began by filling the variable with the highest N, then the next, and so on. Either using this technique or relying on the "filled" designations of the factors listed in the postimputation tables would give the same result.

TABLE A.I
Preimputation N of Iowa, New Hampshire, and primary variables

Variable	N	Minimum	Maximum	Mean	Standard deviation
Primary Popular Vote Share (%)	71	0	0.76	0.16	0.21
New Hampshire Vote Share (%)	71	0	0.50	0.17	0.16
New Hampshire Poll Support (raw data, before Iowa Caucus, %, unfilled[a])	45	0	50	15.58	14.76
National Fund-Raising Share (candidate's percentage of active same-party candidate total money raised, second half of pre-election year, unfilled)	66	0.002	0.56	0.18	0.15
Gallup Poll Support (poll closest to Iowa Caucus, %, raw totals only, includes candidates not reaching Caucus)	61	0.01	0.60	0.15	0.16
Raw Iowa Caucus Vote Share (%, as reported by *Des Moines Register*)	69	0	0.76	0.16	0.17
Share of Field (percentage that candidate represents)	85	0.11	0.50	0.17	0.09
Valid N (listwise)	40				

[a] Unfilled = no imputed data included.

TABLE A.2

Postimputation N of Iowa, New Hampshire, and primary variables

Variable	N	Minimum	Maximum	Mean	Standard deviation
Primary Popular Vote Share (%)	71	0	0.76	0.16	0.21
New Hampshire Vote Share (%)	71	0	0.50	0.17	0.16
Share of Field (percentage that candidate represents)	85	0.11	0.50	0.17	0.09
New Hampshire Poll Support (before Iowa Caucus; %; filled[a] using Gallup Poll Support, itself filled; percentage of National Fund-Raising total, itself filled; and percentage of Share of Field)	69	0	0.53	0.17	0.15
National Fund-Raising Share (candidate's percentage of active same-party candidate total money raised, second half of pre-election year, scaled to account for missing candidates and those not reaching the Caucus, filled using percentage of Share of Field, African American, and Pre-Caucus Straw Poll Support, and normalized back to 100% per cycle)	69	0.002	0.56	0.17	0.14
Gallup Poll Support (before Iowa Caucus; %; normalized based on raw Gallup totals, which were scaled to include only candidates reaching the Caucus then filled using percentage of Share of Field and percentage of National Fund-Raising total and then normalized back to 100% per cycle)	69	0.011	0.66	0.17	0.17
Iowa Caucus Vote Share (%, as reported by *Des Moines Register* but scaled by proportionally factoring in undecided and uncommitted votes)	69	0	0.87	0.17	0.19
Valid N (listwise)	68				

[a] For candidates for whom no data were available, multiple-imputation regression models used other variables to predict, or fill, their missing variable values.

TABLE A.3

Preimputation N of continuous nonsurvey explanatory variables

Variable	N	Minimum	Maximum	Mean	Standard deviation
Iowa Caucus Vote Share (%, scaled, as reported by *Des Moines Register* but proportionally factoring in undecided and uncommitted)	69	0	0.87	0.17	0.19
Share of Field (percentage that candidate represents)	85	0.11	0.50	0.17	0.09
Press Coverage (candidate's percentage of active same-party candidates' total)	25	0.02	0.64	0.15	0.15
National Fund-Raising Share (%, unfilled,[a] candidate's percentage of active same-party candidate total money raised, second half of pre-election year)	66	0.002	0.56	0.18	0.15
Days in Iowa (for candidate in 2 years before Caucus, unfilled)	72	0	15	40.72	32.17
TV Advertising (constant 2004 dollars, unfilled)	35	0	2,813,000	481,149	790,430
Iowa Spending (real total dollars, unfilled, pre-election year, combined third and fourth quarter, including non-FEC sources)	62	0	3,200,000	245,271	515,980
Under 15% Democratic Viability Threshold (unfilled, scaled Iowa Poll Support, factoring out percentage choosing undecided in last *Des Moines Register* Iowa Poll)	68	0	1	0.26	0.44
Valid N (listwise)	16				

NOTE: FEC = Federal Election Commission.

[a] Unfilled = no imputed data included.

Postimputation N of continuous nonsurvey explanatory variables

Variable	N	Minimum	Maximum	Mean	Standard deviation
Iowa Caucus Vote Share (%, scaled, as reported by *Des Moines Register* but proportionally factoring in undecided and uncommitted)	69	0	0.87	0.17	0.19
Share of Field (percentage that candidate represents)	85	0.11	0.50	0.17	0.09
TV Advertising (percentage of total Iowa TV advertising, filled[a] using percentage of Share of Field, percentage of National Fund-Raising, percentage of Iowa Spending, percentage of Days in Iowa, Gallup Poll Support, Iowa Poll Support, and Pre-Caucus Straw Poll Support)	69	0	0.70	0.17	0.15
Press Coverage (percentage of total, based on total number of print articles in four top Iowa-region papers, filled using Ideological Crowding, itself filled; Gallup Poll Support, itself filled; number of candidates; Under 15% Democratic Viability Threshold, itself filled; Democrat; and Campaign Contact with Strong Partisans, itself filled)	69	0	0.82	0.17	0.17
National Fund-Raising Share (percentage of active same-party-candidate total money raised, second half of pre-election year, scaled for missing data, filled using percentage of Share of Field, African American, and Pre-Caucus Straw Poll Support, which was unfilled, then normalized back to 100% per cycle)	69	0.002	0.56	0.17	0.14
Days in Iowa (percentage difference from the average of the candidate's party's candidates reaching Caucus, based on Days in Iowa, filled using Home State Near Iowa; percentage of Iowa Spending, itself filled; Years Out of Power; Gallup Poll Support, itself filled; log of National Fund-Raising, itself filled; Party Holding White House; Open Seat)	69	0	3.50	0	0.70
Iowa Spending (percentage of total, pre-election year combined third and fourth quarter, scaled for missing data, filled using percentage of Share of Field; percentage of National Fund-Raising, itself filled; Home State Near Iowa, normalized back to 100% per cycle)	69	0	0.54	0.17	0.17

TABLE A.4
(*Continued*)

Variable	N	Minimum	Maximum	Mean	Standard deviation
Under 15% Democratic Viability Threshold (dummy variable, based on Iowa Poll Support, filled)	76	0	1.00	0.29	0.46
Valid N (listwise)	69				

[a] For candidates for whom no data were available, multiple-imputation regression models used other variables to predict, or fill, their missing variable values.

TABLE A.5
Preimputation N of continuous survey-based explanatory variables

Variable	N	Minimum	Maximum	Mean	Standard deviation
Iowa Caucus Vote Share (%, scaled, as reported by *Des Moines Register* but proportionally factoring in undecided and uncommitted)	69	0	0.87	0.17	0.19
Rally Attendance (percentage of all respondents of candidate's party ["partisans"] saying they attended a rally [or meeting] for the candidate, unfilled[a])	50	0.003	0.34	0.11	0.08
Campaign Contact (percentage of all partisans saying they were contacted by the candidate)	44	0.03	0.85	0.33	0.23
Viability (percentage of respondents giving candidate any chance to win the Primary)	48	0.40	1.00	0.77	0.19
Electability (percentage of partisans *not* responding that candidate was more likely to lose than win the general election)	50	0.10	0.98	0.50	0.28
Raw Ideological Vote Share (percentage of partisans placing candidate closer than any other ideologically, plus a proportional share of ties)	52	0.05	0.55	0.17	0.12
Valid N (listwise)	41				

[a] Unfilled = no imputed data included.

TABLE A.6

Postimputation N of continuous survey-based explanatory variables

Variable	N	Minimum	Maximum	Mean	Standard deviation
Iowa Caucus Vote Share (%, scaled, as reported by *Des Moines Register* but proportionally factoring in undecided and uncommitted)	69	0	0.87	0.17	0.19
Rally Attendance (percentage of all partisans saying they attended a rally [or meeting] for the candidate, filled[a] using Electability, Share of Field, Ideological Crowding, Party vs. Incumbent, and Years Out of Power)	70	0.003	0.34	0.11	0.08
Campaign Contact (percentage of all partisans contacted by candidate, filled using *t* [number of 4-year increments since 1976]; Share of Field, Iowa Poll Support, itself filled; percentage of Iowa Spending, itself filled; percentage of total Days in Iowa, itself filled; Pre-Caucus Straw Poll Support, itself filled; Ideological Crowding, itself filled; Rally Attendance [Strong Partisans], itself filled)	69	0	0.85	0.26	0.24
Viability (percentage of respondents giving candidate any chance to win the general election, filled using Electability, itself filled, and log of Real Receipts)	70	0.40	1.00	0.75	0.18
Electability (percentage of partisans *not* responding that candidate was more likely to lose than win the general election, filled using Share of Field, African American, Democrat, Gallup Poll Support, itself filled; Iowa Poll Support, itself filled; Party Holding White House)	69	0.10	1.00	0.49	0.26
Ideological Crowding (1 − Ideological Vote Share, percentage of partisans placing candidate closer than any other ideologically, plus a proportional share of ties, filled and scaled)	69	0.49	0.96	0.83	0.11
Valid N (listwise)	69				

[a]For candidates for whom no data were available, multiple-imputation regression models used other variables to predict, or fill, their missing variable values.

TABLE A.7
Preimputation N of Predictive Model variables

Variable	N	Minimum	Maximum	Mean	Standard deviation
Iowa Caucus Vote Share (%, scaled, as reported by *Des Moines Register* but proportionally factoring in undecided and uncommitted)	69	0	0.87	0.17	0.19
Gallup Poll Support (raw %, closest to Iowa Caucus, unfilled[a] and unscaled, including candidates not reaching Caucus)	61	0.01	0.60	0.15	0.16
Iowa Poll Support (raw %, using Iowa Poll from *Des Moines Register* closest to the Caucus)	52	0	0.56	0.14	0.14
Pre-Caucus Straw Poll Support (%, unfilled and unscaled)	49	0	0.71	0.14	0.15
Final Explanatory Model Prediction (%, unscaled, regressing scaled Iowa Caucus Vote Share on the Explanatory Model with percentage of Supporters 2000–2004 Internet Factors included)	69	0	0.82	0.18	0.18
Valid *N* (listwise)	28				

[a] Unfilled = no imputed data included.

Postimputation N of Predictive Model variables

Variable	N	Minimum	Maximum	Mean	Standard deviation
Iowa Caucus Vote Share (%, scaled, as reported by *Des Moines Register* but proportionally factoring in undecided and uncommitted)	69	0	0.87	0.17	0.187386
Gallup Poll Support (%, scaled to include only candidates reaching the Caucus, filled[a] using Share of Field and National Fund-Raising Share, normalized back to 100% per cycle)	69	0.01	0.66	0.17	0.168500
Iowa Poll Support (%, from *Des Moines Register*, scaled to factor out percentage of undecided, filled using percentage of Iowa Spending, itself filled; Home State Near Iowa dummy; Share of Field; Gallup Poll Support, itself filled; normalized back to 100% per cycle)	69	0	0.67	0.17	0.16
Pre-Caucus Straw Poll Support (based on raw Pre-Caucus Straw Poll Support, scaled to factor out omitted candidates, prenormalized to 100%, filled using Gallup Poll Support, Iowa Poll Support, National Fund-Raising Share, percentage of total Days in Iowa, and Share of Field, normed back to 100% per cycle)	69	0	0.72	0.17	0.15
Final Explanatory Model Prediction (%, unscaled, regressing scaled Iowa Caucus Vote Share on the Explanatory Model with percentage of Supporters 2000–2004 Internet Factors included)	69	0	0.82	0.18	0.18
Valid N (listwise)	69				

[a] For candidates for whom no data were available, multiple-imputation regression models used other variables to predict, or fill, their missing variable values.

THE 1976 CHALLENGE

Of the 18 variables in the Final Explanatory Model, only 10 have full data for 1976. Television Advertising and Press Coverage, for instance, come from sources that simply do not go that far back in time.[1] All of the survey data—used to calculate Viability, Electability, Ideology, Rally Attendance, and Campaign Contact—are built on an instrument employed for the first time in 1980. And the *Des Moines Register*'s Iowa Poll on Caucus candidates did not even come into existence until the next cycle, in 1984. For all of these variables, it was necessary to use the multiple-imputation models to fill all of the values in 1976.

How much of a challenge does this present to the overall data? To what extent can we rely on that 1976 cycle, given that perhaps 40 percent of the data in it must be imputed?

To find out, we can use the imputed data within a model aimed at predicting some of the values we actually have for 1976, to see how well those estimates match the data we possess. For Days in Iowa, National Fund-Raising Share, and Iowa Spending (in spite of Iowa Spending's own challenges), for which we have data on every case in 1976, we can see how well the rest of the model estimates each, and get a sense for how far off the imputed values will be with their estimates in that year generally.

For Days in Iowa, the picture is somewhat troubling. On one hand, the rest of the Explanatory Model[2] explains 80 to 85 percent of the variation in candidates' percentage of the total Days in Iowa for that cycle ($R^2 = 0.850$, adj. $R^2 = 0.800$), a highly statistically significant result ($F = 16.951$, $p < 0.001$). On the other hand, the estimates for each 1976 candidate are obviously not spot on (Figure A.1). They raise concerns that the model is not accurately projecting values back to 1976.

Days in Iowa is a particularly troublesome variable to predict in any case or for any year, because the amount of time a candidate spends in a given state is not something closely linked to other factors, at least theoretically. We can see that, in 1988, a year with all of the data present, we can arrive at a relatively convincing approximation of the variable (Figure A.2).

So, granted, the Explanatory Model performs more poorly predicting 1976 Days in Iowa than it does predicting 1988 Days in Iowa. However, it is very likely that the 1976 Days in Iowa values are much more of an anomaly than 1976 values for other variables. The reason is that from 1980

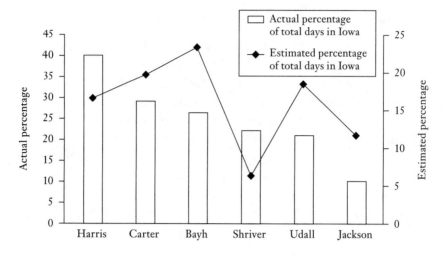

Figure A.1.　Actual versus estimated percentage of total days in Iowa, 1976 Democratic candidates

NOTE: Each candidate's percentage of the total days spent in Iowa, both actual and as estimated by the Explanatory Model excluding the Days in Iowa variable.

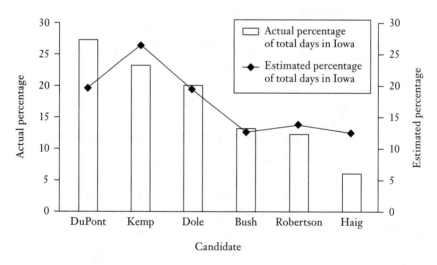

Figure A.2.　Actual versus estimated percentage of total days in Iowa, 1988 Republican candidates

NOTE: Each candidate's percentage of the total days spent in Iowa, both actual and as estimated by the Explanatory Model excluding the Days in Iowa variable.

on candidates adopted Carter's strategy of tackling Iowa first, in person, to establish credibility early in the primary process. It was Carter who first recognized that time spent in retail politicking in the state might propel him ultimately to the nomination and successfully implemented that strategy. By stark contrast, values for the factors on which we do not have 1976 data—viability assessments, ideological placements, or press coverage, for instance—would theoretically conform much more closely to future (and prior) years. Why would they be radically different in 1976 than in 1980 or for that matter 1972? That sets the heavily imputed variables apart from the Days in Iowa variable, at least theoretically.

And bolstering that assertion, we find that the results for estimating 1976 Iowa Spending are far superior. The rest of the Explanatory Model[3] predicts slightly more of the variation in candidates' percentage of total Iowa Spending that cycle than it does of Days in Iowa ($R^2 = 0.861$, $R^2 = 0.815$), a result that is highly statistically significant ($F = 18.636$, $p < 0.001$). And visually it is clear that the 1976 cycle is less anomalous as far as Iowa Spending goes, with the model fairly accurately placing each candidate's percentage of the total that cycle (Figure A.3).

The model's performance for a year with full data appears better still, but not dramatically so. For the 1988 Democratic Primary, the model is relatively accurate for most candidates, but it does underestimate Gore's relative Iowa spending while overestimating Hart's (Figure A.4). Thus in this case the model's performance for 1976 with sparse data and 1988 with full data is roughly analogous, which is modestly reassuring.

The picture is slightly murkier for overall National Fund-Raising Share. The power of the rest of the Explanatory Model[4] to predict National Fund-Raising Share is somewhat less than for the other two factors, which might stand to reason as it is geared to estimate Iowa outcomes, not national outcomes. The model explains about three-quarters of the variation in candidates' National Fund-Raising Share ($R^2 = 0.783$, $R^2 = 0.711$), which is still a highly statistically significant result ($F = 10.818$, $p < 0.001$).

The candidate-by-candidate 1976 predictions appear largely accurate, with the exception of Harris and Shriver, whose relative national fund-raising amounts are badly overestimated by the model—perhaps understandable from an estimate based on Iowa variables, considering that the two candidates, for instance, spent a relatively large number of days in the state (23 and 13, respectively) (Figure A.5).

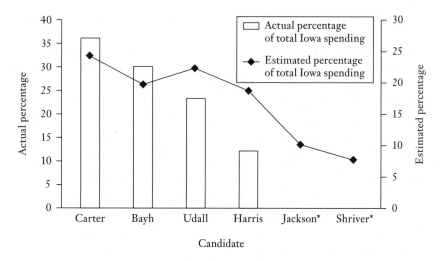

Figure A.3. Actual versus estimated percentage of total Iowa spending, 1976
Democratic candidates

NOTE: Each candidate's percentage of the total amount spent in Iowa that cycle, third and fourth
quarters of pre-election year (1975), both actual and as estimated by the Explanatory Model excluding
the Iowa Spending variable.

*Candidate reported spending nothing in Iowa.

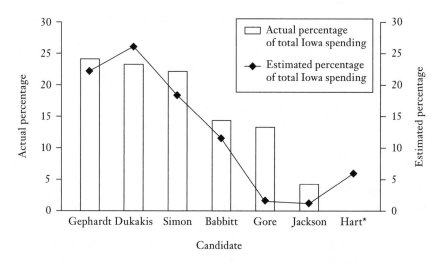

Figure A.4. Actual versus estimated percentage of total Iowa spending, 1988
Democratic candidates

NOTE: Each candidate's percentage of the total amount spent in Iowa that cycle, third and fourth
quarters of pre-election year (1987), both actual and as estimated by the Explanatory Model excluding
the Iowa Spending variable.

*Gary Hart did not report spending anything in Iowa.

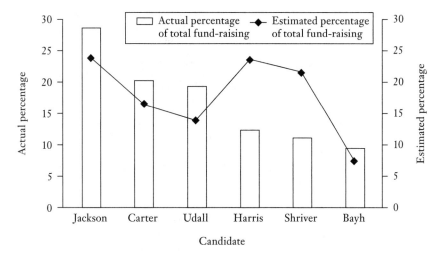

Figure A.5. Actual versus estimated percentage of total national fund-raising,
1976 Democratic candidates

NOTE: Each candidate's percentage of total national fund-raising that cycle, third and fourth quarter of the pre-election year (1975), both actual and as estimated by the Explanatory Model excluding the National Fund-Raising variable.

By comparison, again using a cycle with highly complete data—the 1988 Democratic Primary—we can see a somewhat better level of performance for the model. In that case, the model overestimates the actual percentage for two candidates again, this time Jackson and Gephardt, but to a lesser extent (Figure A.6).

As is the case with Iowa Spending data, the bottom line is that our estimates, while not perfect, appear relatively accurate, and roughly analogous between high-data cycles and the low-data 1976 cycle.

The conclusion appears to be that, given the rest of the data, we are able to predict actual 1976 data with reasonable precision compared to our ability to predict other data-rich cycles, with the exception of Days in Iowa, which may be anomalous in 1976. This should give us some confidence that we may use the 1976 cycle in the full analysis, in spite of the considerable imputation required to do so.

One result of having to work with only sparse data in 1976 is that I tried not to focus on lines of argument about how the Caucus changed in its early years, but rather I mainly restricted my analysis to present-day questions of what appears to be shaping Caucus outcomes, how it may have evolved just in the last few iterations, what actually happened in 2004, and

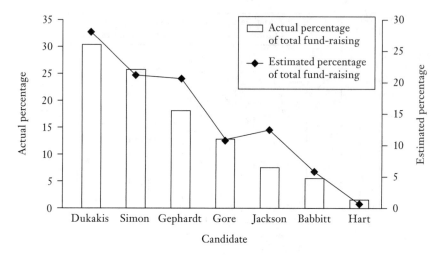

Figure A.6. Actual versus estimated percentage of total national fund-raising, 1988 Democratic candidates

NOTE: Each candidate's percentage of total national fund-raising that cycle, third and fourth quarter of the pre-election year (1987), both actual and as estimated by the Explanatory Model excluding the National Fund-Raising variable.

what we learned as a result of what did happen in 2004. There are certain to be other shortcomings in the results, but since what emerges is a relatively clear picture, I hope it retains its value.

PERCENTAGE-FORM DATA

As mentioned in the variable descriptions, nondummy factors are generally operationalized to account for *relative* effort by a candidate. After all, candidates are boosted not just by spending in Iowa or building a large organization but by spending more and building bigger than their opponents' campaigns. To attempt to capture this truth, most of the factors appear in the models as a percentage of the total for the field. For instance, a candidate's national fund-raising is presented not as a dollar figure (or a logarithm of that figure, as the literature might suggest) but as the percentage that the candidate raised of the total fund-raising for candidates that cycle.

This "percentage of the total" form of the independent variables, as well as the "percentage of the vote" form for the dependent variable, presents a statistical problem. There is a technical literature (see, for instance, Greer and Dunlap [1997]; Tomz, Tucker, and Wittenberg [2002]; Chan [2003]; Cohen, Noel, and Zaller [2004]) on the challenges of analyzing percentage data. According to Cohen, Noel, and Zaller (p. 16), though a model with a percentage as the dependent variable

> would generate unbiased results if estimated by OLS, OLS estimation would encounter two problems. The first is the possibility of out-of-bound estimates. The sum of candidate vote shares is, in fact, bounded by scores of 0 and 100, but OLS estimation could easily generate y-hat estimates outside this range. More important than the out-of-bounds estimates would be the loss of efficiency entailed by an estimation technique that failed to use information about what candidate vote shares must sum to. The second problem is biased statistical inference. OLS estimation would fail to take account of correlated errors within each set of state elections. That is, if one candidate does better than expected in a particular state, other candidates must have done less well. Failure to accommodate this error structure would bias the estimates of parameter precision, even if not the results themselves.[5]

The method prescribed by Tomz, Tucker, and Wittenberg (2002) and updated by Cohen, Noel, and Zaller (2004) for dealing with this problem is to estimate the model with log-ratios rather than the raw percentages themselves, and then perform seemingly unrelated regressions (SURs) for each case. Those regressions produce a figure that can be translated back into an estimate of vote total, estimates that are not constrained by the technical problems plaguing percentage-form data. Though this study does not adopt that reform, I acknowledge both its technical importance and the potentially adverse effects not using it has on the results presented in this study.

IOWA SPENDING

The first question raised by the discussion in Chapter 5 is whether it is feasible to include the variable using only the complete available Federal Election Commission (FEC) data, perhaps using imputation to fill what gaps remain, which might eliminate the systematic errors.

The challenge with doing so is that the FEC data tend to be missing for recent candidates most likely to have ignored Iowa spending limits: those

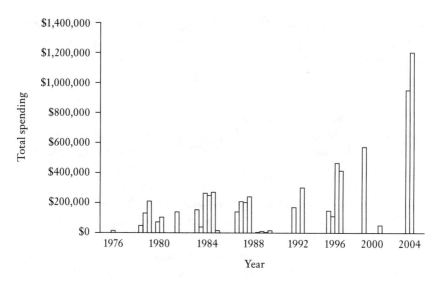

Figure A.7. Candidates' Iowa spending, 1976–2004

NOTE: Amount spent in Iowa (2004 dollars) in third and fourth quarter of year before election year, by election year and candidate, including only FEC sources or imputed values. Gaps indicate that no data were available for a candidate or set of candidates, or (rarely) that reported spending was zero.

who were self-funded or decided to forgo federal matching money. Those candidates would be the top end of the Iowa Spending variable and are those most of interest to recent analyses, including Kerry and Dean in 2004 and Bush and Forbes in 2000. And the 2004 data are especially gap-toothed as current state spending limits cease to bind, and with few estimates, biased or not, to guide. Those missing data are likely to be systematically and significantly—using the term in its technical sense—different from the rest of the data. A glance at Figure A.7 gives an indication of this challenge.

As a result of gaps in the data, modeling FEC-only data for Iowa Spending for multiple imputation is extraordinarily difficult, unlike most of the variables in this analysis. The best models I could devise produce absurd results, even given the substantial data available to build them. For instance, the FEC-only model with the highest predictive power and the most theoretically attractive and significant factors that I could design estimates Ambassador Alan Keyes spending almost twice what George W. Bush spent in 2000 and Senator Alan Cranston (D-Calif.) outspending Walter Mondale by two to one in 1984.

One crucial implication of this analysis is that empirically there is a bright side to the non-FEC data. By combing through as many other sources as possible, we are able to greatly supplement what is available from the FEC alone. Non-FEC data are likely closer to the actual amounts spent by the candidates since they are available mainly for candidates who spent by far the most and who are also those least frequently reporting state totals to the FEC. Accordingly, we find that the results of imputation models based on data including the non-FEC sources are far superior both in explanatory power and credibility of estimates.

Those extra data are also unique. I know of no other compilation of Iowa Spending data of its kind, an argument for exploring its implications, with appropriate caveats for the heterogeneity of its sourcing.

All this raises the question: What difference would it make to exclude the variable from the models in this study? The answer is that excluding Iowa Spending from the model makes a subtle but important difference in the results of the Explanatory Model. Though the factor itself is not statistically significant ($p = 0.089$), excluding it switches the Television Advertising variable from significance ($p = 0.029$) to insignificance ($p = 0.119$).

The difference is easy to explain, especially when one observes that the sign of the Television Advertising coefficient is negative. In both versions of the model, that is, a candidate's percentage of total TV spending in a cycle actually has a negative relationship with that candidate's Iowa performance, holding all else constant. More TV is associated with losing, controlling for Days in Iowa, Ideological Crowding, and so forth.

Thus, the Explanatory Model's conclusions on TV spending are questionable given the data challenges presented by the Iowa Spending factor (and the television data, as documented in the discussion of organization's role in Iowa in the body of the study). However, they are also worth reporting, with appropriate cautions as to their reliability. Otherwise, frankly, we risk misspecifying the model, at least with respect to television.

PRIMARY POPULAR VOTE SHARE

Another question could be raised about whether Primary Popular Vote Share is the ideal operationalization of primary performance. After all, merely using the share of the primary vote a candidate obtains does not reflect *when* that vote was obtained nor does it factor in when the candidate dropped out of the race. A candidate like Dean in 2004 who competed hard and made a significant play for the nomination might drop out midway

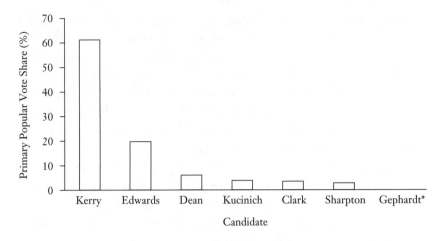

Figure A.8. 2004 candidate Primary Popular Vote Share
NOTE: Percentage of the total primary vote for all 2004 candidates.
*Gephardt had a fraction of a percent of the primary vote.

through the process, for instance, while low-tier candidates like Kucinich and Sharpton remained in the race, winning a small portion in state after state.

Eyeballing the actual 2004 primary vote percentages in Figure A.8, we see some evidence to support this charge as well as some to dismiss it. Below the runner-up Edwards, the candidates all accumulated fairly low percentages of the primary vote share. Thus Dean had only about 6 percent of the final primary vote, while Kucinich had between 3 and 4 percent, Clark a similar amount, Sharpton about half that, and Gephardt only the fraction of a percent represented by his share in the Caucus, after which he dropped from the race.

On the basis of these totals, one could argue that Kucinich and Sharpton were rated too high by the factor, while Gephardt and Clark and potentially Dean were rated too low. However, as much as that argument appeals to a conventional wisdom about the tier of candidates each represented, there is a certain amount of objectivity to the measure. Kerry, the nominee, had the lion's share of the primary vote; the runner-up, Edwards, had another large chunk, and Dean outpaced the rest of the field by what proportionally is a great deal even if it was absolutely a small percentage. And given that Gephardt dropped out after the first contest, on which he had explicitly based his entire presidential bid, could one not make the argument that he was not as strong a candidate as Kucinich, who despite never having had a prayer, did have an activist constituency?

This cursory examination of one cycle lends some anecdotal credibility to the usefulness of the Primary Popular Vote Share factor. Let us be more rigorous, however. After all, what we need are quantitative gauges of the degree to which a variable is filled with noise given candidates' exits at different times of the race over the entire 1976–2004 period. To get one, we can simply examine the models in this study designed to predict Primary Popular Vote Share. Those models' explanatory power and goodness-of-fit statistics of interest—specifically their R^2 and F-statistic—are measures of the extent to which theoretically relevant variables account for Primary Popular Vote Share's variation. If those values are low, we can say at least that Primary Popular Vote Share is difficult to predict and possibly that the difficulty arises because of nearly random variation from the timing of candidates' exits. If those values are high, we can say with some confidence *either* that Primary Popular Vote Share has little noise in it or, at worst, that what noise there is in the variable from candidate exit is predictable and associated with variables we would expect to influence primary performance.

So is Primary Popular Vote Share a noisy variable, by that measure? The answer is probably no. Of the four models presented in this chapter, two are designed to predict and explain primary vote share. One, using the size of the field, Iowa performance, national poll strength, and fund-raising success, accounts for about 60 percent of the variation in Primary Popular Vote Share ($R^2 = 0.622$, adj. $R^2 = 0.598$), an amount that is highly statistically significant ($F = 25.921$, $p < 0.001$), as reflected in Table A.9. Adding New Hampshire performance to the mix improves on that already strong performance; that model accounts for almost 80 percent of the variation in Primary Popular Vote Share ($R^2 = 0.777$, adj. $R^2 = 0.759$), an amount that is even more highly statistically significant ($F = 43.158$, $p < 0.001$).

In other words, only just over 20 percent of the variation in Primary Popular Vote Share is left unexplained when a mere five variables are used to predict it. What is more, none of those five variables explores the time after the New Hampshire Primary, when candidates are dropping out of the race. (And note that this does not include the considerable additional

TABLE A.9
How much variation can we predict in Primary Popular Vote Share?

Model	R^2	Adj. R^2	F-statistic	p
Only Iowa and Exhibition Season variables predicting Primary vote	0.622	0.598	25.921	<0.001
Iowa, New Hampshire, and Exhibition Season variables predicting Primary vote	0.777	0.759	43.158	<0.001

explanatory power of Iowa and New Hampshire's e-mentum.) It appears that Primary Popular Vote Share is at least nonrandom in a way that can be explained by theoretically relevant variables.

All that said, an important second question should be explored: whether a superior alternative exists. Put another way, should we rely on Primary Popular Vote Share *faute de mieux*—for lack of anything better—or is there another option that makes more sense?

Quickly, let's review six potential alternative measures of a candidate's performance in the primary. First, we could use the Primary Popular Vote Total. The data are as readily available as Primary Popular Vote Share, after all. However, the overall vote total is different in each cycle, which is irrelevant variation that is effectively factored out by using a candidate's vote share instead. What's more, using the vote total does not address the concern about random variation from candidates dropping out of the race. The Primary Popular Vote Total factor, therefore, creates more problems than it solves.

The same criticism could be leveled at the second and third alternatives, Number of Delegates as allocated by voters and Number of Delegates as allocated by the convention. With the total number of delegates shifting in ways totally unrelated to each candidate's performance that cycle, both raise more questions than they answer.

Fourth, we could use the percentage of delegates as allocated by voters. This measure would seem attractive because, after all, it is the one technically used by the parties to decide the nomination. However, data on delegate share are surprisingly hard to collect. After all, so many delegates are uncommitted in the process that it is difficult to know when they are actually allocated. A complex process of counting them is necessary, literally involving a review of delegate statements.

Therefore, unlike popular vote share, which is a matter of public record, I found delegate share readily accessible only in recent contests. What's more, because larger states tend to be placed slightly later in the primary process, the data simply have the same characteristics as Primary Popular Vote Share with a slightly greater skew toward the nominee. Figure A.9 lays out the 2004 example. Again, Share of Delegates creates more problems than it solves.

Fifth, we could potentially use candidates' Share of Delegates as allocated by the convention. That solves the problem of counting delegates, as the convention vote is a matter of public record. But as anyone familiar with recent conventions can tell you, today they have little to do with candidate performance and everything to do with promoting the nominee. Therefore the delegate votes are wildly skewed to the nominee, as we can see in Figure A.10. Indeed, in 2004 only Kucinich received any delegate votes in Boston—a grand total of 43 to Kerry's 4,253.

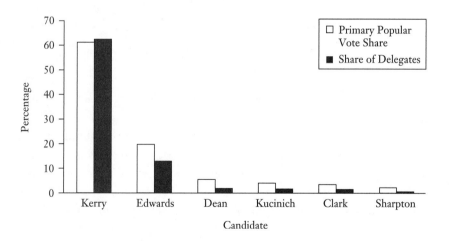

Figure A.9. 2004 candidate Primary Popular Vote Share versus Share of Delegates as allocated by voters

NOTE: Percentage of the total primary vote for all 2004 candidates, with the share of delegates won by each candidate. Gephardt had no vote share or delegates.

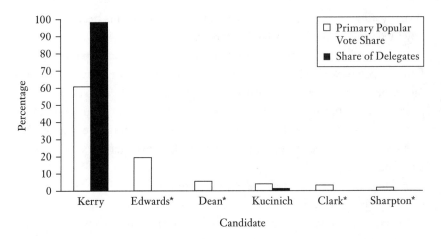

Figure A.10. 2004 candidate Primary Popular Vote Share versus Share of Delegates as allocated by convention

NOTE: Percentage of the total primary vote share for all 2004 candidates, with the share of delegates received by each candidate at the 2004 Democratic National Convention.

*Candidates who won no delegates at the convention.

The final option to consider would be candidate rank of finish. There are some attractive qualities to rank. By definition it is proportional, without the skew toward the nominee that the front-loading of the primary increasingly creates in other measures. And it does not alter with size of the popular vote or number of delegates. However, rank must be based on another factor. If rank is based on the proportion of votes won in the primary, why use it and not use Primary Popular Vote Share, a continuous variable that contains the information in rank with a great deal more variation?

The upshot of this analysis is that, though certainly the timing of candidate exit wounds Primary Popular Vote Share's credibility as a dependent variable, it is at least predictable in theoretically sound ways, and the alternatives appear inferior. Thus it seems reasonable to base the primary models on Primary Popular Vote Share, acknowledging the factor's shortcomings.

PRESIDENTIAL RACES INCLUDED AND EXCLUDED

Note that the database is structured around competitive Iowa races. That leaves out only the 1984, 1992, 1996, and 2004 primaries in which presidents Ronald Reagan, George H. W. Bush, Bill Clinton, and George W. Bush were running for reelection, respectively. It does include the Ford and Carter reelection campaigns, which were competitive in Iowa, defined as those in which the second-place finisher obtained more than 20 percent of the share of the field he represented, given the number of candidates in the race.

(To determine which races were contested, I obtained the "proportional vote share" by dividing the percentage of the vote in Iowa by the percentage of the field the candidate represents (which of course is also the percentage of the vote the candidate would expect to get, ceteris paribus.) Once the proportional vote share statistic was obtained, I used it to measure each cycle by how well the competitor nearest to the winner fared, and I decided that any cycle in which that competitor finished with less than 20 percent of his vote share was uncompetitive and should be excluded.)

In fact, the line for a competitive race could be drawn in a wide range below that figure and still exclude completely uncontested races, while leaving in place 2000, 1976, 1984, and the other more contested races. Except for 1992, in which second-place finisher Tsongas received only 21 percent of his vote share, the least competitive race in the model because Iowa senator Tom Harkin was running, there is also a wide range above the 20 percent threshold in which the line could be drawn. The next-worst fate for a second-place challenger was 2000, when Bradley received 70 percent of his vote share. (By this measure, the most competitive race was the 2004 Democratic contest, when second-place finisher Edwards had more than double his vote share, or 255%.)

Note that a handful of the earliest models in this study used the slightly different threshold of 25 percent of proportional vote share. The implication of that difference is that 1992 on the Democratic side was excluded as well. During that race, as was discussed in Chapter 2, Harkin's presence in the race made moot Iowa's role, leading other candidates to all but bypass the state. Instead, then governor Bill Clinton (D-Ark.) took his struggling campaign to New Hampshire, where he was able to post a stronger-than-expected challenge to Senator Paul Tsongas (D-Mass.). Again, excluding that contest from consideration arguably drops out a race where New Hampshire made an important impact.

The 1992 race on the Republican side is worth mentioning, as well.

Republicans did not even hold an Iowa Precinct Presidential Caucus that year, with commentator Patrick J. Buchanan focusing his primary challenge against incumbent president George H. W. Bush on New Hampshire. Buchanan campaigned aggressively against Bush for the nomination but chose to begin that battle after Iowa. Ultimately, of course, the sitting president Bush was able to capture the nomination, but in the analysis of Iowa's impact on the nomination, leaving out the 1992 Republican New Hampshire results, where Buchanan captured a sizable minority of the Granite State vote, could be seen to skew the results of this analysis.

Early regression models in this study, especially the 2004 Preliminary Predictive Model run before that year's Caucus, did not have enough data to include 1992 in their estimates. Thus, while the database has information from 1976 to 2004, in effect the 2004 Preliminary Predictive Model stretched from 1976 to 1988, and then from 1996 to 2004. Later models were run with additional data from 1992 added in on the Democratic side, as well as significant imputation. As a result, in those newer models, when more of those data were available, I lowered the threshold to 20 percent to include 1992.

In the later models I also added two dummy variables to the model to control for 1992's unique nature: an Iowa Favorite Son variable—for Harkin himself, in this case—and a Running against Iowa Favorite Son variable—for Tsongas, Clinton, Kerry, and Brown. Given this patch and the amount of data available, I feel confident in including the cycle on the Democratic side in the later models.

Most important, adding the 1992 Democratic race did not appear to make a difference to the models—except that the Harkin dummy variable is usually statistically significant, of course (surprisingly, running against Harkin was not statistically significant, likely because the model controls for many level-of-effort variables). So there appears to be little reason to object to some models including the cycle while some do not, as long as it is disclosed where the threshold is set at 25 percent such that 1992 on the Democratic side is not included.

Finally, the most basic element of this appendix: which candidates were included in the models presented in *Grassroots Rules*.

Note that the list is (must be!) devoted to those who competed in the Iowa Caucus. As we have seen, this leads to some startling omissions. For instance, the Bush-Buchanan race in 1992 is not included, as there was no presidential straw poll at the Caucus that year. Most objectionable, perhaps, is that 1976 does not include Senator Edmund Muskie, Senator George McGovern, Governor George Wallace, or Senator Hubert Humphrey, none of whom were reflected in the Caucus results. The 1996 list does not contain Governor Pete Wilson or Senator Arlen Specter, who dropped out of the race before the Caucus took place. The same is true of Senator Bob Smith, former vice president Dan Quayle, Representative John Kasich, former secretary of transportation Elizabeth Dole, and former governor Lamar Alexander in 2000 and Senators Bob Graham and Carol Moseley Braun in 2004.

Though my decision not to enter noncompeting candidates in 1976 may raise questions, I believe that for an analysis of Iowa performance, the list makes good sense.

Candidate	Year	Party	Candidate	Year	Party
Dean	2004	Democrat	Keyes	1996	Republican
Kucinich	2004	Democrat	Lugar	1996	Republican
Clark	2004	Democrat	Taylor	1996	Republican
Kerry	2004	Democrat	Dornan	1996	Republican
Edwards	2004	Democrat	Harkin	1992	Democrat
Gephardt	2004	Democrat	Tsongas	1992	Democrat
Sharpton	2004	Democrat	Clinton	1992	Democrat
Lieberman	2004	Democrat	Kerrey	1992	Democrat
Bush	2000	Republican	Brown	1992	Democrat
Forbes	2000	Republican	Bush	1992	Republican
Keyes	2000	Republican	Buchanan	1992	Republican
Bauer	2000	Republican	Dole	1988	Republican
McCain	2000	Republican	Robertson	1988	Republican
Hatch	2000	Republican	Bush	1988	Republican
Gore	2000	Democrat	Kemp	1988	Republican
Bradley	2000	Democrat	DuPont	1988	Republican
Dole	1996	Republican	Haig	1988	Republican
Buchanan	1996	Republican	Gephardt	1988	Democrat
Alexander	1996	Republican	Simon	1988	Democrat
Forbes	1996	Republican	Dukakis	1988	Democrat
Gramm	1996	Republican	Jackson	1988	Democrat

Candidate	Year	Party	Candidate	Year	Party
Babbitt	1988	Democrat	Crane	1980	Republican
Hart	1988	Democrat	Anderson	1980	Republican
Gore	1988	Democrat	Dole	1980	Republican
Mondale	1984	Democrat	Carter	1980	Democrat
Hart	1984	Democrat	Kennedy	1980	Democrat
McGovern	1984	Democrat	Brown	1980	Democrat
Cranston	1984	Democrat	Ford	1976	Republican
Glenn	1984	Democrat	Reagan	1976	Republican
Askew	1984	Democrat	Carter	1976	Democrat
Jackson	1984	Democrat	Jackson	1976	Democrat
Hollings	1984	Democrat	Harris	1976	Democrat
Bush	1980	Republican	Udall	1976	Democrat
Reagan	1980	Republican	Bayh	1976	Democrat
Baker	1980	Republican	Shriver	1976	Democrat
Connally	1980	Republican			

RALLY ATTENDANCE AND CAMPAIGN CONTACT VARIABLES

Note that for Rally Attendance and Campaign Contact in particular, it is of concern that the early data are not Iowa-specific, though they include Iowa.[6] Also note that for the 1992 data the survey question was whether the respondent had attended a rally *or* a meeting because, as Abramowitz et al. (2001) report, virtually no rallies were held owing to the presence of favorite-son Harkin of Iowa in the race.

Also note that Walter Stone himself suggested to me including the percentage of supporters present at the Caucus who had experienced one of these factors—the measure used in the 2004 Preliminary Predictive Model but not in the Final Explanatory Model.[7] The idea is to control for the fact that surveys of caucusgoers are not random samples but bear the imprint of the percentages of supporters who showed up for a given candidate. Building the percentage of all caucusgoers who received mail or were contacted by a campaign, for instance, would bear indelible marks of the successful campaigns that year—obviously, more Bush and Gore supporters attended the 2000 Caucus, just as more Carter supporters attended the 1976 Caucus.

Using the percentage of supporters present at the Caucus does erase the most ex post facto statistical marks of winners and losers on Caucus night from the data. However, it raises potentially more serious concerns that such a measure mischaracterizes the factor's role in the Caucus. If both of one candidate's 2 supporters at a precinct caucus were contacted by his campaign, while 30 of another candidate's 100 supporters were not, it does not help gauge success in Iowa to operationalize contact as 100 for the first and 70 for the second.

BLOCK *F*-TEST ON ORGANIZATION FACTORS

In the discussion of organization in the Iowa Caucus, I perform a statistical test to measure the joint explanatory power of three retail politics indicators: Days in Iowa, Rally Attendance, and Campaign Contact. That test, known as a block *F*-test, is based on Fisher's *F*-statistic, and I used the following process for conducting it in this specific case.

To test the joint explanatory power of multiple factors in an OLS regression model, we can calculate an *F*-statistic in this way:

$$F = \frac{(R^2_{UR} - R^2_R)/m}{(1 - R^2_{UR})/(n - k)}$$

where R^2_{UR} is the coefficient of determination of the unrestricted model—in this case, the R^2 when including all of the variables in the Explanatory Model, or 0.867; R^2_R is the coefficient of determination of the restricted model—in this case, the R^2 when including all of the variables in the Explanatory Model *except* the three organization variables, or 0.851; m is the number of regressors omitted from the restricted model—in this case, three; n is the number of cases (of course)—in this case 68; and k is the number of regressors in the unrestricted model—in this case, 18.

The calculation of the *F*-statistic in this case follows:

$$F = \frac{(0.867 - 0.851)/3}{(1 - 0.867)/(69 - 18)}$$
$$= 24.07$$

That F-statistic is statistically significant at the $p < 0.05$ level (with a p-value much closer to 0.01 than 0.05, actually), as noted in the text.

FULL-YEAR VERSUS HALF-YEAR NATIONAL FUND-RAISING

The models in the book that include a measure of relative fund-raising all use the candidates' third- and fourth-quarter receipts as filed with the FEC during the pre-election year. A legitimate question could be raised about the use of that statistic: Why not include the entire pre-election year's fund-raising total? Aren't we losing something by excluding that first half of the year during the crucial exhibition season?

After exploring both options, I settled once again on using half-year receipts, at least for the current study. There were three reasons: the first theoretical, the second empirical, the third practical.

The first reason came back to the reason I chose half-year fund-raising in the first place. Theoretically, I chose it as a measure of momentum going into the Iowa Caucus. I did not want to include early spikes in fund-raising for a candidate whose momentum had dwindled as he approached the election year. Theorists currently working on large (and impressive) models of primary forecasting, like Cohen, Noel, and Zaller (2004), have identified the problem of measuring pre-Iowa momentum, so it would seem to benefit them to try to gauge it as accurately as possible.

Thus theoretically and in terms of the model's place in the literature it makes some sense to retain the half-year measure of fund-raising. However, against that point could be leveled the counterargument that the full-year fund-raising measure adds an important theoretical component as well: the resources themselves, which candidates could spend in Iowa and beyond. Put another way, leaving out the first two quarters of the pre-election year fails to capture the full scope of the cash candidates can bring to bear over the course of the primary. And let's not fool ourselves: The Iowa campaign is usually in high gear before the second half of the pre-election year, so first- and second-quarter dollars would certainly come in handy in the Hawkeye State.

That brings us to the second reason to retain the half-year measure: Empirically, including the full-year measure in the model boosts the multi-collinearity problem from which the Explanatory Model suffers. True, it also very slightly nudges up the R^2 of the model (from 0.867 to 0.873) as well as its F-statistic (from 18.153 to 18.267), and it has a considerably higher t-score within the model (from 0.594 to 1.107). But it is still not statistically significant—its multicollinearity with Ideological Crowding boosts that factor's variance-inflating factor (VIF) from 16.615 to 17.175, as well as taking Electability's VIF from 10.043 to 10.372.

While that multicollinearity is very interesting, it further obscures the Explanatory Model's ability to tease out the various effects of the factors, because it renders both Ideological Crowding and Electability statistically insignificant. That may be an important empirical finding, but as long as we make clear that half-year fund-raising is a measure of momentum rather than overall fund-raising prowess, we can see the three effects more clearly by using half-year fund-raising than we can with full-year fund-raising.

Finally, it is worth noting that my data on full-year fund-raising, generously shared with me by Mayer, did not include either 1976 or 2004. As this appendix has laid out, there is already a serious concern about the lack of data in 1976. Using full-year fund-raising under these conditions worsens that concern, because I had to impute the 1976 and 2004 values to run the regression model. Long term, that is no excuse for relying on the half-year value, as gathering the additional data at the FEC is relatively straight-forward. But for the purposes of this study, it is another elbow nudging me toward using the half-year data, which require virtually no imputation, even in 1976.

In the end, therefore, while there are strong arguments on both sides, I decided to include half-year fund-raising data in the final model. I will continue to explore full-year fund-raising data in the future, and it may well be superior. Theorists are encouraged to factor any concerns they have into their reading of the study's results.

One final note: Adkins and Dowdle tell me that an important additional factor with respect to national receipts is the fund-raising costs the candidate incurs. Their point is an astute one: Candidates may raise very large total dollar figures, but if they rely on direct mail to do so, their costs could easily run as high as 50 percent of that amount. Controlling for fund-raising costs would eliminate in the model an apparent advantage that a high-cost candidate would not enjoy. Though I did not include this factor in this study, in future studies I would very much like to explore Adkins and Dowdle's approach, and I encourage other scholars to do the same.

The process for obtaining Ideological Vote Share was as follows. I first obtained the Minimum Ideological Distance (*MID*) for every survey respondent for each cycle simply by calculating

$$MID(IP_A, IP_B, \ldots, IP_k)$$

for candidates A, B, and others up to the final *k*th candidate in the field.

Using that information, I created a dummy variable for each candidate to indicate whether that candidate was at that *MID* to the respondent, making certain that all system-missing values were reset to zero (which makes Ideological Vote Share a slightly more conservative estimate of a candidate's support; however, the final step would not mathematically work otherwise). That is, I designated

$$MID_A, MID_B, \ldots, MID_k$$

where MID_A is a dummy variable for whether or not candidate A is at the *MID* from the respondent, MID_B is a variable for candidate B, and a similar variable is calculated for each candidate up to the final *k*th candidate in the field.

Next, I summed all those dummy variables for each respondent for each cycle to obtain the total number of candidates at *MID* from each respondent that year. That is, I calculated

$$CAM_r = \Sigma(MID_B, \ldots, MID_k)$$

where CAM_r is the number of candidates at *MID* from respondent *r*, for each respondent.

I then obtained a Respondent Ideological Vote Share (*RIVS*) for each candidate for each respondent by dividing the candidate at *MID* dummy variables by the total number of candidates at *MID* variable one at a time. Put in equation form, I obtained this statistic for each candidate for all respondents (the values for each candidate can be computed at once, obviously):

$$RIVS_A = MID_A/CAM_r$$
$$RIVS_B = MID_B/CAM_r$$
$$\vdots$$
$$RIVS_k = MID_k/CAM_r$$

where $RIVS_A$ is the share of the respondent's ideological vote for candidate A, $RIVS_B$ is the share for candidate B, and a similar variable is calculated for each candidate up to the final, kth candidate in the field.

Note the theoretical importance of the $RIVS$ value: It is the share of the respondent's vote the candidate would expect to receive were that vote to be both (1) divisible between candidates, and (2) allocated proportionately to candidates on the basis only of the respondent's ideological placements.

Now the reader will see where this is leading. Taking the cross tabulation between respondents of the candidate's party and the $RIVS$ variable for each candidate yields the percentage of same-party respondents granting that candidate a given share of their vote—100 percent, 50 percent, 33 percent, and so forth.

For example, 4.8 percent of surveyed Democrats in 2004 had a Dean $RIVS$ of 100 percent. In other words, 4.8 percent of Democrats had placed Dean as the candidate closest to them ideologically and placed no other candidate closer or equidistant. Gephardt had the highest percentage of Democrats with an $RIVS$ of 100 percent for him, at 5.3 percent. For Kucinich the figure was 3.6 percent; for Clark, 1.3 percent.

Now note something interesting: For Kerry the figure is only 2.8 percent. So Gephardt's percentage of those placing themselves closest to him was almost double Kerry's. Yet Kerry got more than twice Gephardt's vote. Perhaps electability was at work there.

Finally, multiplying each of these cross-tab percentages by each $RIVS$ value and summing those partial percentages into a single percentage created the final Ideological Vote Share score for each candidate. The results for Dean's 15.07 percent Ideological Vote Share are presented in Table A.10 to clarify the final calculation.

TABLE A.10
Calculation of Dean Ideological Vote Share

Dean 2004 Respondent Ideological Vote Share (*RIVS*; %)	Percentage of Democrats surveyed at that *RIVS* (%)	Calculated Dean Ideological Vote Share (%)
0	53.30	0
12.50	14.47	1.81
14.29	2.79	0.40
16.67	3.55	0.59
20.00	2.54	0.51
25.00	6.09	1.52
33.33	4.82	1.61
50.00	7.61	3.81
100.00	4.82	4.82
Total		15.07

That brings us to the variable used in the Explanatory Model, Ideological Crowding. Ideological Crowding is just $1 -$ Ideological Vote Share, that is, it is calculated as

$$IC_A = 1 - IVS_A$$
$$IC_B = 1 - IVS_B$$
$$\vdots$$
$$IC_k = 1 - IVS_k$$

where IC_A is candidate A's measure of Ideological Crowding, IVS_A is candidate A's overall Ideological Vote Share among surveyed partisans, IC_B and IVS_B are the same measures for candidate B, and a similar variable is calculated for each candidate up to the final, kth candidate in the field.

Models and Estimates Used in the Study

Following are some of the models and estimates discussed in the text.

TABLE B.1
Iowa versus New Hampshire in predicting primary vote

Variable	Unstandardized beta	Standard error	p
New Hampshire Vote Share (%)	0.786***	(0.596)	<0.001
Iowa Caucus Vote Share (%)	0.093	(0.093)	0.320
Controls			
National Fund-Raising Share (%)	−0.229	(0.143)	0.114
Gallup Poll Support (%)	0.637***	(0.114)	<0.001
Share of Field (percentage that candidate represents)	−0.320	(0.185)	0.089
(Constant)	−0.004	(0.027)	0.875

NOTE: Dependent variable is Primary Popular Vote Share. $R^2 = 0.777$; adj. $R^2 = 0.759$; F-statistic $= 43.158$.

***$p < 0.001$.

TABLE B.2
Iowa versus the exhibition season in predicting New Hampshire

Variable	Unstandardized beta	Standard error	p
Iowa Caucus Vote Share (%)	0.155*	(0.074)	0.040
Controls			
National Fund-Raising Share (%)	−0.089	(0.125)	0.478
Gallup Polling Support	−0.107	(0.113)	0.349
Share of Field (percentage that candidate represents)	0.079	(0.154)	0.612
New Hampshire Polling Data	0.937***	(0.152)	0
(Constant)	0.003	(0.022)	0.906

NOTE: Dependent variable is New Hampshire Vote Share. $R^2 = 0.729$; adj. $R^2 = 0.708$; F-statistic $= 33.960$.

*$p < 0.05$; ***$p < 0.001$.

Iowa versus New Hampshire, controlled for Harkin

Variable	Unstandardized beta	Standard error	p
Iowa Caucus Vote Share (%)	0.244*	0.113	0.035
Favorite Son (Harkin 1992)	−0.282*	0.129	0.032
New Hampshire Vote Share (%)	0.718***	0.121	0.000
Controls			
Share of Field (%)	−0.331	0.179	0.070
National Fund-Raising Share (%)	−0.257	0.139	0.069
Gallup Poll Support (%)	0.607***	0.112	0.000
(Constant)	−0.002	0.026	0.926

NOTE: Dependent variable is Primary Popular Vote Share. $R^2 = 0.793$; adj. $R^2 = 0.773$; F-statistic = 38.961.

*$p < 0.05$; ***$p < 0.001$.

TABLE B.4
Iowa versus New Hampshire, controlled for Harkin and Home State Near Iowa

Variable	Unstandardized beta	Standard error	p
Iowa Caucus Vote Share (%)	0.253*	0.115	0.032
Favorite Son (Harkin 1992)	− 0.292*	0.131	0.029
Home State Near Iowa	− 0.019	0.031	0.547
New Hampshire Vote Share (%)	0.702***	0.124	<0.001
Controls			
Share of Field (%)	− 0.344	0.182	0.063
National Fund-Raising Share (%)	− 0.264	0.140	0.064
Gallup Poll Support, (%)	0.619***	0.114	<0.001
(Constant)	0.004	0.028	0.879

NOTE: Dependent variable is Primary Popular Vote Share. $R^2 = 0.794$; adj. $R^2 = 0.770$; F-statistic = 33.100.

*$p < 0.05$; ***$p < 0.001$.

TABLE B.5
Iowa e-mentum and New Hampshire in predicting primary vote

Variable	Unstandardized beta	Standard error	p
New Hampshire Vote Share (%)	0.681***	(0.129)	<0.001
Iowa e-mentum	0.316*	(0.129)	0.018
Controls			
National Fund-raising Share (%)	−0.453**	(0.133)	0.001
Gallup Poll Support (%)	0.708***	(0.108)	<0.001
Share of Field (%)	−0.245	(0.161)	0.135
Online Support (%)	−0.001	(0.005)	0.856
(Constant)	−0.002	(0.023)	0.933

NOTE: Dependent variable is Primary Popular Vote Share. $R^2 = 0.842$; adj. $R^2 = 0.825$; F-statistic = 49.585.

*$p < 0.05$; **$p < 0.01$; ***$p < 0.001$.

TABLE B.6
Iowa e-mentum and exhibition season in predicting New Hampshire

Variable	Unstandardized beta	Standard error	p
Iowa e-mentum	0.395***	0.079	<0.001
Controls			
National Fund-Raising Share (%)	−0.206*	0.970	0.039
Gallup Poll Support (%)	−0.094	0.085	0.273
Share of Field (%)	−0.013	0.113	0.910
New Hampshire Poll Support (%)	0.901***	0.110	<0.001
Online Support (%)	0.000	0.003	0.992
(Constant)	0.000	0.016	0.999

NOTE: Dependent variable is New Hampshire Vote Share. R^2 = 0.860; adj. R^2 = 0.846; F-statistic = 58.517.

*p < 0.05; ***p < 0.001.

TABLE B.7
Explanatory Model—campaign effects variables

Days in Iowa (percentage difference from the average of the candidate's party's candidates reaching Caucus)

Rally Attendance (percentage of all partisans saying they attended rally)

Campaign Contact (percentage of all partisans saying they were contacted by candidate)

TV Advertising (estimated percentage of the total spent by same-party candidates that cycle)

Press Coverage (percentage based on total number of print articles in four top Iowa-region papers)

Controls

Under 15% Democratic Viability Threshold (Democrats not reaching 15% in the Iowa Poll dummy variable)

National Fund-Raising Share (candidate's percentage of active same-party candidates' total money raised, second half of pre-election year)

Iowa Spending (percentage of total in pre-election year combined third and fourth quarter)

Electability (percentage of partisans *not* responding that candidate was more likely than not to lose the general election)

Ideological Crowding (1 − Ideological Vote Share, or the total percentage of all partisans for whom candidate is closer than any other plus proportional share of ties)

Share of Field (%)

Viability (percentage of partisans giving candidate any chance)

Home State Near Iowa dummy variable

African American dummy variable

Incumbent President dummy variable

Favorite Son (Harkin 1992) dummy variable

Running vs. Favorite Son (non-Harkin 1992) dummy variable

Running vs. Incumbent President dummy variable

NOTE: Dependent variable is Iowa Caucus Vote Share (%, scaled), as reported by *Des Moines Register* but proportionally factoring in undecided and uncommitted.

TABLE B.8

Estimate of Explanatory Model—campaign effects variables

Variable	Unstandardized beta	Standard error	p
Days in Iowa (percentage difference from average)	0.061*	(0.028)	0.034
Rally Attendance (all partisans)	−0.273	(0.239)	0.258
Campaign Contact (all partisans)	−0.026	(0.068)	0.709
Press Coverage (percentage of total)	0.060	(0.101)	0.553
TV Advertising (%)	−0.406*	(0.191)	0.039
Controls			
Under 15% Democratic Viability Threshold	−0.075**	(0.027)	0.008
Electability	0.248*	(0.118)	0.041
Ideological Crowding	−0.849*	(0.369)	0.025
Share of Field (%)	−0.111	(0.326)	0.736
Viability	0.068	(0.140)	0.631
National Fund-Raising Share (percentage of total)	0.088	(0.148)	0.555
Iowa Spending (percentage of total)	0.254	(0.158)	0.114
Home State Near Iowa	−0.003	(0.028)	0.913
African American	0.033	(0.049)	0.514
Incumbent President	0.095	(0.090)	0.296
Favorite Son (Harkin 1992)	0.242	(0.123)	0.054
Running vs. Favorite Son (non-Harkin 1992)	−0.034	(0.048)	0.477
Running vs. Incumbent President	0.045	(0.070)	0.521
(Constant)	0.775	(0.388)	0.051

NOTE: Dependent variable is Iowa Caucus Vote Share. $R^2 = 0.867$; adj. $R^2 = 0.820$; F-statistic = 18.152.

*$p < 0.05$; **$p < 0.01$.

TABLE B.9
Explanatory Model—strategic voting variables

Ideological Crowding (1 − Ideological Vote Share, or the total percentage of all partisans for whom candidate is closer than any other plus proportional share of ties)

Electability (total percentage of partisans *not* responding candidate more likely to lose the general election)

Viability (percentage of partisans giving candidate any chance to win the nomination)

National Fund-Raising (percentage of active same-party candidate total money raised, second half of pre-election year)

African American dummy variable

Controls

Under 15% Democratic Viability Threshold (Democrats not reaching 15% in the Iowa Poll dummy variable)

Days in Iowa (percentage difference from average of the candidate's party's candidates reaching Caucus)

Rally Attendance (percentage of all partisans saying they attended rally)

Campaign Contact (percentage of all partisans saying they were contacted by candidate)

TV Advertising (percentage of estimated total spent by opponents)

Press Coverage (percentage of total number of print articles in four top Iowa-region papers)

Iowa Spending (percentage total, pre-election year combined third and fourth quarter)

Share of Field (percentage that candidate represents)

Home State Near Iowa dummy variable

Incumbent President dummy variable

Favorite Son (Harkin 1992) dummy variable

Running vs. Favorite Son (non-Harkin 1992) dummy variable

Running vs. Incumbent President dummy variable

N O T E : Dependent variable is Iowa Caucus Vote Share (%, scaled), as reported by *Des Moines Register* but proportionally factoring in undecided and uncommitted.

TABLE B.10

Estimate of Explanatory Model—strategic voting variables

Variable	Unstandardized beta	Standard error	p
Ideological Crowding	−0.849*	(0.369)	0.025
Electability	0.248*	(0.118)	0.041
Viability	0.068	(0.140)	0.631
National Fund-Raising (percentage of total)	0.088	(0.148)	0.555
African American	0.033	(0.049)	0.514
Controls			
Under 15% Democratic Viability Threshold	−0.075**	(0.027)	0.008
Days in Iowa (percentage difference from average)	0.061*	(0.028)	0.034
TV Advertising (percentage of total)	−0.406*	(0.191)	0.039
Share of Field (%)	−0.111	(0.326)	0.736
Rally Attendance (all partisans)	−0.273	(0.239)	0.258
Campaign Contact (all partisans)	−0.026	(0.068)	0.709
Press Coverage (percentage of total)	0.060	(0.101)	0.553
Iowa Spending (percentage of total)	0.254	(0.158)	0.114
Home State Near Iowa	−0.003	(0.028)	0.913
Incumbent President	0.095	(0.090)	0.296
Favorite Son (Harkin 1992)	0.242	(0.123)	0.054
Running vs. Favorite Son (non-Harkin 1992)	−0.034	(0.048)	0.477
Running vs. Incumbent President	0.045	(0.070)	0.521
(Constant)	0.775	(0.388)	0.051

NOTE: Dependent variable is Iowa Caucus Vote Share (%). $R^2 = 0.867$; adj. $R^2 = 0.820$; F-statistic $= 18.152$.

*$p < 0.05$; **$p < 0.01$.

TABLE B.11
2004 Preliminary Predictive Model

Iowa Poll Support[a] (%)
Days in Iowa[b] (percentage of total spent by all candidates of the candidate's same
   party since the prior general election)
TV Advertising[c] (percentage of total)
Iowa Spending[d] (percentage of total)
Pre-Caucus Straw Poll Support[e] (%)
National Polling Data against primary challengers
Press Coverage[f] (percentage of total in four top Iowa-region papers among active
   same-party candidates)
National Fund-Raising Share (percentage of total fund-raising by same-party
   candidates in the second half of pre-election year)
Share of Field (percentage that candidate represents)
Forbes–TV Advertising interactive term
Democratic Pre-Caucus Straw Poll Support interactive term (%)
Favorite Son–Home State Near Iowa dummy
African American dummy variable
1976, 1980, 1984, 1996, and 2000 dummy variables to control for fixed effects
   for time

NOTE: Dependent variable is Iowa Caucus Vote Share (%).

[a] Imputed using percentage of Share of Field, percentage of total National Fund-Raising for the second half of the year before the election, percentage of total Iowa Spending (filled; i.e., for candidates for whom no data were available, multiple-imputation regression models used other variables to predict, or fill, their missing variable values), National Poll Support, organizational strength scaling factor (the factor to translate straw poll results to the same scale as Caucus results, when more candidates were in the field for straw poll than reached the Caucus), amount of fund-raising receipts (2004 dollars), Iowa Spending (2004 dollars), Pre-Caucus Straw Poll Support (filled), percentage total Days in Iowa (filled), and the dummy variable for Favorite Son (candidates with a home state near Iowa).

[b] Imputed using percentage of Share of Field that the candidate represents, percentage of National Fund-Raising total, and National Poll Support to create index for 1980 Republicans.

[c] Imputed using percentage of the Share of Field the candidate represents, percentage of National Fund-Raising total, National Poll Support, scaled organizational strength, national receipts (2004 dollars), Iowa Spending (2004 dollars, filled), percentage of total Days in Iowa (filled), the Forbes dummy variable, and the Democratic 15% Viability Threshold dummy variable.

[d] In 2004 dollars, imputed using Forbes–Days in Iowa and Forbes–National Fund-Raising interactive terms, as well as the average Days in Iowa of all candidates, percentage of Share of Field that the candidate represents, the Under 15% Democratic Viability Threshold dummy variable, National Poll Support, the number of years that the candidate's party had spent out of power, and National Fund-Raising receipts for the second half of the year before the election (2004 dollars).

[e] Imputed using percentage of the Share of Field the candidate represents, percentage of total money raised for the second half of the year before the election, National Fund-Raising receipts (2004 dollars), percentage total Iowa Spending for the second half of the year before the election (filled), Iowa Spending for the second half of the year before the election (2004 dollars, filled), National Poll Support, and the organizational strength scale.

[f] Imputed using percentage of same-party candidates' total Days in Iowa, National Poll Support, Iowa Poll Support (filled), Pre-Caucus Straw Poll Support (filled), number of candidates in the race on Caucus day, National Fund-Raising (2004 dollars) for the second half of the year before the election, the Forbes dummy variable, the Under 15% Democratic Viability Threshold dummy variable, spending on TV Advertising (real, filled), percentage of total TV advertising spending (filled), Iowa Spending for the second half of the year before the election (real, filled), percentage of total Iowa Spending (filled).

TABLE B.12

Estimate of 2004 Preliminary Predictive Model

Variable	Unstandardized beta	Standard error	p
(Constant)	0.036	0.029	0.223
Iowa Poll Support (%)	1.178***	0.244	0.00004
Days in Iowa (percentage of total)	−0.301*	0.124	0.022
1984 dummy variable	−0.076*	0.037	0.048
TV Advertising (percentage of total)	0.248	0.139	0.084
Iowa Spending (percentage of total)	−0.311	0.196	0.124
Pre-Caucus Straw Poll Support (%)	0.192	0.146	0.197
National Poll Support	−0.212	0.165	0.208
Democratic Pre-Caucus Straw Poll Support (%) interactive term	0.079	0.079	0.324
Press Coverage (percentage of total in four top Iowa-region papers for same-party candidates)	−0.108	0.167	0.525
National Fund-Raising (percentage of total by same-party candidates in the second half of pre-election year)	0.102	0.175	0.565
Favorite Son–Home State Near Iowa dummy	−0.016	0.029	0.584
Share of Field (percentage that candidate represents)	0.082	0.17	0.633
Forbes–TV Advertising interactive term	−0.044	0.213	0.837
African American dummy variable	0.003	0.033	0.926
1976, 1980, 1996, and 2000 dummy variables to control for fixed effects for time	Various	Various	None significant

NOTE: $R^2 = 0.928$; adj. $R^2 = 0.881$; F-statistic = 19.918.

*$p < 0.05$; ***$p < 0.001$.

TABLE B.13
Final Predictive Model

Final Explanatory Model Factor, %, unscaled, regressing scaled Iowa Caucus Vote
 Share on the Explanatory Model with 2000–2004 Internet metrics included
Iowa Poll Support (normed to 100% per cycle, imputed using percentage of Iowa
 Spending, Home State Near Iowa dummy, percentage of Share of Field, and Gallup
 Poll Support, scaled to factor out the percentage of those who chose undecided in
 last *Des Moines Register* Iowa Poll)
Pre-Caucus Straw Poll Support (scaled, normed to 100% per cycle, imputed using
 Gallup Poll Support, Iowa Poll Support, percentage of total National Fund-
 Raising, percentage of total Days in Iowa, and percentage of Share of Field)
Gallup Poll Support (percentage based on raw Gallup totals, scaled to include only
 candidates reaching the Caucus, then filled[a] using percentage of Share of Field and
 percentage of National Fund-Raising, then normed back to 100% for each field of
 candidates)

NOTE: Dependent variable is 1976–2000 Iowa Caucus Vote Share (%, scaled), as reported by *Des Moines Register* but proportionally factoring in undecided and uncommitted.

[a]For candidates for whom no data were available, multiple-imputation regression models used other variables to predict, or fill, their missing variable values.

TABLE B.14
Final Predictive Model results for 1976–2004

Variable	Unstandardized beta	Standard error	p
Final Explanatory Model factor	0.633***	(0.097)	<0.001
Iowa Poll Support (%)	0.412**	(0.116)	0.001
Pre-Caucus Straw Poll Support (%)	0.213**	(0.075)	0.006
Gallup Poll Support (%)	−0.188**	(0.060)	0.003
(Constant)	−0.013	(0.010)	0.205

NOTE: Dependent variable is Iowa Caucus Vote Share (%, scaled). $R^2 = 0.920$; adj. $R^2 = 0.915$; F-statistic $= 183.116$.
**$p < 0.01$; ***$p < 0.001$.

TABLE B.15
Final Predictive Model results for 1976–2000

Variable	Unstandardized beta	Standard error	p
Final Explanatory Model factor	0.630***	(0.102)	<0.001
Iowa Poll Support	0.399**	(0.123)	0.002
Pre-Caucus Straw Poll Support	0.220**	(0.079)	0.007
Gallup Poll Support	−0.187**	(0.064)	0.005
(Constant)	−0.011	(0.011)	0.343

NOTE: Dependent variable is 1976–2000 Iowa Caucus Vote Share (%, scaled). $R^2 = 0.920$; adj. $R^2 = 0.914$; F-statistic $= 161.024$.
**$p < 0.01$; ***$p < 0.001$.

Reference Matter

Notes

CHAPTER ONE

1. Note that I use the terms *retail politics, grassroots,* and *organization* more or less interchangeably throughout the book, despite their referring to subtly different concepts. The specific operationalization of the factors used to measure the concept is laid out in more detail in Chapter 5.

2. See, for instance, John McCormick and Jonathan Roos, "Some see Iowa's leadoff role in jeopardy," *Des Moines Register,* January 24, 2000.

3. U.S. Census Bureau data.

4. See, as the monolithic centerpiece of an entire body of works, Robert D. Putnam, *Bowling Alone: The Collapse and Revival of American Community* (2000).

5. This is the approach taken by Parent, Jilson, and Weber (1987) in applying the Michigan Model of individual vote choice to aggregate-level data at the full primary level.

CHAPTER TWO

1. Except, of course, in Nebraska, which has a nonpartisan legislature.

2. Booser 1935, 222–23, quoted in Key 1946, 371, cited in Bass 1998, 227.

3. David Yepsen, "Iowa's caucuses: An introduction and history," *Des Moines Register* (http://desmoinesregister.com/extras/politics/caucus2004/history.html [accessed May 13, 2007]).

4. See also *Des Moines Register,* "Winners and losers" (http://desmoinesregister .com/extras/politics/caucus2004/pastresults.html [accessed May 13, 2007]).

5. Yepsen, "Iowa's caucuses."

6. Details came from Ralph Brown in an e-mail communication with me, June 11, 2007.

7. See also *Des Moines Register,* "Winners and losers." Winebrenner attributed his data, which match the *Register*'s, to the Republican Party itself, and he notes that national media sources "reported less complete results that had Bush leading Reagan by 4 to 6 percentage points."

8. Yepsen, "Iowa's caucuses."

9. Though without being able to cite the exact date, I heard President Bush say as much in a speech in Iowa City, despite his having placed a distant third in the 1988 Caucus.

10. Yepsen, "Iowa's caucuses."

11. *Des Moines Register,* "Winners and losers."

12. The data on the last New Hampshire poll before the Iowa Caucus took place were generously provided to me by presidential primary scholar William G. Mayer.

13. Primary: New Hampshire, "Past New Hampshire Primary Election Results" (http://www.primarynewhampshire.com/new-hampshire-primary-past-results .php [accessed May 15, 2007]).

14. Scott Berkowitz, interview with the author, November 1, 2006.

15. Yepsen, "Iowa's caucuses."

16. Yepsen, "Iowa's caucuses."

17. For an amusing vignette about Gephardt's ad mocking Dukakis's promotion of Belgian endive, see Cramer 1993, 914.

18. Carl Weathers and Robbie Robertson, "Democratic Debate '88" (Saturday Night Live transcripts, season 13, episode 10).

19. Poll by PSI Research/Capitol Communications, 300 likely caucusgoers, ±5.5%, cited in *Des Moines Register,* March 10, 1999.

20. See note 11.

21. Fox News/Opinion Dynamics Poll, conducted January 7–8, 2004; Fox News/Opinion Dynamics Poll, conducted January 21–22, 2004. In 2004 the Caucus was held January 19. In another, less frequently conducted poll, Kerry's support also rose from 7% before the Caucus to 53% after the results of the early states, including New Hampshire and South Carolina, were in. (The New Hampshire Primary was held January 27; the South Carolina Primary was held February 3.) See CBS News Poll, January 12–15, 2004, and CBS News Poll, February 12–15. All polls are available at http://www.pollingreport.com/who4dem.htm (accessed May 15, 2007).

22. Cook quoted in U.S. Department of State, "A Look Ahead: The New Hampshire Primary" (*Election Focus 2004* 1, no. 2 [January 21, 2004], p. 1. http://usinfo .state.gov/dhr/img/assets/5796/elections01_21_04.pdf [accessed July 17, 2007]).

23. Kevin Landrigan, "NHPrimary.com: Why Iowa Caucuses mean so little in New Hampshire" (CNN.com, January 21, 2000, http://archives.cnn.com/2000/ ALLPOLITICS/stories/01/21/iowa.nh/index.html).

CHAPTER THREE

1. Note that "time-series" is something of a misnomer here—the data occur over time, but they in no way are panel data, going back to the same subjects or even the same number of subjects, at each time *t*.

2. That is not to imply that all data stretch from 1976 to 2004. See Appendix A for more information on limitations in the amount and quality of information in various areas of the database.

3. I am indebted to my colleague Andrew Dowdle for underscoring the importance of this flaw in my data.

4. Much of Gregg's data are available at http://www.politicallibrary.org/Tall State/listing.html.

5. The figures used to calculate 2004-dollar figures come from the U.S. Department of Labor, Bureau of Labor Statistics. I used the Consumer Price Index for All Urban Consumers (CPI-U), U.S. city average, which puts 1982–1984 = 100. Note that to get real 2002 dollars, for instance, the number is divided by the CPI for the year it occurred, then multiplied by 179.9, the 2002 index.

6. Defined as those who had nonzero results after rounding in either national polls or the Iowa Caucus. Al Sharpton is the only candidate included who does not meet this definition; he is included exclusively because of his high profile.

CHAPTER FOUR

1. Note that Mayer makes the point that Carter was the only one campaigning in Iowa in 1976 (Mayer 1996a, 63).

2. I am once again indebted to my colleague Andrew Dowdle for pointing out the importance of this factor.

3. The last name is also reported "Rassman" in various sources.

4. One of many personal testaments to this argument can be found at http://www.statenews.com/op_article.phtml?pk=23256.

5. Short for "Web log," a *blog* is a journal or diary that is posted on a website and updated on a regular basis. The content of the blog reflects the personal opinion of the site's owner. Blogs are an increasingly popular source of political information.

6. Reading articles on the Internet about a candidate is actually significantly associated with that candidate's performance in the Caucus—but in a negative direction—when controlling for other Internet factors.

7. Note that, in fact, I used a scaled Iowa Caucus vote total, eliminating "Uncommitted" and "Undecided," which count for large proportions of especially early cycles. I am indebted to Wayne Steger for pointing out the importance of doing so.

8. More precisely, those e-mentum factors were constructed by regressing Primary Popular Vote Share on both Iowa Caucus Vote Share and the Internet metric and saving the model's estimates.

9. Note that for the lightly contested 1992 Iowa Democratic race and those in 1988 and before, this study assumes no Internet activity at all. That is almost certainly a false assumption. However, given the minuscule amount of Internet activity reported in 1996, I believe it is safe to assume no Internet activity in those early

cycles. In fact, relative to the 2000 and especially 2004 cycles, 1996 itself probably makes no difference in the estimates in the models that follow, because Internet penetration was so limited. I feel very comfortable with the 1992 cutoff, but theorists who disagree may take issue with the results on that score.

10. Note that I employed the same Iowa online e-mentum factor in both models in this chapter, even though the factor was generated by regressing Online Support and Iowa Caucus Vote Share on Primary Popular Vote Share, not New Hampshire Vote Share. If anything, of course, that should understate the size of the explanatory power, which as the reader will find is considerable in the model. Still, in the future, I will be using each dependent variable to create its own e-mentum factor, to be technically accurate.

CHAPTER FIVE

1. Author's interview with David Den Herder, May 12, 2003.

2. As mentioned in Chapter 1, the terms *organization, retail politics*, and *grassroots* are used more or less interchangeably throughout this study. The specific operationalization of the three factors used to measure the concept and the Retail Politics Index intended to measure this concept are laid out in detail below and in Appendix A.

The "time on task" statement is from David Yepsen, *Des Moines Register* columnist. It is a frequent statement by him and others, but in this case it comes from a personal conversation with the author.

3. Keith Fortmann interview, April 19, 2003.

4. Brian Kennedy interview, April 8, 2003.

5. Brian Kennedy interview, April 8, 2003.

6. Wayne Steger, e-mail to author, February 3, 2007.

7. See http://www.bowlingalone.com/data.htm.

8. Or as they put it, "Long term retrenchment in voter turnout is partly attributable to the decline in face-to-face political mobilization" (Gerber and Green 2000, 653).

9. Author's interviews with David Den Herder, May 12, 2003; Tim Hyde, April 16, 2003; Jeff Link, June 10, 2003; Sara Taylor, April 22, 2003; and John Stineman, April 10, 2003.

10. Author's interviews with Keith Fortmann, April 19, 2003; Bob Haus, April 15, 2003; Jeff Link, June 10, 2003; Tim Hyde, April 16, 2003; and Tom Synhorst, April 11, 2003.

11. Author's interviews with David Den Herder, May 12, 2003; Bob Haus, April 15, 2003; John Stineman, April 10, 2003; Sara Taylor, April 22, 2003; and Eric Bakker, May 13, 2003.

12. Author's interviews with Jeff Link, June 10, 2003; and Eric Bakker, May 13, 2003.

13. Author's interview with Jeff Link, June 10, 2003. As an aside, Link dismisses the criticism that the process is too complicated and might break down. "Breakdowns are rare and take place in rural areas, in people's living rooms," in places like Lyon County, Link quips, "where there are ten Democrats in the whole county." With nine campaigns in 2004, Link points out, there will be "seasoned campaign staff" in all of the major precincts, which prevents "any significant skew in the numbers." In every precinct he has been in, Link says, "people are standing around checking on the person who makes the call in."

14. Author's interviews with Jeff Link, June 10, 2003; and Eric Bakker, May 13, 2003.

15. Author's interview with Keith Fortmann, April 19, 2003.

16. Author's interview with Jeff Link, June 10, 2003.

17. Author's interview with Eric Bakker, May 13, 2003.

18. Author's interview with David Den Herder, May 12, 2003.

19. Author's interviews with Keith Fortmann, April 19, 2003; John Stineman, April 10, 2003; and Sara Taylor, April 22, 2003, who is the operative who suggested that grassroots organizing could overpower a candidate with greater financial wherewithal.

20. Author's interview with John Stineman, April 10, 2003. Note that I investigated these interactions extensively in an earlier paper, "Theory and Practice in Testing Models of the Iowa Caucus" (conference paper, Midwest Political Science Association Annual Meeting, Section 12: Elections and Voting Behavior, Panel 2: The Presidential Nominating Process, April 15, 2004); also presented as "Theory and Practice: Can Political Professionals Shed Light on Primary Election Models?" (Western Political Science Association Annual Meeting, Section 12: Elections and Voting Behavior, Panel 22:02: Wimp or Shrimp? How Voters Decide, March 18, 2005).

21. Descriptions of pre-Caucus activities for Democrats are found on pp. 58, 60–63, 65–66 for 1976; 87–90 for 1980; 110–20 for 1984; 137–44, 146–52 for 1988; 191, 193–94 for 1992; and 233–35 for 1996. Descriptions of pre-Caucus activities for Republicans are found on pp. 66–67 for 1976; 81–87 for 1980; 120 for 1984; 153–63 for 1988; 194 for 1992; and 204–33 for 1996.

22. The 2000 Democratic figures were echoed in the *Washington Post*, January 25, 2000.

23. For 2004 the data are from the *Des Moines Register* website, http://desmoines register.com/extras/politics/caucus2004/days.html. Republican and Democratic 2000 data come from Winebrenner, "Individual Candidate Days in Iowa 1997–00," unpublished data. Democratic 1976 data come from Winebrenner (1998, 66). Republican 1976 and Democratic 1988 data come from Squire (1989, 5). The rest come from the unpublished Winebrenner data.

24. All 2004 data are from a University of Wisconsin study by Ken Goldstein of 2004 candidate airings in the largest 100 markets from the beginning of the

election cycle until November 30, 2003. The study's summary used to develop these data, "Iowa Presidential Campaign Spending Doubles New Hampshire," is available at http://polisci.wisc.edu/tvadvertising/Press_Releases/Press_Release_PDFs/Release%202003%20December%204th.pdf. The 2000 Forbes and Bush data are an estimate from Sanders and Redlawsk (2000). The data on 2000 Democrats are from the *Washington Post,* January 25, 2000. For all 1988 and 1996 Republicans, television spending data are drawn from Winebrenner (1998).

25. Author's interview with Tim Hyde, April 16, 2003.

26. As noted in Appendix A, the exception is the Under 15% Democratic Viability Threshold dummy variable, which is derived from candidates' performance in the Iowa Poll. I believe the exception is theoretically important and does little empirical damage to the model.

CHAPTER SIX

1. Author's interview with Tim Hyde, April 16, 2003.

2. Author's interview with Bob Haus, April 15, 2003.

3. Author's interviews with Eric Bakker, May 13, 2003; Keith Fortmann, April 19, 2003; Brian Kennedy, April 8, 2003; and Bob Haus, April 15, 2003.

4. Author's interviews with Keith Fortmann, April 19, 2003; Brian Kennedy, April 8, 2003; Tim Hyde, April 16, 2003; and John Stineman, April 10, 2003.

5. I am indebted to Clyde Wilcox for pointing this out to me.

6. Defined as those who had nonzero results after rounding in either national polls or the Iowa Caucus. Al Sharpton is the only candidate included exclusively because of his profile.

CHAPTER SEVEN

1. Fox News, January 19, 2004.

2. This summary of Bartels's work draws on the one in Cohen, Noel, and Zaller 2004.

3. Wayne Steger recommended that I gather these data, and I gratefully acknowledge the assistance of my colleague Irina Papkov in helping me do so.

4. Polling data for 2004 were from "Iowa Poll finds surge by Kerry, Edwards," *Des Moines Register,* January 17, 2004, available at http://miva.dmregister.com/miva/cgi-bin/miva?extras/iowapoll/poll.mv+file=prez0401. Note that Carol Moseley Braun (D-Ill.) withdrew from the race on the Thursday before the Caucus. During the 2004 Iowa Poll, as a result, her name was dropped from the candidate list during polling on Thursday and Friday nights before the Tuesday, January 19, Caucus. The 2000 Republican and Democrat, 1992 Democrat, and 1988 Republican and Democrat polling are all results from the Iowa Poll conducted closest to the Iowa Caucus in those years and come from my January 21, 2004, interview with

Anne Selzer of Selzer & Co., Inc., which conducted those polls for the *Des Moines Register*. The 1984 Democratic Iowa poll data are results from the Iowa Poll closest to the 1984 Caucus, and come from my interview with Glen Roberts, former pollster for the *Des Moines Register*, January 21, 2004.

5. See Squire 1989, 9–10. Data for the 2000 Republicans are from the ABC/ *Washington Post* Poll, December 1999. Data for the 1996 Republicans are from the *New York Times*, January 23, 1996, two weeks before the Iowa Caucus. (Note that I used a 1% estimate from that poll for those that the *Times* reported got 2% or less.) Though I sought to find polling as close to the Caucus as possible, the 1988 Democrats are from December 1987, and the 1988 Republicans are from October 1987. Because these 1976–2004 national polling data are neither standardized nor sourced so as to be replicable, during the course of this study I replaced the data with a single poll, the Gallup Poll, at the closest point to the Caucus, the practice more common in the literature. The models that use each are clearly marked, with a description of any (minor) differences the switch caused.

6. For which, as I mention elsewhere, I am indebted to Wayne Steger, who gathered the data in the first place, and was generous enough to provide them to me.

7. The Gallup Poll data were mostly obtained from Wayne Steger (to whom I am much indebted) in December 2004 and can also be found in the Gallup Opinion Index/Gallup Poll publications. The polls included are November 1975, Democratic; January 1976, Republican; December 1979, Republican; January 1980, Democratic; October 1983, Democratic; October 1987, Democratic; October 1987, Republican; November 1991, Democratic; November 1995 (second wave), Republican; December 1999 (second wave), Democratic; December 1999 (second wave), Republican, and January 2–5, 2004, Democratic.

8. In earlier versions of the Explanatory Model, one exception was organizational strength as measured by the proxy of early straw poll performance. To be consistent, a direct measure of organizational strength—such as number of offices and staff in Iowa, as was suggested by one commentator—should be selected for the Explanatory Model, and Pre-Caucus Straw Poll Support should be used only in predictive models. The three proxies for organizational strength listed in Chapter 5 were substituted for straw poll performance in all explanatory models in this study, and straw poll performance was used exclusively for predictive models.

APPENDIX A

1. See Chapter 5 for a detailed description of both the sources and methodology underlying both Television Advertising and Press Coverage.

2. That is, the entire Explanatory Model except for the Days in Iowa variable, used to predict a candidate's percentage of the total Days in Iowa.

3. That is, the entire Explanatory Model except for the Iowa Spending vari-

able, used to predict that Iowa Spending variable. (Note that for this estimation, instead of using the percentage difference from the average Days in Iowa as does the Explanatory Model when used to predict Iowa Caucus Vote Share, I used the candidates' percentage of the total Days in Iowa, which has a more linear relationship with Iowa Spending. I believe the two factors are more or less theoretically interchangeable.)

4. That is, the entire Explanatory Model except for the National Fund-Raising variable, used to predict that National Fund-Raising variable. (Again, note that for this estimation, instead of using the percentage difference from the average Days in Iowa as in the Explanatory Model when used to predict Iowa Caucus Vote Share, I used the candidates' percentage of the total Days in Iowa, which has a more linear relationship with National Fund-Raising. As I said above, I believe the two factors are essentially theoretically interchangeable.)

5. I am indebted to Hans Noel for explaining both this challenge and its solution.

6. Note that other waves within Abramowitz et al.'s (2001) Republican and Democratic 1984–1996 ICPSR (Inter-university Consortium for Political and Social Research) panel data (for instance, 84b, 88b, 88c) had different point values than the first wave (84a and 88a) and took place later in the election. Only the first wave's value should be used in a study of the primary.

7. Author's interview with Walter J. Stone, April 27, 2003.

Bibliography

Abboud, Alexandra M. 2004. A Look Ahead: The New Hampshire Primary: Candidates prepare for January 27 race. U.S. Department of State, International Information Programs, January 21. http://usinfo.state.gov/dhr/Archive/2004/Jan/21-43106.html.

Abramowitz, Alan I. 1989. Viability, Electability, and Candidate Choice in a Presidential Primary Election: A Test of Competing Models. *Journal of Politics* 51:922–92.

Abramowitz, Alan I., John McGlennon, Ronald B. Rapoport, and Walter J. Stone. 2001. Activists in the United States Presidential Nomination Process, 1980–1996. Inter-university Consortium for Political and Social Research 6143, Second ICPSR Version.

Abramowitz, Alan I., and Walter J. Stone. 1984. *Nomination Politics: Party Activists and Presidential Choice.* New York: Praeger.

Adams, Williams C. 1987. As New Hampshire Goes. In *Media and Momentum*, edited by Gary R. Orren and Nelson W. Polsby. Chatham, NJ: Chatham House.

Adkins, Randall E., and Andrew J. Dowdle. 2001. How Important Are Iowa and New Hampshire to Winning Post-Reform Presidential Nominations? *Political Research Quarterly* 54 (2): 431–44.

Adkins, Randall E., Andrew J. Dowdle, and Wayne P. Steger. 2002. Before the Primaries: Modeling Presidential Nomination Politics during the Exhibition Season. Conference paper, American Political Science Association Annual Meeting, Boston.

Arterton, Christopher F. 1978. Campaign Organizations Confront the Media Environment. In *Race for the Presidency: The Media and the Nominating Process*, edited by James David Barber. Englewood Cliffs, NJ: Prentice Hall.

Bartels, Larry M. 1988. *Presidential Primaries and the Dynamics of Public Choice.* Princeton, NJ: Princeton University Press.

———. 1989. After Iowa: Momentum in Presidential Primaries. In *The Iowa Cau-*

cuses and the Presidential Nominating Process, edited by Peverill Squire, 121–48. Boulder, CO: Westview Press.

Bass, Harold F., Jr. 1998. Partisan Rules, 1946–1996. In *Partisan Approaches to Postwar American Politics*, edited by Byron E. Shafer. Chappaqua, NY: Chatham House.

Booser, James H. 1935. Origins of the Direct Primary. *National Municipal Review* 24:222–23.

Brady, Henry E. 1989. Is Iowa News? In *The Iowa Caucuses and the Presidential Nominating Process*, edited by Peverill Squire, 89–119. Boulder, CO: Westview Press.

Brown, Clifford W., Lynda W. Powell, and Clyde Wilcox. 1995. *Serious Money: Fundraising and Contributing in Presidential Nomination Campaigns*. New York: Cambridge University Press.

Busch, Andrew E. 2000. New Features of the 2000 Presidential Nominating Process: Republican Reforms, Front-Loading's Second Wind, and Early Voting. In *In Pursuit of the White House 2000: How We Choose Our Presidential Nominees*, edited by William G. Mayer. New York: Chatham House.

Campbell, Angus, Philip E. Converse, Warren E. Miller, and Donald E. Stokes. 1960. *The American Voter*. New York: Wiley.

CBS News Poll. Conducted January 12–15, 2004. http://www.pollingreport.com/who4dem.htm (accessed May 15, 2007).

———. Conducted February 12–15, 2004. http://www.pollingreport.com/who4 dem.htm (accessed May 15, 2007).

Chan, Wai. 2003. Analyzing Ipsative Data in Psychological Research. *Behaviormetrika* 30 (1): 99–121.

Cohen, Marty, Hans Noel, and John Zaller. 2004. From George McGovern to John Kerry: State-level Models of Presidential Primaries, 1972 to 2004. Conference paper, Midwest Political Science Association Annual Meeting, Chicago.

Cramer, Richard Ben. 1993. *What It Takes*. New York: Vintage Books.

Fiorina, Morris P. 1980. The Decline of Collective Responsibility in American Politics. *Daedalus* 109 (Summer): 25–45.

Fox News/Opinion Dynamics Poll. 2004a. Conducted January 7–8. http://www .pollingreport.com/who4dem.htm (accessed May 15, 2007).

———. 2004b. Conducted January 21–22. http://www.pollingreport.com/who4 dem.htm (accessed May 15, 2007).

Geer, John G. 1989. *Nominating Presidents: An Evaluation of Voters and Primaries*. New York: Greenwood Press.

Gerber, Alan S., and Donald P. Green. 2000. The Effects of Canvassing, Telephone Calls, and Direct Mail on Voter Turnout: A Field Experiment. *American Political Science Review* 94:653–63.

Goldstein, Ken. 2003. Iowa Presidential Campaign Spending Doubles New Hampshire. polisci.wisc.edu/tvadvertising/Press_Releases/Press_Release_ PDFs/Release%202003%20December%204th.pdf.

Greer, Tammy, and William P. Dunlap. 1997. Analysis of Variance with Ipsative Measures. *Psychological Methods* 2 (2): 200–7.

Gregg, Hugh. 1993. *A Tall State Revisited: A Republican Perspective.* Nashua, NH: Resources of New Hampshire, Inc.

Grush, John E. 1980. Impact of Candidate Expenditures, Regionality, and Prior Outcomes on the 1976 Democratic Presidential Primaries. *Journal of Personality and Social Psychology* 38:337–47.

Hagen, Michael G., and William G. Mayer. 2000. The Modern Politics of Presidential Selection: How Changing the Rules Really Did Change the Game. In *In Pursuit of the White House 2000: How We Select Our Presidential Nominees,* edited by William G. Mayer. New York: Chatham House.

History Learning Site, The. The Primaries and Elections in America. http:// www.historylearningsite.co.uk/primaries.htm.

Hull, Christopher C. 2004. Kerry-ing the Hawkeye State: The Iowa Caucus' Impact on the Presidential Race, 1976–2004. Conference paper, Northeast Political Science Association Annual Meeting, Special Symposium, NPSA Program Sections Congress, Presidency, and the Courts and Parties, Interest Groups, and Electoral Behavior, Boston, MA, November 11–13.

———. 2005. The Big Mo from 1980 to 2004: Is Technological "e-mentum" Amplifying Key Events in Presidential Races? Conference paper, Midwest Political Science Association Annual Meeting, Panel 21-5: Defining Moments and Significant Stories in the 2004 Presidential Campaign Cycle, Chicago, April 7.

———. 2007. The Iowa Caucuses. In *Encyclopedia of Political Communication,* edited by Lynda Lee Kaid and Christina Holtz-Bacha. Thousand Oaks, CA: Sage.

Hutter, James L., and Steven E. Schier. 1984. Representativeness: From Caucus to Convention in Iowa. *American Politics Quarterly* 12:431–48.

Key, V. O., Jr. 1946. *Politics, Parties, and Pressure Groups.* New York: Crowell.

King, Gary, James Honaker, Anne Joseph, and Kenneth Scheve. 2001. Analyzing Incomplete Political Science Data: An Alternative Algorithm for Multiple Imputation. *American Political Science Review* 95 (1): 49–69.

Lengle, James I. 1981a. Changing the Rules Changes the Game. *Commonsense* 4 (2): 13–20.

———. 1981b. *Representation and Presidential Primaries: The Democratic Party in the Post-Reform Era.* Westport, CT: Greenwood Press.

Lengle, Jim, and Byron Shafer. 1976. Primary Rules, Political Power, and Social Change. *American Political Science Review* 70 (1): 25–40.

Mayer, William G., ed. 1996a. *In Pursuit of the White House: How We Choose Our Presidential Nominees,* Chatham, NJ: Chatham House.

———, 1996b. Caucuses: How They Work, What Difference They Make. In *In Pursuit of the White House: How We Choose Our Presidential Nominees*, edited by William G. Mayer. Chatham, NJ: Chatham House.

———. 1996c. Forecasting Presidential Nominations. In *In Pursuit of the White House: How We Choose Our Presidential Nominees*, edited by William G. Mayer. Chatham, NJ: Chatham House.

———, ed. 2000. *In Pursuit of the White House 2000: How We Choose Our Presidential Nominees*. New York: Chatham House.

———. 2004. The Basic Dynamics of the Presidential Nomination Process: An Expanded View. In *The Making of the Presidential Candidates, 2004*, edited by William G. Mayer, 83–132. Lanham, MD: Rowman & Littlefield.

Mayer, William G., and Andrew E. Busch. 2004. *The Front-Loading Problem in Presidential Nominations*. Washington, DC: Brookings Institution Press.

McCormick, John, and Jonathan Roos. 2000. Some See Iowa's Leadoff Role in Jeopardy. *Des Moines Register.* January 24.

Nie, Norman H., Sidney Verba, and John R. Petrocik. 1976. *The Changing American Voter.* Cambridge, MA: Harvard University Press.

Norrander, Barbara. 1993. Nomination Choices: Caucus and Primary Outcomes, 1976–1988. *American Journal of Political Science* 37:343–64.

———. 1996. Presidential Nomination Politics in the Post-Reform Era. *Political Research Quarterly* 49 (4): 875–915.

Orren, Gary R., and Nelson W. Polsby. 1987. *Media and Momentum*. Chatham, NJ: Chatham House.

Parent, Wayne, Calvin Jilson, and Ronald Weber. 1987. Voting Outcomes in the 1984 Democratic Party Primaries and Caucuses. *American Political Science Review* 81:67–84.

Patterson, Samuel C. 1984. Iowa. In *The Political Life of the American States*, edited by Alan Rosenthal and Maureen Moakley, 83–98. New York: Praeger.

Patterson, Thomas. 1980. *The Mass Media Election: How Americans Choose Their President*. New York: Praeger.

Polsby, Nelson W. 1983. *Consequences of Party Reform*. New York: Oxford University Press.

———. 1989. The Iowa Caucuses in a Front-Loaded System: A Few Historical Lessons. In *The Iowa Caucuses and the Presidential Nominating Process*, edited by Peverill Squire, 149–61. Boulder, CO: Westview Press.

Putnam, Robert. 2000. *Bowling Alone: The Collapse and Revival of American Community*. New York: Simon & Schuster.

Ranney, Austin, ed. 1981. *The American Elections of 1980*. Washington, DC: American Enterprise Institute.

Robinson, Michael J. 1981. The Media in 1980: Was the Message the Message? In *The American Elections of 1980*, edited by Austin Ranney. Washington, DC: American Enterprise Institute.

Rosenthal, Alan, and Maureen Moakley. 1984. *The Political Life of the American States.* New York: Praeger.

Sanders, Arthur, and David Redlawsk. 2000. Outside Money in the Presidential Nominating Process: The Iowa Caucuses. Conference paper, American Political Science Association Annual Meeting, Washington, DC.

Scammon, Richard M., Alice V. McGillivray, and Rhodes Cook. 1996. *America Votes 22: A Handbook of Contemporary American Election Statistics.* Washington, DC: Congressional Quarterly Press.

———. 2000. *America Votes 24: A Handbook of Contemporary American Election Statistics.* Washington, DC: Congressional Quarterly Press.

Schattschneider, E. E. 1942. *Party Government.* New York: Rinehart.

Schier, Steven E. 1980. *The Rules of the Game: Democratic National Convention Delegate Selection in Iowa and Wisconsin.* Washington, DC: University Press of America.

Shafer, Byron E., ed. 1998. *Partisan Approaches to Postwar American Politics.* Chappaqua, NY: Chatham House.

Squire, Peverill. 1989. *The Iowa Caucuses and the Presidential Nominating Process.* Boulder, CO: Westview Press.

Stone, Walter J. 1982. Party, Ideology, and the Lure of Victory: Iowa Activists in the 1980 Prenomination Campaign. *Western Political Quarterly* 35:527–38.

Stone, Walter J., and Alan I. Abramowitz. 1983. Winning May Not Be Everything, but It's More Than We Thought. *American Political Science Review* 77: 945–56.

Stone, Walter J., and Ronald B. Rapoport. 1994. Candidate Perception among Nomination Activists: A New Look at the Moderation Hypothesis. *Journal of Politics* 56:1034–52.

Stone, Walter J., Ronald B. Rapoport, and Alan I. Abramowitz. 1989. How Representative Are the Iowa Caucuses? In *The Iowa Caucuses and the Presidential Nominating Process,* edited by Peverill Squire, 19–49. Boulder, CO: Westview Press.

———. 1992. Candidate Support in Presidential Nomination Campaigns: The Case of Iowa in 1984. *Journal of Politics* 54:1074–97.

Tolkien, J. R. R. 1994. *The Lord of the Rings.* Boston: Houghton Mifflin.

Tomz, Michael, Joshua A. Tucker, and Jason Wittenberg. 2002. An Easy and Accurate Regression Model for Multiparty Electoral Data. *Political Analysis* 10 (1): 66–83.

Winebrenner, Hugh. 1983. The Evolution of the Iowa Precinct Caucuses. *The Annals of Iowa* 46:618–35.

———. 1985. The Iowa Precinct Caucuses: The Making of a Media Event. *Southeastern Political Review* 12:99–132.

———. 1998. *The Iowa Precinct Caucuses: The Making of a Media Event.* 2nd ed. Ames: Iowa State University Press.

Wodehouse, P. G. 1983. *Jeeves and the Tie That Binds.* New York: Harper & Row.

Wolfinger, Raymond E. 1989. Who Is Vulnerable to the Iowa Caucuses? In *The Iowa Caucuses and the Presidential Nominating Process,* edited by Peverill Squire, 163–68. Boulder, CO: Westview Press.

Yepsen, David. Iowa's caucuses: An introduction and history. *Des Moines Register.* http://desmoinesregister.com/extras/politics/caucus2004/history.html (accessed May 13, 2007).

Index

Page numbers in italics refer to figures and tables.